MW00776501

"Few people in my fairly [...] have the combination of spiritual insight that Larr[...] lays out a wide view of the massive changes that business [...] and the inclusion of professionals into the work of God's mission have made. Specifically, he solidifies the biblical and missiological foundation for BAM, shares a multitude of real-life BAM stories (motivation and impact), and posits a path forward for those seeking to see Jesus Christ made known to the world. I encourage anyone with a heart for missions and business to read this book!"

—Mike Baer, BAM Author, Speaker, Practitioner

"As a long-time missionary himself, Larry does a wonderful job offering a bold new plan for rethinking the way churches send missionaries into the world. A careful reading of this book, however, will also be disruptive to the way we think about church! Churches that take his message to heart will realize that in addition to the few they send as 'missionaries,' they are already sending the whole congregation out the door with missional intent every week."

—Albert Erisman, Co-chair, Theology of Work Project
Author, *The Accidental Executive* and *The ServiceMaster Story*

"Larry has done the kingdom a great service with *Missions Disrupted*. He opens our eyes to the issues of integrating faith and work, and he urges us to make the changes needed to meet the challenges of the times. This book includes more than two dozen real businesses as mission stories that anyone can relate to. These are stories of people scattered around the world, people like you and me, using their education and skills to disrupt their local communities for the glory of Jesus. From them, you learn from practitioners about their failures and struggles, their victories, and God's guidance. I highly recommend this book!"

—Patrick Lai, Entrepreneur, B4T Mentor and Speaker
Author of *WORKSHIP: Recalibrate Work and Worship*

"The business press is replete with articles describing the Fourth Industrial Revolution's transformative impact on business and society in the coming years. In *Missions Disrupted*, Larry Sharp uses his storytelling skills to present a transformative approach to missions in our changing world. This compelling message draws energy from engaged Christian men and women across the globe using biblically based commerce to transform lives. This is a game-changer!"

— Ken Leahy, VP Finance
Johnson & Johnson Pharmaceutical Services

"I am grateful for Larry's careful recovery and authentic presentation of the ancient truths of our missional Triune God at work in his world in this generation. Its application to all Christ-followers wherever the Spirit takes them is made tangible through diverse, real-time stories. My prayer is that the Father may speak to all readers, giving them knowledge of his calling and equipping for the glorious task they share together."

—Peter Shaukat, Co-founder of a Global BAM Investment Fund

"Holy disruptions! A burning bush redirected Moses and changed history. A fish disrupted Jonah, and it impacted a whole nation. And now, Larry Sharp writes brilliantly about holy disruptions in our generation. The changes needed are profound as we do business with a mission: missional professionals can change history and impact nations. Rooted in a Judeo-Christian tradition, this book is relevant and serves as a guiding star for the future—a must-read."

—Mats Tunehag, Chair, BAM Global
International Speaker, Writer, and Consultant

James Sharp
I Kings 8:60

Missions
Disrupted

From PROFESSIONAL
MISSIONARIES

to MISSIONAL
PROFESSIONALS

HENDRICKSON
PUBLISHERS
an imprint of Hendrickson Publishing Group

THEOLOGY OF WORK   PROJECT

Missions Disrupted: From Professional Missionaries to Missional Professionals

© 2022 Larry Sharp

Published by Hendrickson Publishers
an imprint of Hendrickson Publishing Group
Hendrickson Publishers, LLC
P. O. Box 3473
Peabody, Massachusetts 01961-3473
www.hendricksonpublishinggroup.com

ISBN 978-1-68307-414-4

Printed in the United States of America

First Printing — August 2022

Library of Congress Control Number: 2022933996

Contents

Preface

*An intelligent man is open to new
ideas. In fact he looks for them.*

—King Solomon (Prov. 18:15 TLB)

The purpose of this book is to provide compelling evidence to recalibrate the way we think about how God is working in the twenty-first-century world. The narrative for that shift lies in the stories of lives and communities transformed through men and women living out their faith in the workplace. They are not professional missionaries, but they are missional professionals.

Leo Tolstoy wrote that "the only question important to us is, 'what shall we do and how shall we live?' " The central presupposition is that God is at work in the world in accordance with the definition of *missio Dei*—"the sending of God"—and followers of Jesus are first and foremost "called" to him. To quote Os Guinness, "Our secondary calling, considering who God is as sovereign, is that everyone, everywhere, and in everything should think, speak, live and act entirely for him."[1]

In short, this means that our work matters to God because he made us in his image as beings with unique abilities, gifts, and characteristics that bring creative glory to God. All such work is in the spirit of Paul's letter to the Colossians: "Whatever you do, work at it with all your heart, as working for the Lord, not for human masters" (Col. 3:23). Practically speaking, if God bestowed gifts to a person to be a farmer, then that farmer works for the glory of God; if as a business entrepreneur, that businessperson too works for the glory of God. It's the same for a teacher, a nurse practitioner, or an engineer.

There is no higher calling than serving God's mission using the resources given to us, and the secondary calling gives a dignity and spiritual significance to everyday work. In the spirit of the Reformers, William Tyndale wrote, "If our desire is to please God, pouring water, washing dishes, cobbling shoes, and preaching the Word 'is all one'" (the support theology for this is summarized in chapter 1).

In our ever-changing times, we can look at Disruptive Innovation Theory as a practical support theory for the changes we're seeing in missional thinking in the church and in the hearts of the current generation of believers. The proposition here is that change will come as a "diffusion of innovation," meaning on the tails of the normal curve via early adopters who are willing to see things differently and adjust to a new way of doing "missions." According to this theory, church and mission leaders need to work with those in the marketplace to creatively realize how they can proclaim the gospel through godly living in the workplace.

The real-life narratives that you will read in chapters 6, 7, and 8 show how followers of Christ have combined their God-given gifts, talents, and work experiences with their faith and sharing the gospel in word and deed. They include those working overseas, citizens of other countries, and those who migrated abroad as entrepreneurs to start what are now successful businesses, bringing glory to God and their communities through their talents. They include those from a wide range of professions and skills: musicians, health-care providers, engineers, agriculturalists, business entrepreneurs, English teachers, coffee gurus, and many more.

If you already understand the apologetics of faith and work, as well as disruptive business theory, you may find some of this material redundant. In this case, I encourage you to go immediately to the stories (chapters 6, 7, and 8) to enjoy reading about God at work in other cultures via the workplace. If questions arise concerning theology and theory, you can return to the apologetics in chapters 1 through 5 for the rationale for using your gifts in the marketplace.

As pastor, professor, and author J. D. Payne writes, "Kingdom citizens should glorify God by serving the nations with differing skills and advocating for social justice issues."[2] With this perspective in mind, we direct our attention to God as a sending God, our primary and secondary calling, disruption via the diffusion of innovation, and some models to emulate from a wide range of professions. The hoped-for conclusion is that all of God's people in the twenty-first century will discover and then take up their place in *missio Dei*.

Note: While all of the following stories are real, because of security considerations, many individuals and companies featured in this book have requested the use of pseudonyms for any details that could identify them.

Acknowledgments

No book is ever truly written alone, and I have found that to be true for me.

I am immensely grateful for those who helped extend my understanding of the faith and work movement, such as Albert Erisman, co-chair of the Theology of Work Project. During my time as a Pollard Research Fellowship Scholar, he encouraged me and shared some of his writings on the subject with me.

Much of my understanding of Business as Mission is because I have been privileged to associate with leaders in the movement who have challenged and mentored me, such as Mats Tunehag, Patrick Lai, Peter Shaukat, and Mike Baer among others. I also want to thank my colleagues in the BAM consulting group, IBEC Ventures, who contributed many ideas for this book as we learned together. Thanks especially to Ken Leahy, Gary Willett, Robert Johnstone, and Robert Bush.

Thanks to Crossworld global mission agency for its support of this endeavor with its policies, and Dale Losch and Jim Lapinski who were particularly encouraging.

I am also thankful for the leaders of the many businesses whose stories are told here. It has been a privilege to hear about their experiences and write about a small part of each.

This book would not be possible without the amazingly competent and encouraging Patricia Anders and her editing team at Hendrickson Publishers. This would not have happened without them, and I am most thankful.

Finally, I am grateful to my wife, Vicki, who commented on the manuscript and supported and encouraged me during the many hours of interviews, research, and writing.

Introduction

The very notion that there is such a thing as "full-time ministry" is one of the great disservices we in the West have done to the body of Christ. We have marginalized the vast majority of believers from actively participating in the Great Commission by essentially saying, "You can pray, you can give us money, and you can even take a short-term trip. But leave the full-time missionary task to us professionals."

—Dale Losch, *A Better Way: Make Disciples Wherever Life Happens*

In April 1972, my wife and I showed up at the Brazilian consulate in New York City. We had been appointed by a mid-sized mission agency, Unevangelized Fields Mission (now called Crossworld), to serve in their Amazon region of Brazil. We did not have an appointment, and I was not even an American citizen, but we needed a resident visa for their country.

The consular officer asked some simple questions: "Who are you? What would you like? Why do you want to live in Brazil? How long do you wish to stay? Do you have your passports with you?" That same afternoon, we left the consulate with a missionary visa, good for an indefinite period. With occasional updates and minimal effort, we were able to maintain permanent residency in Brazil for the next twenty-one years. Such a story is rare today, and soon it will be untrue anywhere in the world. Those days are essentially gone!

Unlike the couple of decades following the Second World War, modern-day missionaries are no longer allowed free and open access to most of the world's countries. More than two-thirds of the world's population (over four billion people) live in over seventy countries that no longer grant religious worker (missionary) visas. The field of missions, as it was once understood, is dying. In fact, the words *missionary* and even *Christianity* have become pejorative in many parts of the world. In the words of Bob Dylan's 1964 anthem, "The times they are a-changin'!"

In the final few years of my tenure as a vice president of Crossworld, two of the organization's best church-planting missionary couples living in two different countries in Asia resigned from the mission but stayed in their country! No, they were not dismissed; and no, they had not become dissatisfied with the mission. There were no family issues and no obvious reason for their decision to leave the mission while remaining where they were.

When I met with them to hear their reason, it was simple yet profound: They no longer wanted to be deceitful in countries that denied visas to missionaries. One said, "I want to look any government official in the eye who is asking if I am a missionary or if I receive funds from a church in America and say no. I just want to live as a missional professional businessperson."

What is the big deal about this word *missionary* anyway? Imagine that you live in North Africa, the Middle East, or Asia, and are unfamiliar with Christian terminology. Then imagine that you hear someone mention "missionary." Although the official definition is that it's a person sent on a mission (usually religious), a quick internet search may tell you that it also means "to persuade or convert." You may then read that a missionary is a person specifically sent to promote Christianity—and, of course, you may take issue with this if you're an adherent of another faith.

Rick Love, an expert on Islamic studies, says it this way:

> How do Muslims understand the term "missionary?" Since colonialism coincided with missionary activity throughout Asia, the Middle East, Africa and Latin America, Muslims understand a missionary to be someone who moves to their country to engage in brainwashing, and culture-changing activities that pave the way for Western ideas, immoral lifestyles, and at times foreign governments, to conquer their lands and people.[1]

Certainly, nothing could be farther from the hearts and minds of God's missional disciples.

If you continue with your curiosity and research the word *evangelism*, you will read that "evangelism refers to our human efforts of proclaiming this message to nonbelievers. . . . We proclaim the gospel with the hope that our audience responds by trusting, repenting, and following and obeying Jesus."[2] There are quick links to proselytism, propaganda, and the making of converts. Even traditional dictionaries such as Merriam-Webster suggest "militant or crusading zeal." None of those terms are useful to missional followers of Jesus today.

While you and I may use words such as *missions, missionary, Christian*, and *evangelism* in reference to our rich and meaningful tradition, the meaning of the word *mission* is different. As suggested by many theological scholars, the term describes God at work, not something done by Christians or the church. The Latin word *mitto* has its roots in the sending of Jesus by the Father and the sending of the Holy Spirit by the Father and the Son (John 17:18). In the sixteenth century, however, Jesuits changed this historical and theological meaning to describe the spreading of the Christian faith to those who were not Roman Catholics. It was then that missions came to be understood as the sending function of the church.

In chapter 1 we will look further at the meaning and historical understanding of the mission of God (*missio Dei*). For now, suffice it to say that *missio Dei* describes that which God does as an expression of his nature, love, and purpose in the world. Mission is more than just making converts and planting churches. Likewise, it is not a reference to radical theologies that provide a hermeneutic expressed in terms of liberation theology or the social gospel. It moves beyond a "giving" culture and doing good things. It moves toward solving real problems in the world while bringing the truth of the gospel to listening hearts.

The idea that social action is a partner with evangelism, one propelled by John Stott and others, recognizes the second part of the Great Commandment to love our neighbor as linked to Jesus' Great Commission command to make disciples. Mission then is more holistic, more inclusive, and more transforming than the definition of missions in the twentieth century. Theological reflection demands a more precise and accurate hermeneutic.

With all of the various historical understandings that accompany these theological and missiological terms, we have to ask ourselves if there are better ways to serve God's mission. Do we really want to perpetuate a view that it is more about the mission of the church than what God is up to in the world? Do workers in the Islamic world really want to be associated with the Christian Crusades? Do unbelievers know enough to differentiate between the pure and holy unadulterated church and individual local Christians with their particular assembly of believers? Do we want to violate the laws of countries that prohibit missionaries? Do we want people to think of us as proselytizers when Jesus simply wants humble followers?

Missiologists and cross-cultural workers remind us that reading the Scriptures is an interpretive act that is highly dependent on the Holy Spirit. Could it be that the Holy Spirit is nudging twenty-first-century believers toward a historic understanding of *missio Dei*, one less dependent on structures and ideologies and more sensitive to God's mission? In our search for a first-century Jesus-follower, could we simply live the incarnational gospel in everyday work and life?

Chapter 2 shifts from the theological to the theoretical sociological construct: of Disruptive Innovation Theory, as developed by the late Harvard business professor, Clayton Christensen. His impact on the business world has been enormous, influencing the likes of Andy Grove at Intel and Jeff Bezos at Amazon. Leaders in health care and education have also applied the principle to their industries.

Disruptive innovation describes the process by which a product or service initially takes root in simple applications at the bottom of the market and then relentlessly moves "up market," eventually displacing established competitors. It describes the progress and results of well-known disruptive innovations such as Japanese vehicles, the transistor radio, personal computers, mobile phones, and distance education. Jeff Bezos's mantra helps to provide context: "If you are going to invent, you are going to disrupt."[3]

Chapter 3 presents the proposition that Disruptive Innovation Theory describes the changes in mission today. Missional professionals are gradually challenging the professional missionary as God's modus operandi—not to replace them in all cases, but with at least equal potential in God's mission. Missionary work is being disrupted by a return to the theological *missio Dei*, to a holistic gospel, to blessing the nations instead of converting them, and to involving all believers, not just the professional clergy class. The summation of this thesis is therefore: "From professional missionaries to missional professionals."

Chapter 4 begins the process of transitioning from the theology of *missio Dei* and Disruptive Innovation Theory to the practical, starting with testimonials of those who are faithful followers of Jesus and active in the workplace today. Some of these represent the children of the "Greatest Missionary Generation,"[4] with other examples of professionals in the North American workplace who understand the intricacies of faith and work. The testimonials of understanding and praxis in North America pave the way for the cross-cultural stories of international missional professionals that follow.

Several authors and organizations have suggested that the disconnect between faith and the workplace as an unbiblical perspective has its roots in the philosophy of Plato and Aristotle. These early Greek philosophers essentially taught that work is inferior, while affirming that the highest form of work was intellectual and certainly not manual. Sadly, the church today has come to believe that a dichotomy exists between faith (spiritual, of the mind) and work (secular, of the body). Thankfully, there have been serious efforts to write and speak on the theology of work and theology of vocation to move the church toward a more biblical, integrative understanding.

This biblical understanding is based in the Genesis record, which asserts that God created man in his own image with a mandated job description to further his image in the world (Gen. 1:26–28). This is often called the Cultural Mandate or the Creation Mandate. From the beginning, all work has been considered to have dignity and everyone a calling to serve their neighbor and community in all forms of work. There is no dissonance, as Paul affirms, "Let each person lead the life that the Lord has assigned him and to which God has called him" (1 Cor. 7:17 ESV).

Martin Luther argued that God calls every believer equally to all kinds of work, with the primary calling to holiness, sanctification, and to Christ himself. Luther then argued that everyday work is imbued with spiritual significance. In *The Babylonian Captivity of the Church*, he writes, "The works of monks and priests, however holy and arduous they may be, do not differ one whit in the sight of God from the works of the rustic laborer in the field or the woman going about her household tasks. . . . All works are measured before God by faith alone."[5] Such a view of calling gives everyday work dignity and spiritual significance. This idea is founded in God being a God of work, giving humanity the task of working in the garden and beyond. In *Why Work?*, Dorothy Sayers writes, "What is the Christian understanding of work? . . . It is that work is not, primarily, a thing one does to live, but the thing one lives to do. . . . It is the medium in which he offers himself to God."[6] Likewise, R. Paul Stevens's reference to the Hebrew words *abad* (work) and *shamar* (take care) in Genesis as also meaning service to God, worship, and keeping his commandments, implies no distinction between sacred and secular work.[7] He even suggests that profession is a choice and that what is important is "vocational holiness."

In chapter 5, we will look at anecdotal stories as a way to understand the Business as Mission (BAM) movement and its quadruple bottom line (profitable business, job creation, creation care, and the making of disciples). That meaning is then interpreted in real-life narratives that help us visualize how all professions can and must be part of *missio Dei* in the twenty-first century.

Chapters 6, 7, and 8 provide multiple narratives of international missional professionals primarily in Asia and Africa, such as business owners, engineers, educators, musicians, and managers. They all have the heart of God and a passion for his great mission in the world in the workplace. These stories represent people who have proven to be profitable over time, usually ten years or more, while, by the grace of God, demonstrating a cross-cultural integration of faith and work in the marketplace of their profession and industry. Their sectors include agriculture, the arts, education, retail, real estate, manufacturing, law, medicine, consulting, and service domains.

The narratives in chapter 6 focus primarily on what has often been called "tentmaking" or "marketplace ministry" and include the stories of those who have taken jobs in impoverished and unreached areas of the world. In chapters 7 and 8, the stories are primarily about business start-ups that have scaled to reach profitability and sustainability along with clear metrics of job creation, disciple-making, and creation care. Each understands the historical transition from the professional missionary as God's epitome of service to the equally valid role of missional professionals, especially in the twenty-first century. Chapter 9 reminds us that all followers of Jesus are called to participate in the *missio Dei* from all professions, talents, and levels of skills and abilities. Standing on the shoulders of those who have gone before us, whether from the first century or the twentieth, we remember that the Great Commandment of Jesus applies to the kingdom of God "here and now" and that his Great Commission to make disciples means those today as well as "not yet." This chapter reminds us that this togetherness means working in partnership with churches, the agency world, and the academy of the colleges and universities. It involves the whole body of believers, taking the whole gospel to the whole world.

Chapter 10 concludes with a reminder that there is still a place for the professional missionary, but missional professionals living out their faith in the marketplace must no longer be neglected as key players in *missio Dei*. It is argued that the word *missionary* as a noun referring to a professional cross-cultural religious worker may have limited use in the future; for most cultures, it has served its usefulness and should be abandoned for better expressions of how God has called us to live, love, and serve. For large numbers of people, the term carries with it images of imperialism, white dominance, and a "we/them" mentality. Although we will always hold the banner of the gospel high as followers of Jesus, theologically, missiologically, and practically, it is unnecessary to use these damaging and ambiguous terms.

This chapter challenges us to see the world differently, to be involved with our God-given wiring as in the parable of the talents. All have responsibility to serve the kingdom of God with integrity, authenticity, faithfulness, and truth. If the Christians of the first century could spread the good news efficiently by living out the message of Jesus without a sending salary, a professional training program, mission agency structures, or having a professionalized term such as "missionary," certainly the same could be true in the twenty-first century.

Please note that this book is not an attempt to deconstruct (a popular term these days) the gospel or the Great Commission, or to suggest a new paradigm (another overused term). It simply wrestles with the idea of what it could look like for us to behave in a first-century manner while living in our twenty-first-century reality.

The success of twentieth-century missionary activity was unique to two millennia of Christian history, as it took advantage of conditions that for the most part no longer exist. Thus it is likely that the twenty-first century should and will be more akin to the first century, with God's people committed to God as the real sender as they live out their faith locally and go to the ends of the earth as God's image-bearers. Only as faith is integrated with life where most of life happens (at work) will any real and long-lasting change be effected in individuals and in communities. Indeed, the times they are a-changin'!

CHAPTER 1

The Age of Missions Has Ended, the Age of *Missio Dei* Has Begun

*Simply stated: mission is not first something the
church does but describes the being of God.*

—John G. Flett, *A Theology of* Missio Dei

In my recent book, following after Tom Brokaw's *The Greatest Generation*,[1] I proposed that the missionary generation that began their work after the Second World War was the "Greatest Missionary Generation." Evidence for this included the sheer size of the missionary force, the relative openness of almost every country of the world, the overwhelming response by numerous people groups, the missionaries' commitment to be obedient to the Great Commission of Jesus, and the increased affluence that gave rise to the professionalization of the missionary careers in the last half of the twentieth century. In the introduction to my book, I mentioned that historian George Marsden said that this time saw the "greatest spurt of growth in the two-century tenure of modern missions."[2] I concluded that these were the greatest missionaries in the greatest generation, and I meant it.

This is not to negate the fact that Christianity expanded to numerous regions in the Mideast, North Africa, the Mediterranean, and Asia in the five centuries after the times of the apostles, with plenty of evidence of the thriving churches which resulted. Beginning in the late fifteenth century, Roman Catholic missionaries accompanied the Spanish and Portuguese explorations. The missionary exploits of the Jesuits, Franciscans, and Dominicans are well known in India, China, and Latin America. Most missiologists propose that the modern Protestant missionary movement began

with William Carey, who founded the Baptist Missionary Society
in 1792 and sailed for China a year later. This "Father of Modern
Missions" not only responded to Jesus' call to "make disciples of all
nations," but he also demonstrated Jesus' love with various educational, translation, publishing, and practical achievements.

David Livingstone's goal was to draw attention to the evils of
the slave trade and to open the African continent to Christianity,
trade, and Western civilization. The names of Taylor, Townsend,
Judson, Carmichael, Roseveare, Moffat, Zinzendorf, Jones, Sles-
sor, and Jaffray are well known as faithful and fruitful missionaries.
There was certainly significant missionary activity in the centuries
prior to the rise of the postwar generation.

It must be noted at this point that the thesis of this book is not
to deconstruct the Great Commission, or that my discussion of innovation suggests that the call to make disciples needs an innovative
reframing. In their recent writings, Ed Stetzer and Patrick Lai use
the word *recalibrate*, which the Cambridge Dictionary defines as a
change in the way one thinks about something or, as the Free Dictionary says, to check or adjust by comparison with a standard. The
standard of the Great Commission to make disciples is unchange-
able. Perhaps, therefore, the propositions offered in this book would
be more kindly referenced as a rediscovery, refocus, or recalibrating.

Because the terms "mission," "missions," and "missionary" are
extrabiblical terms, they are often nuanced to align with a writer's
biases and perspective, my own included. All uses of them here are
intended to have biblical concepts assigned to them. Stetzer suggests that *missio Dei* is God focused and that he is on a mission to
glorify himself. It is what God is doing in the world. *Mission* is for
everyone and it's something we participate in—joining in what God
is doing, including gospel proclamation and demonstration. *Missions* focuses on the particular calling to engage in cross-culturally.
Christians are being *missional* when they join Jesus' work of serving the hurting and saving the lost.[3]

In this work, I suggest that the future is a future of the mission of God, meaning God's revelation of love for the world and
involvement in the world, something in which the church is

privileged to participate. "It is not the church which undertakes mission; it is the *missio Dei* which constitutes the church."[4] Or in the words of Christopher Wright in his review of the grand narrative of the Bible, "The primary agent of the mission of God is the people of God."[5]

God is a sending God, who first demonstrated this by sending Adam and Eve as regents on earth to fill and bless the earth. He then sent the nation of Israel to bless the nations, beginning with Abraham. Much later, he sent his Son as the servant, the "sent one" and redeemer of the world. He then sent the Holy Spirit to continue his mission in the world, rounding out the understanding of the mission of God sourced in a trinitarian God. Mission is the purpose and action of the Triune God. All of these sendings were evidence of God on mission in the world. The New Testament church of today continues to exist because of God's mission and is the result of his grand purposes.

Our understanding of God's mission must then move from something that churches do for the sake of God to understanding the very nature of God as missionary and sending. It changes "missions" in the plural, as if every church has a mission, to "mission" in the singular. Because God is one, mission is one. In 1964, British mission historian Stephen Neill wrote in his pivotal history, "The age of missions ended. The age of mission began."

In Genesis 1–2, *missio Dei* begins with *imago Dei*, which is sometimes referred to as the Creation Mandate or the Cultural Mandate. Theologians of the past thirty years have gone to great lengths to understand the meaning and to connect the *imago Dei*, the "image of God," to the *missio Dei*, the "mission of God"; the latter being a natural response to the first. The two terms should not be dichotomized; there is unity in image and mission, sacred and secular, faith and work. Every believer is made in the image of God and has received the mission of God; thus both work and mission should be central to our existence as Christians.

While it is true that we cannot achieve a complete and accurate understanding of God's nature, the idea of *imago Dei* suggests that it is possible to act on what we do know. We know that every

human represents God's divine image, is created with certain quali-
ties, characteristics, or endowments (spiritual, rational, volitional,
etc.) that make them like God. We are made in the image of a relational God (the internal workings of the Trinity and God's desire
to relate to humanity), and we most naturally live in community, as
God does. Humans are also creators, just as God is a creator; therefore, the functions of our lives are representative of God's intent.
We reflect his image (Gen. 1:26–27, 9:6; Col. 3:10; James 3:9). Old
Testament scholar J. Richard Middleton summarizes:

> What ties together this whole trajectory from Genesis 1 to the New
> Testament is the consistent biblical insight that humanity from the
> beginning, and now the church as the redeemed humanity, is both
> gifted by God with a royal status and dignity and called by God ac-
> tively to represent his kingdom in the entire range of human life, that
> is, in the very way we rule and subdue the earth. If Genesis 1 focuses
> on the gift of *imago Dei* (although not to the exclusion of the call), in
> contrast to dehumanizing ancient Near Eastern alternatives, the New
> Testament makes both gift and call crystal clear. In gratitude for God's
> gracious mercy in gifting us with salvation, the community of faith
> is called upon by Paul in Romans 12:1–2 to stop mirroring passively
> the culture in which it lives ("conformed to the world") and instead
> to mirror God in and to the culture. But a mirror, although a tradi-
> tional symbol for the *imago Dei*, is too flat to capture the full-orbed
> character of the human calling to be God's royal representatives in
> creation. A more adequate symbol might be the prism. Humanity
> created in God's image—and the church as the renewed *imago Dei*
> is called and empowered to be God's multi-sided prism in the world,
> reflecting and refracting the Creator's brilliant light into a rainbow of
> cultural activity and socio-political patterns that scintillates with the
> glory of God's presence and manifests his reign of justice.[6]

R. Paul Stevens notes that mission is what God is doing in the
world through the people of God, his image-bearers and his primary agents; it is God moving toward the world and in the world.
Believers have been included in this activity of God; thus mission is
not a human activity undertaken because of obedience to the Great
Commission.[7] To follow this logic, mission is not motivated by the

need of the world, but by God who sends his people. Missionary activity is not the work of the church and its missions committees but is more accurately the church itself at work.

To understand *missio Dei* is to understand God's desire for a relationship with humans, just as he had in mind at creation when he made man in his image (Gen. 1:26–27). The mission of God is simply an extension of the Creation Mandate: the work God did and gave humanity to do, which continues with the Great Commandment (Matt. 22:36–40) and Great Commission (Matt. 28:18–19). Combined, they form a holistic mission that includes matters of the heart and eternity as well as the whole of society; it also includes bringing righteousness, justice, and empowerment to those on the margins of society—indeed the whole of creation. It is concerned with the kingdom of God in the "here and now" as well as the "not yet." Here, Stevens quotes Réne Padilla:

> Every human need . . . may be used by the Spirit of God as a beachhead for the manifestation of his kingly power. That is why in actual practice the question of which comes first, evangelism or social action, is irrelevant. In every concrete situation the needs themselves provide the guidelines for the definition of priorities. As long as both evangelism and social responsibility are regarded as essential to mission, we need no rule of thumb to tell us which comes first and when.[8]

The many references to the kingdom of heaven and the kingdom of God in Matthew's Gospel appear equally concerned with the "here and now" (living out the kingdom of God on earth) as with the "not yet" (eternity in heaven). Stevens continues:

> The Church's mission is not to "bring in" the church, or even to extend it. The Church's mission is to "bring in" the Kingdom. In this way the people of God participate in, embody, and serve what God is accomplishing by creation, salvation, sanctification and consummation. . . . The church is God's primary agency in fulfilling his sending.[9]

If, as the Gospel of Matthew suggests, the mission of God is to bring God's kingdom to this earth as well as bring God's people to their heavenly kingdom, then such a mission must connect with an imperfect world—a world in pain, poverty, war, distress; a world without justice and the *shalom* that Jesus provides.

In the Old Testament, God affirms the ability of man to create wealth (Deut. 8:18) and to ensure justice for the needy (Ps. 140:12), and he instructs us to "give to the poor," share our food, and be "kind to the poor" (Prov. 28:27; 22:9; 19:17). Moses required Israelites to be "open-handed" and generous to those in need (Deut. 7–8; 10–11), and God promised prosperity and refreshment to the generous person (Prov. 11:25); the prophets declare the importance of taking up the cause of the fatherless, widowed, and victims of injustice; and Micah 6:8 defines what is good in terms of acting justly, loving mercy, and walking humbly with God.

Similarly, the New Testament expresses practical good news for the poor as well as spiritual good news (Luke 4:18–19). James (2:15–16), Paul (Rom. 12:13), and John (1 John 3:17) all make it clear that action is required. Caring for others is more than theological doctrine; it is praxis for the believer. It is connected to loving our neighbor. The physical and social condition of humanity is one side of the coin, which is linked to the Great Commandment of Jesus—to love our neighbor—and it is a crucial and mandatory side of *missio Dei*.

Therefore, it is incorrect to say that the church has a mission; it *is* the mission. Mission should be the full-time preoccupation of the people of God; not just delegated to a few designated missionaries. Because every believer is made in the image of God and has received the mission of God, then work *and* mission should be central to our existence as Christians. We undertake this full-time missional activity in our occupations, in our individual lives, in church community, and as it relates to the "here and now" and to the eternity of "not yet." All Christians are to be missional, on mission with God—but not all are missionaries, as the term has been used in the recent past.

The problem of the past several centuries, which was exacerbated in the last half of the twentieth century, is that the church has configured itself into a bifurcated society: that is, believers are either laity or clergy. In addition, Christians have been conditioned to see themselves as living their sacred lives separate from their secular lives. This version of ancient Gnosticism has done immeasurable damage to the everyday believer's understanding of *missio Dei*. A 2014 survey by LeTourneau University's Center for Faith and Work revealed that 70 percent of churched people are unsure how their work serves God, and 78 percent say their work is less valuable than a pastor's.

In the twenty-first century, we are a long way from the ancient Hebrew meaning of the word *avodah* (ah-vod-ah), which is translated in the English Bible to mean work and worship. Its meaning is equally "service," "worship," and "common labor." In its simplest explanation, we can say that work is worship and that we need to connect with the mission of God in all we are and in all we do. Patrick Lai uses the term "workship" as the title of his 2021 book.[10] Dallas Willard explains this distinction as follows:

> There truly is no division between sacred and secular except what we have created. And that is why the division of the legitimate roles and functions of human life into the sacred and secular does incalculable damage to our individual lives and the cause of Christ. Holy people must stop going into "church work" as their natural course of action and take up holy orders in farming, industry, law, education, banking and journalism with the same zeal previously given to evangelism or to pastoral and missionary work.[11]

Missiologists of the past century taught that all mission is essentially obedience to God's commands, which resulted in the massive missionary movements of the twentieth century. However, if one looks at mission as being God's endeavor, we will see ourselves as going with him into the world. It is first and foremost his work to make disciples, rather than the ecclesiastical framework of today's missionary efforts, which focus on getting people into the church and on church planting, the mantra of nearly every missionary agency today. From the viewpoint of the rest of the world, this is proselytism and conversion and hardly what the term *missio Dei* has in mind.

Therefore, it may be fair to suggest that the theology and structures of our Western churches today are not truly missional. They are shaped by the tradition and legacy of Christendom, and thus these structures and traditions mitigate an optimum potential of being relevant in the world. How long has it been since you saw a local church intentionally commission public school teachers, university graduates, or professional people in front of the entire church as true missional workers in the marketplace? For most of us, the answer is never. Why not?

H. A. Snyder differentiates between church people and kingdom people:

> Kingdom people seek first the kingdom of God and its justice; church people often put church work above concerns of justice, mercy and truth. Church people think about how to get people into the church. Church people worry that the world might change the church; kingdom people work to see the church change the world.[12]

In short, God's goal is that the whole people of God engage the whole mission of God in the whole world.

My purpose here is not to be critical or insensitive of the strong emphasis on the proclamation dimension of missionary activity in the last century, but rather to provide an increased focus on the incarnational or demonstration dimension. I have the greatest respect for the missionary efforts and successes of the twentieth century, which certainly include the demonstration dimension in practice, although less so in its theology. However, an understanding of *missio Dei* certainly would lead us to the conclusion that Jesus equally lived and taught the good news. Today, that means a 24/7 approach to the gospel. The cultural mandate suggests we work in such a way as to be image-bearers of God in the world (Gen. 1–2). Life was not meant to exist in a spiritual bubble; we are to be creative in our work as we bring dignity to ourselves and others, being prosperous in our work in ways that brings glory to God.

At risk of appearing reductionistic, a look at this succinctly in terms of Jesus' "commands" might provide perspective.

> "Thou shalt *love the Lord thy God* with all thy heart, and with all thy soul, and with all thy mind. This is the first and great commandment."
> (Matt. 22:37–38 KJV; italics mine)

To love God as described in this and other passages of Scripture brings us to a deep relationship with the creator of the universe and releases us as co-creators. It requires a grand love affair, so that we are so enraptured with him that our world centers in all respects with his desires, beauty, perspectives, and passion. In other words, to understand the mission of God as revealed from Genesis to Revelation is to be a committed agent of his mission, which started with each of us as a representative, or image, of God in the world. What follows is a renewed understanding of the Creation Mandate:

> "And the second is like unto it, '*Thou shalt love thy neighbor* as thyself.' On these two commandments hang all the law and the prophets." (Matt. 22:39–40 KJV; italics mine)

To love our neighbor asks the question of what love means in a local and worldwide sense. What does love look like when the single parent across the street is struggling? What does it mean if we live in a dysfunctional family? How about loving gay colleagues at our workplace? What does it look like in a world of poverty, unemployment, and racial injustice? What does love look like when unjust social structures and systems strip the dignity from men and women? What about the human trafficking industry that plagues our world, or when endemic racism is alive and well? As Martin Luther stated, "A gospel that does not address the issues of the day is not the gospel at all."

Certainly, *missio Dei* in perspective and praxis for individuals and the church suggests a demonstration of love in the context of the human condition of the day. As vice-regents over both natural and human resources, Christians have a social responsibility; and, as John Stott suggests, "not primarily in order to give the gospel visibility or a credibility it would otherwise lack, but rather simple uncomplicated compassion. Love has no need to justify itself. It merely expresses itself in service wherever it sees need."[13] Stott continues by saying that both the Great Commandments and the Great Commission include compassion and social action as well as evangelistic responsibility. They all belong together as partners in the mission of God.

Certainly, Jesus preached, proclaiming the good news of the kingdom of God and teaching about the coming and the nature of the kingdom, how to enter it and how it would spread. But he served in deed as well as in word, and it would be impossible in the ministry of Jesus to separate his works from his words. He fed hungry mouths and washed dirty feet, he healed the sick, comforted the sad and even restored the dead to life. [14]

In Matthew 28:19, Jesus gave us the Great Commission when he said, "Go and *make disciples of all nations*" (italics mine). To make disciples of all nations highlights the *missio Dei* as discussed earlier in this chapter. A search for understanding leads us to the fact that most people do not worship God, and that it is the passion of God himself to solve the problem. God's way of solving the problem is that his image-bearers are to live like Jesus by loving and serving and as "little Christs," drawing people to the Savior of the world. David Bosch states, "Mission is not primarily an activity of the church, but an attribute of God. God is a missionary God."[15] And Jürgen Moltmann says, "It is not the church that has a mission of salvation to fulfill in the world; it is the mission of the Son and the Spirit through the Father that includes the church."[16]

Darrell Guder summarizes these terms in his succinct manner:

> We have come to see that mission is not merely an activity of the church. Rather, mission is the result of God's initiative, rooted in God's purposes to restore and heal creation. "Mission" means "sending," and it is the central biblical theme describing the purpose of God's action in human history. . . . The biblical message is more radical, more inclusive, more transforming than we have allowed it to be. . . . The church of Jesus Christ is not the purpose or goal of the gospel, but rather its instrument and witness. . . . God's mission is calling and sending us, the church of Jesus Christ, to be a missionary church in our own societies, in the cultures in which we find ourselves.[17]

By definition, the term "missions" suggests propagating the Christian faith with evangelistic techniques and planting churches. The proposition behind this book is not about reforming missions but about *missio Dei*. It does not just represent another missionary methodology; it represents *missio Dei* in the context of God the Creator. Our work is a worshipful expression of our sacred calling to live a holy life, serve others, and bring others to do the same. Although it sounds simplistic, most believers in the early church were not called to be church planters or missionaries—both of which imply a missionary order, structure, and system. All were called to be witnesses of the good news. Bob Roberts is clear on this point: "Faith as a program is intrusive. . . . Faith as a lifestyle and principles to live by is powerful and engaging." He says that we make a mistake when we start with ecclesiology. "We should start with Christology. . . . If you focus on mission, churches will follow, but if you focus on churches, mission often gets lost."[18] Surely, wherever we go, we do not go to proselytize or to plant Christianity. We go to live and love like Jesus; and through our relationships as God's image-bearers, bring others to do the same. We are Jesus-followers, image-bearers of the king—not missionaries. Some practitioners in this realm have entered their unreached, impoverished world with a view to "blessing the community" in the spirit of God's commission to Abram in Genesis 12:3. In fact, it is a matter of integrity, authenticity, and credibility that more and more missionaries no longer want to be a called "missionaries."[19]

In his book *Glocalization: How Followers of Jesus Engage a Flat World*, Roberts dares to provide chapter titles such as "It's All about the Kingdom, Not Missions," "Get Over Your Call to Preach," and "Serve Not to Convert but Because You Have Been Converted." He writes, "Sadly, what we have done to 'missions' is to make it only the gospel of proclamation regarding accepting Jesus as Savior." He reminds us that it is much more than that.[20] Quoting Ray Bakke, he says, "You don't start by planting churches. You plant ministry that 'scratches where people itch' in the name of Jesus."[21] Is that not exactly what Jesus did? He started where the person was—in sickness, in hunger, with theological questions, with the need or issue of the moment. Roberts believes that "for us to engage the world and be effective, we are going to have to hold on to what we know is the truth and yet do it in a different way. The gospel is the good news of Christ bringing the kingdom that transforms us personally—giving us a new way to live here and now, and a new home in the future as well."[22]

Is it possible to return to a first-century understanding? If we did, then we would see our lives centered practically around our work that God ordained. Out of our work emerge relationships and opportunities to demonstrate who God is and proclaim the good news (1 Thess. 2:8–9). As in the first century, Christians will just "go" and bring blessing to individuals and nations, serving as in the model of Jesus, and making disciples through relationships wherever life happens. Churches will be the inevitable result (Matt. 16:18), not the product of a church-planting strategy.[23]

Although such a model is not unique to the first century, it is embodied in the worldwide missional endeavor of the Moravian church, which began in the first half of the eighteenth century. As early as 1732, they began sending out missionaries; and over the years, developed a far-flung mission movement that lives on today in Moravian churches, schools, and communities in Europe, the Caribbean, Central America, North America, South America, Nepal, and Africa. They are of interest here because they were not only the first large-scale Protestant missionary movement, but they were also the first in modern times to send non-ordained lay people to the missions field rather than professional clergymen. Their first missionaries were a potter and a carpenter sent to the Caribbean Island of St. Thomas.

Perhaps the best-known vestiges of Moravian missions are Bethlehem, Pennsylvania, and the country of Suriname in South America, where the country today is nearly 50 percent Christian, largely due to Moravian missions. The leader of the initial 1758 efforts, Jonas Paul Weis, states, "Demonstration is as important as proclamation in the Christian World Mission." Businesspeople practiced their "faith active in love" in the marketplace where daily affairs were lived out. The example of the tentmaking missionary, the apostle Paul, was their model for identifying with the community through economic activities.

The Basel Mission followed a similar missionary-commerce philosophy as both entities considered business as not just a strategy but the mission itself. William Danker quotes an 1854 missionary letter that provides further understanding of the integration of faith and work:

> A mission . . . through the power of example, a mission of revealing Christianity in practical life situations, a mission doing everything possible to make godliness visible, a mission that shows Christianity to have promise not only for the life to come but also for this life.[24]

Long-time mission agency leader and president of Peace Catalyst International, Rick Love, prefers to use the term "gospel planting" as more biblically accurate. He asserts that nowhere does the New Testament imply that we are to plant a church. He suggests that the term "church planting" implies that we bring the church from the outside. He recommends an examination of all vehicles of communication, because so many of our cherished terms are stumbling blocks to followers of other religions—such as "Christian," "missions," "missionary," and "church planting" (Appendix A provides suggestions for "New Terms" for Jesus followers of the twenty-first century).

We noted earlier that God in his providence set in motion various "sendings," beginning with the creation of humans. One of those "sendings," subsequent to the sending of the Holy Spirit, was the scattering of Jesus' followers after the stoning of Stephen: "On that day a great persecution broke out against the church in Jerusalem, and all except the apostles were scattered throughout Judea and Samaria" (Acts 8:1). As they were going (i.e., living their lives at work and in community), they were instructed to "make disciples of all nations" (Matt. 28:19). Their work was an opportunity for spiritual living and making disciples.

The book of Acts also indicates various accounts of believers who migrated up the eastern seaboard of the Mediterranean, throughout Asia Minor (modern-day Turkey), to the Mediterranean islands and over into what is now the country of Greece. They "preached the word wherever they went" (Acts 8:4). The word *preach* means that as common Jewish or Gentile Christians, they were simply announcing the good news wherever they went: in their home, in the synagogue, in the marketplace, on their jobs.

It is improbable that most of these were "ordained" to preach or commissioned as missionaries. They were Christians scattered by persecution who communicated to others the love and teaching of Jesus with their lifestyle and conversation. They were so successful that by the time Paul and Silas arrived in Thessalonica, people were realizing that Christians were causing "trouble all over the world" (Acts 17:6).

The Great Commandment of Jesus is one aspect that is linked to loving our neighbors in their physical and social condition. The Great Commission aspect relates to the spiritual hopelessness of the majority in the world. The most ambitious of statistics suggest that only one-third of the world's population are followers of Jesus and that upwards of three billion people are considered unreached—41 percent of the world's population.[25] The goal is that more and more of these will become disciples of Jesus and worshipers of the true God of the universe. As believers in an increasingly hurting world, where are we in our quest to understand the mission of God in the twenty-first century? *Missio Dei* describes that which God does as an expression of his nature, love, and purpose in the world, in the establishing of his kingdom. Mission is more than just making converts and planting churches. It moves beyond the giving culture of charity and aid, as good as this is. It is holistic in every way and moves toward solving real problems in the world, transforming lives into kingdom communities, as well as preparing them for an eternity with Jesus. The idea that social action is a partner with evangelism recognizes the Great Commandment to love our neighbor as linked to the Great Commission to make disciples. Mission then is more holistic, more inclusive, and more transforming than the definition of "missions" of the past two centuries. The *missio Dei*, as God intended it, will bring the kingdom of God to earth today as well as peace for all eternity living with Jesus.

Patrick Lai quotes Os Hillman in his study on work in the Gospels, pointing out:

> Of Jesus' 132 public appearances in the New Testament, 122 were in the workplace. Of the 52 parables Jesus told, 45 had a workplace

context. Jesus never addressed the sacred and secular divide because such a divide never existed in Jewish thinking. The Jews understood that everything they did in work and in the synagogue was to be done to God's glory. This is why quality is so important to Jewish workers. They are not working solely for themselves, but also as worship to God.[26]

Work and worship occur most naturally in everyday life. From Genesis to Revelation, it is what God intended. The mission of God suggests that everyone should live out God's mission in every aspect of life—all the time, and in every way and in every place.

In summary, *missio Dei* is not the church sending; it is God sending. It is not just loving God; it is loving all humanity. It is not only spiritual and eternal; it is physical and temporal. It is not just the salvation of the soul; it is transformation of social conditions. It is not just aid to the poor; it is dignity and empowerment. It is not unidimensional; it is holistic.

Andrew Kirk affirms that "the church is by nature missionary to the extent that if it ceases to be missionary, it has not just failed in one of its tasks, it has ceased being Church."[27] The church is needed in solving injustices and providing innovative solutions that lead to human flourishing in societies. Clark G. Fobes writes,

> When we recover the biblical dignity of work in the *imago Dei*, we will come to see the biblical value of work in the *missio Dei*. As we fulfill our duties as priests made in God's image, keeping and guarding God's presence, extending the boundaries of Eden, and multiplying and filling the earth, we will fulfill our mission until all the earth is filled with worshipers, rejoicing under God's reign in the restored New Heavens and Earth.[28]

In 1964, British mission historian Stephen Neill wrote in his pivotal history, "The age of missions ended. The age of mission began.[29]

CHAPTER 2

Disruptive Innovation
Theory Understood

*The theory goes that a smaller company with fewer
resources can unseat an established, successful business
by targeting segments of the market that have been
neglected by the incumbent, typically because it is
focusing on more profitable areas. As the larger business
concentrates on improving products and services for its
most demanding customers, the small company is gaining
a foothold at the bottom end of the market or tapping
a new market the incumbent had failed to notice.*

—Rosamond Hutt, World Economic Forum

We have established that *missio Dei* provides a unique, albeit biblically historic, look at the mission industry, and thus helps to align
it more closely with God's intent as demonstrated in the Scriptures.
It may be useful to suggest a modern business theory as a means
of understanding our proposed shift in perspective, while maintaining that linking faith with work, or mission with business, is
fundamentally a return to biblical theology and praxis. Scientific
historian Thomas Kuhn popularized the term "paradigm" when
he used it to describe scientific shifts from one model or pattern of
thinking to another. A paradigm is a distinct set of concepts, theories, postulates, and so on, that provide a pattern for thinking about
a subject. It became a useful term for thinking of change.

As already mentioned, disruptive innovation, a term coined
by Harvard University professor Clayton Christensen in 1995, describes a process by which a product or service initially takes root
in simple applications at the bottom of a market before relentlessly
moving "up market," eventually displacing established competitors.

The innovation creates a new market and value network. Christensen has applied this principle to business, health care, education, and technology, providing enormous insight into what companies and organizations need to do to move off the sidelines and into the top tier of their field.

Christensen's ideas have gained wide acceptance, having been applied in business schools as both an analytical tool and a way of thinking. Christensen asserts that if we rely on data (which looks to the past) for decision-making, then we are not going to be ready for the future or prepared for change. He suggests that the way to look into the future (because there is no data) is to develop theories. In the business world, as in the world of education as well as mission, we need to learn "how" to think and rely less on tradition and "what" to think. What interests us for this proposition is this: What are the implications for *missio Dei* and the idea that every believer is at work in that mission of God?

But first, let's look at a few examples of disruptive innovation in the commercial world.

Jeff Bezos did not just improve book sales when he started Amazon. He disrupted everything—networking and delivery systems, and then brought in other products to become the world's largest online shopping retailer. His latest "disruptive" talk concerned drone deliveries and outer space warehouses. His mantra is: "If you are going to invent, you are going to disrupt."

Looking back a few decades, some of us can remember the advent of the transistor radio. People first thought of them as poor-quality junk, but they met a need not yet recognized: they were portable, and teenagers could easily take them to the beach or to parties. Gradually the sound improved, and the product totally disrupted and made redundant the old cabinet radios.

I remember when a visitor showed up at our school in Brazil in the early 1970s with a portable electronic calculator. Our bookkeeper was using a manual adding machine—which did the job but was big, clumsy, slow, and noisy. I took a leap and asked to purchase this calculator from the visitor before he left the country. I paid $180.00 for what today can be bought in Walmart for

$5.99. Portable calculators were disruptive, because they didn't just improve on existing technology; they disrupted it by introducing simplicity, convenience, accessibility, and eventually affordability.

Disruptive Innovation Defined and Applied

Disruptive Innovation Principles and Features	Application 21st-century Business/Technology Examples	Application 21st-century Missiology Example
Incumbent industry tends to neglect other market segments; they focus on improving existing products; change requires disruption.	• Mainframes were expensive and served only the elite. • Detroit automakers dominated the auto industry. • New products developed for use in different ways.	Mission industry is costly and complicated, inconvenient, and dominant; the tradition is that God uses professionally trained gospel stewards, not the everyday person.
Disruptive innovation originates in low-end or in a new-market foothold; it then starts to disrupt existing markets.	• Dominant mainframe computers were disrupted by home computers. • Toyota and other Japanese cars disrupted the Detroit industry.	A new market is the marketplace person; business owner/manager or professional who is missional while on the job and independent of an organization and structure.
Provides a "Proof of Concept" and creates a new market and value network.	• New computer market in homes and schools creates a new set of customers. • Japanese cars were cheaper and eventually better.	New market is the everyday believer with his/her skill and profession; new missional customers as purveyors of the gospel are proving the concept.
Tends to provide a different set of values; therefore, it is a new business model.	• New value that everyone needs a computer; ease of use. • Auto affordability, quality, convenience, and choices; economy cars.	Simplicity, convenience, accessibility, affordability means every believer can get involved. It is a new model of "missions."

Disruptive Innovation Principles and Features	Application 21st-century Business/Technology Examples	Application 21st-century Missiology Example
Normal business environment does not allow for the pursuit of disruptive innovators; therefore, disruption is led by outsiders.	• Difficult for historical businesses like IBM and GM to accommodate innovation. • Bias against the Japanese outsiders.	Church defines missions as run by the church and/or agency with their rules of operation; outsiders must rise to the occasion, with market workers with innovative faith-work theory.
Initially disruptive innovation is considered inferior.	• Early desktops were considered inferior. • Everything Japanese was considered inferior.	Church hierarchy does not recognize *missio Dei* as given to individuals; only to the "church"; Business as Mission (missional professionals) is considered inferior and not biblical by many in the church hierarchy.
Displaces established leading market forms and products.	• "A computer in every home" and affordable. • Japanese cars went from a disruption to quality and preferred autos.	Will twenty-first-century, kingdom-minded, everyday believers displace agency-driven missions and be more like the first century AD?
"Disruptive innovation" term defined and analyzed by Clayton Christensen, beginning in 1995.	• Think radios, computers, automobiles, education, telephones, marketing, and health care.	"Business as Mission" term coined in 1999 and developed over next ten years by Lausanne committee (Mats Tunehag, Jo Plummer, Mike Baer, Craig Shugart, and others).

Perhaps one of the best examples of disruptive innovation is the development of the personal computer, when the big mainframes ruled the day in the 1950s and '60s. Even the chairman of IBM, Thomas Watson, is famously quoted: "I think there is a world market for maybe five computers." The personal computer formed a niche market that appeared unattractive and inconsequential at first but eventually proved their concept and the new product completely redefined the computing industry.

Mobile phones are the same story. The idea is that while the historic technology industry concentrated on improving their product, innovative disruptors focused on the bottom end of the market, tapping into customers with new and different needs. They created new demand and found overlooked customers. Think how Blockbuster was disrupted by the likes of Netflix.

The Diffusion of Innovation Theory developed by E. M. Rogers in 1962 helps to understand how the adoption of new ideas takes place, and it provides additional theory to complement Disruptive Innovation Theory.[1] Regarding our *missio Dei* discussion, the case could be made that it is not new at all, but simply a rediscovery of biblical truth. Nevertheless, one could still consider change in this regard to be innovation because of the length of time the church has been immersed in modern missions.

The Diffusion of Innovation Theory helps us understand the "up market" move of innovation change in consumer products, but it may also be helpful in explaining how the mission of God may be functioning in the twenty-first century.

1. *Innovators.* These are people who want to be the first to try the innovation. They are venturesome and interested in new ideas. These people are willing to take risks and are often the first to develop new ideas. Very little, if anything, needs to be done to appeal to this population.

2. *Early Adopters.* These are people who represent opinion leaders. They enjoy leadership roles and embrace change opportunities. They are already aware of the need to change and so are comfortable adopting new ideas. Strategies to appeal to this population include how-to manuals and information sheets on implementation. They do not need information to convince them to change.

3. *Early Majority.* These people are rarely leaders, but they do adopt new ideas before the average person. That said, they typically need to see evidence that the innovation works before they are willing to adopt it. Strategies to appeal to

this population include success stories and evidence of the innovation's effectiveness.

4. *Late Majority.* These people are skeptical of change and will only adopt an innovation after it has been tried by the majority. Strategies to appeal to this population include information on how many other people have tried the innovation and have adopted it successfully.

5. *Laggards.* These people are bound by tradition and very conservative. They are skeptical of change and are the hardest group to bring on board. Strategies to appeal to this population include statistics, fear appeals, and pressure from people in the other adopter groups.[2]

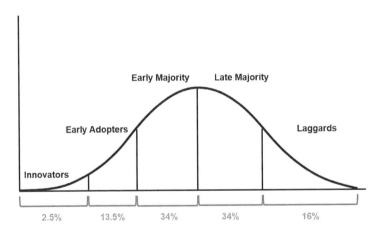

Disruptive innovation[3] is a theory that has been useful in the explanation of change in the twentieth century, and quite likely will be predictive of the change that has begun in the world of missions, as we forge toward the future of "mission" being descriptive of God at work and including all of us as children of God. In a manner somewhat analogous to how changes in computers, education, and electronics developed from the bottom of the market, could it be that change is beginning at the bottom of the "body of Christ" (the nonclergy) and will disrupt everything?

Foreign and church aid to the needy is an example of the importance of disruption. The need to move from aid to trade provides an understanding of how Disruptive Innovation Theory can be applied. While aid is an important response for Bible believers when there is a crisis, disaster, or similar unique need, it has a history of continuing for far too long, resulting in the creation of dependency and loss of dignity in many situations, both in the developed and the developing world. There are many examples across cultures of how international churches, government, and private aid has suffocated dignity and the successful growth of job-creating businesses.[4]

What if we combined the historic meaning of *missio Dei* with disruptive innovation and applied it to the future of God's grand purposes in the world? Could it be that such a revolutionary innovation has already begun in the world of mission? Could it be that the coming decades may be described as so disruptive, to a reformative extent, that coming generations will expect the gospel to thrive because of the integration of faith with the marketplace, with mission linked with every believer and his/her profession? As Gea Gort suggests, "Five hundred years ago we had a Reformation of dogma. Now we have a reformation of mission."[5]

The net result of the early adopters' (people in the marketplace) awareness to the necessity of change is that they and others like them will feel less disenfranchised from God's work in the world. It is well established that marketplace people feel like second-class citizens in their churches; Disruptive Innovation Theory helps us understand the importance of a robust theology of work driving this up-market change.[6] As more and more people in business see the intrinsic value of their work to God's kingdom, that kingdom will grow, and the church will see the connection between its pastor and the workplace of the congregants (Eph. 4:12). God's *shalom* will descend on all of life and the "kingdom [will] come on earth as in heaven" (Matt. 6:10).

CHAPTER 3

Missions Disrupted, *Missio Dei* Exalted

The illiterate of the twenty-first century will not
be those who cannot read and write, but those
who cannot learn, unlearn, and relearn.

—Alvin Toffler

Is it possible for the consideration of *missio Dei* and the theory of disruptive innovation to become the formative apologetic for missional professionals? And if so, disruptive of what? Of whom? Business as Mission spokesperson Mats Tunehag likens kingdom business today to a twenty-first century reformation. The Protestant Reformation was disruptive because it focused Jesus' followers on simpler, easier forms of faith—reading their own Scriptures, the priesthood of individual believers and faith over works as the way of salvation, among other things.

Missional organizations that have started up in the past fifteen years tend to stress an integration of spiritual, social, and economic development in an eclectic fashion. Mission statements include marketplace terminology and praxis that meet physical and spiritual needs, business wisdom, and biblical discipleship. The outcomes include kingdom impact, profitable businesses, entrepreneurial mindsets, and community transformation.

All of this is disruptive! It disrupts the traditional mission industry. It disrupts the pure social enterprise sector. It is disruptive of traditional business. It is disruptive of church missions. It disrupts the sacred-secular divide. Disruptive innovation has been described as insanely creative, rule-breaking, and leading to entrepreneurial change.

Could God's mission, a part of which constitutes the church with all of its programs and structure, and individuals with all of their skills, professions, and abilities change the world in the way that mini mills disrupted the integrative steel industry? Like Toyota disrupted the Detroit auto industry? Like personal computers challenged the mainframes and won? Like online education is disrupting traditional universities? Like retail medical clinics are disrupting traditional doctor's offices?

In the following quote, Tom Bassford, CEO of *SATTalks*, describes "prophetic imagination," a concept somewhat aligned with disruptive innovation:

> Change comes in a thousand different ways but never in a hurry or by unanimous consent. That may be one of the most valuable lessons I've learned over the past 15 years. I used to think the best strategy for effecting change was through critical mass; get more and more people to buy-in to an idea and change will follow. The problem is, critical mass is generally content with the status quo, no matter how much they complain and dream otherwise. It's as true of the church as it is of business, politics or any other endeavor; the middle of the bell curve, with all its critical mass, will never champion radical change.
>
> What I have seen, both historically and in my own experience, is that most paradigm shifts come not from critical mass but from *critical yeast*. They come from individuals with an idea that is "too intellectual," "too idealistic," or just "too complicated" for the critical mass. But that doesn't matter to *critical yeast*—they just plug away, usually in isolation, through countless iterations of trial and error on their way to what Walter Brueggemann called "futures that are genuinely new and not derived."
>
> When it comes to the idea of church missions and sustainable solutions the answers we seek are not derived from the safe and co-opted practices of traditional church missions. Those practices have served a legitimate purpose and must now learn to serve an even higher purpose. Unfortunately, most churches will be content to simply mend and fund their mission efforts as part of their "brand management" in order to demonstrate that they are a caring church and keep their market share of a seeker-sensitive population demanding positive volunteer experiences.[1]

Bassford is talking about disruptive innovation with the metaphor of yeast! I distinctly remember one of the examples Clayton Christensen provides. The RCA radio had a prominent place in our home, just as it did in young Christensen's. But about sixty years ago, the Sony transistor radio began to peck away at the bottom of the radio market. It was inferior and could not compete with the quality performance of my parents' RCA, so it was rightfully ignored. However, Sony began to redefine the standard of performance by providing a product that was readily available and portable. All of a sudden, I could listen to Elvis and classic country music without my parents' knowledge and take the radio wherever I wanted. What started out as an inferior product quickly improved and became industry standard from the bottom up.

Could disruptive innovation be describing the future of God at work in the world? Could challenging historical categories and providing an integrated solution to spiritual, social, economic, and political problems be described as missional disruptive innovation? Could this really be a demonstration of the kingdom of God "here and now" as Jesus said?

Today, marketplace Christians are at the margins of the dominating church and mission agency institutions. I have heard Fortune 500 executives who are Christian tell me so; I have had small business owners say it; and I have had professional sports athletes tell me their role is to give to the cause and pray for outcomes. I believe that the common believer in the pews of our churches views their church community in terms of a sociological spiritual hierarchy with pastors and missionaries at the top of the pyramid. These people feel they have nothing to offer, since they have been conditioned to look at the mission of God as something that has been outsourced to the professional minister and missionary. I once knew a business owner in a major city who had a firm with dozens of employees. He was very involved in a local church, but he told me over breakfast one morning, "I don't see that I have anything to offer the world of missions." Imagine!

Appendix B (What Do You Have to Offer?) constitutes a response to any believer living and working in the business community who is tempted to think they have nothing to offer, or that they're not prepared for kingdom living on the job. The practical things they have learned are directly applicable to an integrated kingdom life. "Whatever you do, do it all for the glory of God" (1 Cor. 10:31).

Similarly, it is common for "undercover missionaries" in limited access countries to ask tentmaker or BAM workers when they have time for ministry. However, workers who understand *missio Dei* and how the gospel spread in the first century and beyond respond by saying, "My work is my ministry." They are not inhibited by the sacred-secular divide mentality that is endemic with most evangelical believers today.

This history of elevating the ministry industry (the sacred) over everyday work (the secular) in other domains demonstrates ignorance toward a theology of work and vocation, further evidence that our Greek heritage is still with us. This dualism has become a gigantic barrier to living a holistic, integrated life of integrity in our generation. The Great Commission has been separated from the Great Commandment, so that loving our neighbor is not united in focus with making disciples. We are a long way from God's intent as represented by *missio Dei*.

Throughout the centuries, Greek influence continued to be felt in the church even though many church leaders fought against it. The Benedictine *ora et labora*, meaning "pray and work," reminds us of the dignity of work maintained by this 1,500-year-old order. Luther, Calvin, and other Reformers wrestled with the doctrine of the priesthood of the believers as an attempt at challenging the sacred-secular dichotomy to bring orthopraxy in line with biblical orthodoxy.

Ken Eldred states that the sacred-secular dualism is so prevalent in the church that it leaves the majority of the body of Christ marginalized from *missio Dei*, and so they lack joy and fulfillment in their daily work.[2] Twentieth-century preacher and author A. W. Tozer reflects that the "sacred-secular antithesis has no foundation in the New Testament." In *The Pursuit of God*, Tozer remarks:

The layman never need think of his humbler task as being inferior to that of his master. Let every man abide in the calling wherein he is called, and his work will be as sacred as the work of the ministry. It is not what a man does that determines whether his work is sacred, it is why he does it.[3]

To be sure, the work of church apostles, prophets, evangelists, pastors, and teachers is an important one for the "equipping of the saints for works of service" (Eph 4:12). Perhaps that is the reason the apostles stayed in Jerusalem in Acts 8, while everyone else seemed to scatter throughout the Mediterranean world. The majority left Jerusalem and lived with their trade, while they "preached Jesus." And we know the amazing results! Could this first-century model be the model of the twenty-first century? "And whatever you do, whether word or deed, do it all in the name of the Lord Jesus" (Col. 3:17).

The church of the twentieth century (with some notable exceptions) greatly exacerbated the sacred-secular divide with its focus on the kingdom of God as "not yet" on evangelistic rescue, and by the polarization of social issues as distinct from fundamentalism. Thankfully, by the end of the century, several voices (such as John Stott, R. Paul Stevens, Os Guinness, Dale Losch, Tim Keller, and Darrow Miller) began to recover evangelical thought, alternatively providing a kingdom theology focusing on the "here and now" being lived out in our lives, in addition to the "not yet."

The aberration of the gospel based on this sacred-secular divide suggests that the mission of God requires a special call and training. Any challenge to the prevailing approach is seen as taking an end-run around the system of outsourcing the missionary task to the agency. Numerous questions and reactions often surface. Is living out my faith in the marketplace a calling rooted in the church? Do marketplace workers have Bible and cross-cultural training? Who is responsible for accountability? These are useful questions to be sure, but not to the exclusion of acknowledging that of "the whole church taking the whole gospel to the whole world" as expressed by John Stott and the Lausanne Committee.

The root of our English word *vocation* is the Latin verb *voca*, which means "to call." The historic understanding of calling includes every type of work. For the believer, the primary calling is to be called to someone (God) not something (work)—which is a secondary calling. Secondary callings matter, but only because of our primary calling to follow God in all his ways; this understanding of calling gives everyday work dignity and spiritual significance. As stated in Ephesians 2:10, "We are God's handiwork, created in Christ Jesus to do good works, which God prepared in advance for us to do."

This statement by the Puritan leader William Perkins is similar to many other Protestant Reformers: "The action of a shepherd in keeping sheep, performed as I have said in his kind, is as good a work before God as is the action of a judge in giving sentence, or of a magistrate in ruling, or a minister in preaching."[4] For the Christian, work is a calling, no matter what it is; we work because it glorifies God.

The English poet Percy Bysshe Shelley suggests that "we are all Greeks" in that we inherited the gnostic view with a dualistic distinction between an imperfect material world and a higher spiritual one. There is hardly an author on this subject who has not acknowledged the sacred-secular divide as the most detrimental obstacle to understanding how people who work in the marketplace are just as integral to disciple-making and church planting as professional clergy.

Martin Luther reminds us that our primary calling is to holiness and to Christ himself. In everyday work and profession our calling is to sanctification and service:

> Monastic vows rest on the false assumption that there is a special calling, a vocation, to which superior Christians are invited to observe the counsels of perfection while ordinary Christians fulfil only the commands; but there simply is no special religious vocation since the call of God comes to each at the common tasks.[5]

Such a view of calling gives everyday work a dignity and spiritual significance. It is sourced in God being a God of work and giving humanity the task of working in the garden and beyond. Gene

Veith states that "the priesthood of believers did not make everyone into church workers, rather it turned every kind of work into a sacred calling."[6] Likewise, R. Paul Stevens's reference to the Hebrew words *abad* ("work") and *shamar* ("take care") in Genesis as also meaning service to God, worship, and keeping his commandments implies no distinction between sacred and secular work. He even suggests that profession is a choice and that what is important is "vocational holiness."[7]

As such, *missio Dei*, and its ancillary implications in our times, is disruptive in the following ways:

1. It provides a theological basis and practical evidence that the faith-work movement is ordained as descriptive of God's mission—integrating faith with the place of activity and in the meaningful structures of the culture. Just as Jesus utilized the marketplace and parables related to the "known" to discuss esoteric spiritual truth, so also does mission.

2. Business and the marketplace are the modern means ordained by God to address the issue of poverty. Business is the only institution that creates wealth through job creation, and it gives dignity, honor, and empowerment to individuals, families, and communities. Jesus gave the Great Commandment, requiring believers to love God and love their neighbor. Today, loving our neighbors may mean creating jobs for them, which can be seen as the modern equivalent of feeding the five thousand or healing lepers.

3. Most Christians of the twentieth century became accustomed to outsourcing missional work to professional clergy. Faith-work integration, marketplace mission, Business as Mission, and related forms are a huge change to this mindset. It is disruptive by offering simplicity, accessibility, and convenience as a new model of living and sharing our faith. It suggests that the incarnation and proclamation of Jesus' gospel is the work of all believers in the workplace, not just the clergy or those paid to be missional with their faith.

4. Mission is innovative by being cost effective. It is not contingent on charity, which has the tendency to attract corruption and destabilization. It addresses issues of declining mission funding and penetrates the thoughts and actions of the millennial generation. Note authors such as Robert Lupton[8] and Steve Corbett and Brian Fikkert,[9] who among others describe toxic charity, helping that hurts, and dead aid. When mission touches the human condition as it does and must, it leads us to focus more on trade and less on aid.

5. Jesus was considered disruptive in almost every situation. His was an upside-down kingdom approach; one not of a conquering hero but a suffering servant (Isa. 53; Mark 10:32–34). He was not the sacerdotal professional clergy, but the everyday servant in cohort with fishermen, tax collectors, and other marketplace people. He drew from the margins of society. His followers were the early adopters and the early majority. They disrupted their world.

Missio Dei was certainly disruptive for my friend Jeff, a multi-talented guy who succumbed to the prevailing church-missions modality of the late twentieth century. Jeff and his wife, Lori, loved Jesus and wanted to make the greatest impact for the kingdom of God, so they did what spiritual followers of Jesus did back then: they sold most of their possessions, joined a mission agency, and were assigned to work in a native village in northern Canada.

Jeff and Lori followed mission protocol as they witnessed, tried to be a testimony, and preached faithfully to the few attendees in the small church they planted. As an outgoing young man, Jeff made friends in the village including the chief, who one day posed a question to him: "Do you really want to help us here in this village?" Jeff readily responded that he did and asked what the chief had in mind. "What we really need is someone to teach some trades and skills to the young people of the village so they can find work and provide for their families." Jeff thought "Yes, I can do that" and got in touch with mission leadership with his plan.

Not long afterward, they said to him, "No, Jeff, you cannot do that. You were assigned to your village to preach the good news, not to start training programs for the youth." Jeff had to tell the chief that he was not able to meet the village's need for a vocational teacher. Jeff and Lori soon realized that there was something inherently wrong with this picture: It lacked an integrated view of how Jesus viewed the kingdom of God. It wasn't as concerned with the "here and now" human condition as much as with the eternal view of the "not yet." After leaving the mission, they studied the Scriptures, and Jeff began to develop his God-given entrepreneurial bent. Today, Jeff is the CEO of Fair Flies, a missional company serving in several poverty-stricken locations in Africa and Asia, offering dozens of jobs where the employees hear the good news of the gospel and are learning to follow Jesus. Thankfully, more and more people are realizing that the old modality of missions needs disruption, and that it needs to be replaced by a more biblical understanding of *missio Dei*, the *real* mission of God.

Of course, change theory can be a complicated, convoluted, and controversial topic. A case can be made that change in the church and change related to *missio Dei* is a function of a major crisis in society and requires radical intervention. Some historical examples include the persecution of the church in the first century, Constantine's Edict of Milan, the Reformation of the sixteenth century, and perhaps the great wars of the twentieth century. Perhaps some of today's sociopolitical divisions, pandemic upheavals, and international conflicts could be God's way of disrupting the evangelical church even now. Perhaps by blessing our world neighbors, instead of "proselytizing" them, our mission will again be more aligned with *missio Dei*.

In *The Coming Revolution in Church Economics*, Mark Deymaz analyzes cultural changes that mandate disruptive innovation in church economics.[10] Without some serious pivots, the church may not survive growing financial burdens on the middle class, fewer increases in contributions to religious organizations, or shifting generational attitudes toward giving, and changing demographics.

Loss of revenue is going to lead to a reshaping in the way churches and mission programs will be funded.

Funding is therefore a fundamental concern in the study of missiology's future. Put simply, money will not be available for the old missions paradigm. Churches and mission agencies will need to learn to leverage assets, bless the community, empower entrepreneurs, and create multiple streams of income to fund mission. As is already happening, Jimmy Scroggins and Steve Wright suggest co-vocational pastors who embrace a calling to serve God both in the church and in the marketplace, which is an interesting return to a first-century model and one that is normative in poorer countries of the world.[11]

Disruptors define, refine, and ultimately create new realities by helping people see things differently. As disruption grows and gains momentum, it will help create the future. Today, faith-work marketplace people, Business as Mission, and related means such as tentmaking are disrupting the missional market.[12] They slowly but surely have the potential (as the little guy at the bottom of the market) to replace the multi-trillion-dollar aid industry and make traditional professional mission groups redundant in much of the world.

Kingdom-marketplace activity by God's missional people makes the "product" (that is, loving your neighbor and making disciples) simple, accessible, convenient, and affordable. It doesn't just improve on what's been done in the past; it disrupts the status quo in modern times by remembering that "faith without works is dead," creating wealth and promoting dignified sustainability. In one sense, it is an ancient idea; but because it has been largely forgotten, it may be considered innovative and certainly disruptive.

CHAPTER 4

Missional Professionals in North America Today

*You never change things by fighting the existing
reality. To change something, build a new model
that makes the existing model obsolete.*

—Buckminster Fuller

Since the publishing of *The Greatest Missionary Generation*, I have
been challenged to listen to the children and grandchildren of that
generation in an effort to understand not only the past but also
practical implications of what the future could and should be. The
context of this earlier work, which valued and praised the post-
Second World War generation for their missionary efforts, was very
different from the world of the 2020s. More than two-thirds of the
world's population now inhabit countries that refuse to grant missionary visas. There seem to be no "calls" today for missionaries to
travel to foreign lands, and the words *missionary* and *missions* tend
to have a negative connotation.

For us in the West, technology has totally reengineered our
communication, entertainment, travel, education, and even relationships. In our culture, young people today are coming of age
with a more affluent and entitlement-oriented mindset, which is
a long way from the Depression era of their great-grandparents
(or even their great-great-grandparents!). Adults in the West seem
propelled by job mobility, while the developing world is moving to
the cities in search of a good job.

Sociologically, multiculturalism has integrated many cultures
and ethnicities of the world, while elsewhere it has propelled some
toward increased insular and nationalistic thinking. The church
in the West seems to have succumbed to increased secularization,

materialism, a bifurcated mindset, and an insular perspective on the mission of God. However, the majority-world church seems to be becoming more and more mission-minded, with countries like Korea and Brazil sending missionaries abroad.

Despite there being much to be encouraged about, the Christian church worldwide continues to view the mission of God with the lens of earlier generations. While most everything around them has changed, God's people fail to realize that all is God's mission and that he is at work in the world. Believers must join him in the context of where he is working, rather than continuing to follow old models of church planting and evangelization.

Adult MK Perspective for the Twenty-First Century

Whereas the "Greatest Missionary Generation" grew up in simpler times—traveling by boat (rather than airplanes), living in huts, and learning languages and cultures very different from their own—their children grew up between two cultures and built unique relationships, values, and identities. They became known as "third culture kids" (TCKs). I became interested to discover how they see the world today, especially as it relates to *missio Dei*.

In the 1980s, I studied adult missionary children of the "Greatest Missionary Generation" and found that most of them had maintained the basic values of their parents (i.e., following in the faith and valuing their intercultural experiences), but most did not follow their parents' vocation of the professional missionary. Those who did join the mission agency community did so in a specialized sense—administration, medicine, education, and so on.

After some reflection on their parents' ministry and their own socialization experiences, my interviews focused on what *missio Dei* looks like today and might look like in the next decade or two. I asked questions like: "If you had grandkids asking how they could best obey Jesus' commands, what would you say?" and "If you were a mission leader today, where would you put the missional emphasis of your organization?" Following are a few of their comments.

Retired surgeon Bill Piepgrass's parents were career missionaries in Haiti who later served in mission leadership in the United States. Bill is representative of an MK's view of what *missio Dei* looks like for his children and grandchildren today. He was quick to affirm that people need to utilize their profession to find points of need or to start a conversation. For him, the catalyst was the medical field after he read *The Saline Solution: Sharing Christ in a Busy Practice* by Walt Larimore and Bill Peel. He considered every patient to be a divine appointment, which he put into practice through his work in hospitals and clinics. "No one wants to be preached at," he told me. "It's about building bridges."

Bill emphasized that every believer is on a mission for God and that the church needs to understand that all believers have different God-given wiring, abilities, education, and experiences, all of which should connect for missional effectiveness. He talked about his daughter and her husband, who have law degrees and work for the US State Department. Every day, they seek to determine where God is in their work and then join him there. For Bill and his children, "work is ministry."

Ken McMillan was seventeen years old when he was shot by the Congo Simbas during the uprisings of 1964 (see *The Greatest Missionary Generation* for the full story). He recovered, became a surgeon, and served in a mission hospital in the Democratic Republic of Congo. He now works for the Bureau of Indian Affairs as a physician. Ken affirmed the thesis of this current book: Missional Christians should aim high and "be good at something valued by the community." He can identify with people because he can help meet their real needs. In Africa, the people wanted schools, churches, and health centers. They wanted more than easy solutions; they needed help addressing systemic issues, not just the symptoms. The medical profession is a metaphor for all other needs in the world.

Ken quotes here Matthew Parris, an atheist who praised the missionaries who not only brought religion but tied it to real needs:

Christianity, post-Reformation and post-Luther, with its teaching of a direct, personal, two-way link between the individual and God, unmediated by the collective, and insubordinate to any other human being, smashes straight through the philosophical/spiritual framework I've just described. It offers something to hold on to for those anxious to cast off a crushing tribal groupthink. That is why and how it liberates.

Those who want Africa to walk tall amid 21st-century global competition must not kid themselves that providing the material means or even the knowhow that accompanies what we call development will make the change. A whole belief system must first be supplanted. And I'm afraid it has to be supplanted by another. Removing Christian evangelism from the African equation may leave the continent at the mercy of a malign fusion of Nike, the witch doctor, the mobile phone and the machete.[1]

In his article, Mr. Parris inadvertently reminded his readers that there indeed is a *missio Dei* and that God is at work in the world. In fact, it is all the work of God; his followers are only stewards of what he is doing.

Born and raised in New Guinea, Larry Cole is the son of a couple who careered pioneer mission work in what is now Papua, Indonesia. He grew up among the Dani people, who were headhunters and warriors living what was then considered to be a "stone age" culture—not an inappropriate term, since the tips of their spears and their digging tools were indeed made from stone. Although he was sent off to a boarding school far away when he was six years old, he always knew his parents loved him. As he got older, he loved visiting his parents—the long treks with his father and camping for weeks in the mountains never before explored by Westerners.

Larry went to LeTourneau University and became an aviation technician, which was a legitimate choice for someone whose first early years depended on supplies delivered by missionary airplanes. While he was in college, however, he began to sense what has become the obvious. "The world is changing so fast," he said. "When my parents went to New Guinea in the 1950s, the people wanted the gospel first and foremost, but today they want education and skill training." Just as Jesus started with physical needs and moved on to the spiritual, so must we.

The mission of God today centers on meeting people where they need to be met. For Larry, that meant helping them prepare for their changing world. This centers on honing practical skills like agriculture, mechanics, teaching, and small business. "We have to work in a new and different way," he says, all the while helping people follow Jesus.

Steve Kearns delivers a similar message: "People respect you because of what you have to offer them." Steve and his twin brother Dan grew up in Brazil and returned to Canada for high school and university, both going on to play professional football in the Canadian Football League. After playing for the BC Lions and the Hamilton Tiger-Cats, Steve joined Athletes in Action. His work today is largely built on his faith integrated with his skill on the gridiron. As he explains, sports are a key way to live and share one's faith. He has gained respect in his job as a chaplain of the Toronto Raptors, Hamilton Tiger-Cats, and Toronto Argonauts, because he has been where the players currently sit—grappling with the issues of life against the backdrop of a professional sports career.

Steve cites stories of trips to Europe, Latin America, and Asia, where people were eager to listen to him because of his professional sports career: "It is the same thing for all professions. Be authentic, care about people, understand who God is." He went on to talk about how faith and life skills go together, which is what God expects of us. His skills and interests were in sports, and he simply asked God to show him the way to use them for his purposes.

As we entertained visions of what the future could look like, Steve shared that in the future, missional believers should take their profession to the ends of the earth and expect churches to provide prayer and encouragement. The age of asking for financial support is coming to a close.

Jeanette Amundsen Klodt was born and raised in Unalakleet and Nome, Alaska, where her parents were career missionaries. Roald and Harriet Amundsen were classic pioneers and are credited with starting high schools, radio stations, a flying service, and a vocational school, as well as churches. While Roald saw himself as a traditional missionary, he also created jobs, educated native Alaskans, and served them with his aviation business. His charismatic personality endeared him to just about everyone in western Alaska.

Jeanette embraced the values she grew up with by learning the local culture, living in the community as servants of the people, and providing services in line with the needs of the area. While she whole-heartedly affirmed her parents' ministry, she acknowledged that the world has changed. Missionaries like her parents who raised their own funding from churches in the lower forty-eight states tended to see those churches as their bosses, looking to them for their needs. It is better nowadays, she said, for missional workers to have a salaried job. This ensures that they are more like the people around them rather than a revered cleric who is expected to be different.

She talked about the Moravians, who philosophically and practically integrated their occupation with their Christian faith. The motto of the Moravian Church is: "In essentials, unity; in nonessentials, liberty; and in all things, love." The Moravian missionaries constituted the first large-scale Protestant missionary movement and were the first to send laypeople on missions rather than clergy. Jeanette noted the positive influence of the Moravians who arrived in Bethel in 1885 who integrated their faith with the culture around them and provided jobs for people.

She summarized how she sees the future with a quote from Exodus 4, where God instructs Moses to utilize what was already in his hand. So should kingdom missional workers. They should use their skills and training, while serving the needs around them like Jesus did. In this way, they will follow God in his mission.

Joanne Laskowski Ryan had a positive experience growing up in Brazil, both in the big city where she lived with her family and in the missionary school that she attended on a spacious campus just outside the city. After attending college in the US, she married Dave, a chiropractor in Seattle, and together they made many mission trips to Eastern Europe and Brazil, utilizing Dave's medical skills and Joanne's social and linguistic skills. As the years rolled by, she has observed how the world of missions continues to morph.

She highlights the importance of relationships in the making of disciples, and she commented on the advantages of the social media world and the increasing number of valuable online resources. This is so much more compared with what missionaries had access to fifty years ago. Regardless, Joanne notes that "humans everywhere still need that personal touch no matter where the country is." She says that many media distractions today mitigate the development of important relationships, especially in cultures like those in Latin America, which highlight the "teaching of the word and discipleship as even more important." Not only do new believers need to experience cognitive learning and skill development, but they also need the relationships of mentorship and friendship, which are integral to *missio Dei*.

Elisabeth Berger is a theologian, mission administrator, and educator who also grew up with career missionary parents in Brazil. Her reflections and observations are a mix of theology and practical analysis. She notes with keen rumination that her parents' generation were oftentimes motivated by the planting of a church or the "saving" of people from hellfire. For her, the biblical alternative goal is that a person knows and reflects God. She stated that as Jesus followers, our task is to represent God's love in a hurting world.

The logical result of such kingdom theology of the "here and now" is not to focus on the "not yet," but to simply make disciples of Jesus in the everyday world today and do that with one's education and experiences (similar to Jeanette's "what is in your hand" metaphor). Elisabeth sees her role in the mission industry as providing resources to help God's people flourish in their jobs, living out the mission of God where the gospel is least known. Rather than joining an agency, individuals join a movement of God representing the mission of God.

With these transitional understandings in mind, it is important to remember that God is still sovereign and wants all people to worship him; he sees his people as the means to fulfill *his* mission of pursuing the kingdom of heaven here on earth. The mission of

God is still the heart of God's passion for his people. Although our immediate reaction to our world may be discouragement, there are indeed signs of people awakening to God in the twenty-first century.

One such encouraging sign is the faith-work movement, which builds the theoretical basis for the integration of our faith with everyday life, clearly defining that God is a God committed to a holistic life for all humanity. Here, there is no sacred-secular divide, no compartmentalization, no bifurcated life, no dualistic mindset!

Much has been written in the past ten years on a theology of work and theology of vocation. These and others dispute historic unbiblical perspectives on God's design for work, such as the notion that work is a necessary evil and something to be endured, only a means to wealth, acquisition, and power, or is primarily concerned with self-actualization. Many believers still think along these lines; for those who do, it is unlikely that they will view their work as a place of ministry and mission.

A more biblical viewpoint specifies that work is not a curse (Gen. 1:26–28), but that it brings economic growth and development (Deut. 8:18), is designed to serve others (1 Pet. 4:10), builds character and capacity (2 Tim. 2:6), enables us to be generous (2 Cor. 9:6–8), and is a source of fulfillment of God's desires (Col. 3:23–24).

While we affirm the advances of the faith-work movement, it is important to recall that God has always been concerned with faith and work integration. The Hebrew word *avodah* unites the ideas of our work with worship of God. Jesus also linked his spiritual teaching with the marketplace of life, such as after healing a boy and then speaking spiritual truth to the crowd (Luke 9); and in the story of the miraculous catch of fish, Jesus integrates biblical truth about love and discipleship (John 21).

Rev. Dr. Art Lindsley (vice president of theological initiatives at the Institute for Faith, Work, and Economics) suggests seven key propositions that can help us understand a theology of work:

1. Work is not a result of the Fall. . . . We were all created to work. In Genesis 1:26–28, image-bearers of God (male and

female) are called to exercise dominion or rulership over the whole creation. Only God can create something out of nothing. We are to create something out of something. We are what Francis Schaeffer and J. R. R. Tolkien called "sub-creators" . . . but it is made harder because of the Fall (Gen. 3:17).

2. Work is more than a place to make money to give to the church or a place to evangelize. It is certainly appropriate to give to the church or, when the appropriate situation presents itself, to share the gospel, but these purposes are not the central reason to work. Work is valuable in itself.

3. The ministerial calling is not higher than other professions, such as business, medicine, law, or carpentry. Jesus was a carpenter, or general contractor, for about 18 years. It is estimated that he worked in this manner from age 12 or 13 to "about 30," according to Luke 3:23. God's kingdom can be advanced from all valid professions. We are all "priests" called to offer spiritual sacrifices and proclaim his excellency in a world of darkness (1 Pet. 2:5; 2:9–10).

4. Redemption extends to all of life, including our work. In creation, we were made to respond to God (personally), respond to each other (corporately), and respond to the creation (cosmically). The Fall impacts all three of these areas. However, redemption influences every area the Fall impacts: Redemption extends to the whole cosmos. Acts 3:21 speaks about the "restoration of all things." Romans 8:19–21 indicates that the whole creation "will be liberated from its bondage." God will restore the cosmos through a new heaven and a new earth. This means our work can participate in the redemption of all of life. In fact, it is an important means of expressing that redemption.

5. There are indications that some of our work will be present in the new heavens and new earth. In Revelation 21:24–26, it says twice that the kings of the earth will bring the "glory of

the nations" into the new heavens and new earth. This seems to indicate that there is something to the unique cultural creativity of each nation that will be present for people to appreciate for all eternity.

6. We are called to glorify God in our work. First Corinthians 10:31 indicates that we are to give glory to him in how we eat and drink and surely in how we work. Our work is to be done for the Lord (Col. 3:23). Work—whether in business, medicine, law, carpentry, construction, garbage collection, or the arts—can all be done to the glory of God and for our Lord. If our work is done well, he may say, "Well done, my good and faithful servant" (Matt. 25:23).

7. Recovering a theology of work can encourage a flourishing society. Throughout the ages, people have desired a path that leads to flourishing. When we work together with other people and serve customers, giving them good products and services, we increase the well-being of our society. We are to use our talents for the good of the kingdom—God's rule and reign on earth, as well as in heaven (Matt. 25:14–30). The Bible encourages "shalom" or flourishing in every direction. The kind of peace desired is pictured in Micah 4:4.[2]

One might wonder why something so fundamental as a theology of work should still consume so much debate several centuries after the time of Christ. At the risk of being charged with intellectual reductionism, I propose that all such tensions are ultimately sourced in a thought system that functionally combines biblical principles, Greek philosophy, post-Enlightenment modernism, and Western individualism. With such an unfortunate integrated evolution of faith, philosophy, and pragmatism, is it any wonder that so many maladies exist that we must overcome in the best interest of facilitating a true *missio Dei*?

There is a tendency to think of the purveyors of God's will in the world as professionally spiritual or ecclesiastical. Biblical history presents the opposite, with most of the obedient Old Testament heroes continuing in their profession, such as farmers, ranchers, political leaders, businesspeople, and soldiers. Indeed, some professionals were called to the clergy or priestly function, but it was not considered normative to see that as a higher calling. Similarly, in the New Testament, one finds tentmakers, administrators, artisans, farmers, and fishermen. The apostles were called to be the leaders of the growing church, not a class to be aspired to by the everyday follower of Jesus. The idea of the professional clergy did not emerge until the second century.

If *missio Dei* describes the heart of God's mission for the world, and if disruptive innovation is a possible theory to help us understand the future of God at work in the world, and if the biblical narrative is profession-centric, is there any evidence that change could be imminent in our times? Is there any evidence of innovative action and even early adopters for such innovation? Is there a demonstration of *missio Dei* in our times? I conclude this chapter with potential evidence at least in North America today.

Dave Kier is the long-time CEO of DFS Feeds Animal Nutrition in Newell, Iowa. He is also a board member of IBEC Ventures, which began in 2006 to provide coaching to missional start-up businesses in developing countries. Dave understands himself to be sent by God to help establish the kingdom in the "here and now," beginning first in northwest Iowa and then to the world. He does so via his company, which has over $100 million in sales per year and produces more than 500,000 metric tons of animal feed each year. The company mission statement is prominently placed in all four production plants: "DFS desires to be an indispensable ally in delivering value through knowledge, honoring God in all we do."

Each of the more than one hundred employees understands that they are to give their best all of the time because, like Dave, they exist to make a difference in the world. Every day, more than twenty semi-trailer trucks drive more than forty-five hundred miles to deliver feed for animal nutrition (primarily hogs and turkeys). Dave sees his practical mission to help feed the world, and in so doing bring glory to God in all that he does. When I visited the Newell plant in 2018, I heard several testimonies from employees and customers who credit Dave with fulfilling God's mission by bringing personal change to their lives. At this writing, Dave is busy developing a feed mill in Zambia to help feed the world and give glory to God!

Barnhart Crane and Rigging Company is an American company founded in 1969 in Memphis, Tennessee. Richard and Nancy Barnhart started with a single location with one pickup truck, a welder, and a ladder. The office was a kitchen table in the family home of current CEO Alan Barnhart.

The purpose of Barnhart Crane and Rigging Co. is to glorify God by providing an opportunity for his people to use their skills and gifts in his service through constructive work, personal witness, and ministry funding. According to their mission statement, Barnhart determines to continuously improve and grow to be the best heavy lift and heavy transport company.[3] Almost sixty years later, the company has grown from that single office to forty-four locations across the country into one of the largest heavy lift and transport companies in the United States.

But a company is only as good as its employees. CEO Alan Barnhart is grateful to have assembled gifted leaders and talented team members who work diligently, solve problems, and uphold company standards. The employees represent all regions of the country and reflect different political persuasions, cultures, and ethnicities. These employees possess talents that are indispensable to the company's success, from engineers to crane operators to truck drivers.

Alan affirms that he does not consider himself to be the owner but a steward for God, who is the real owner of the company. Their three primary values are:

1. To work hard and do a good job, doing everything with excellence.

2. To witness in both deed and faith to who Jesus is and what he has done.

3. To make a profit in order to help others.

As a young man, Alan studied Scripture to find out what God had to say about money. He had two main takeaways from that study. First, "Everything that I have and everything that I am comes from God and belongs to God, and I am a steward of it. My job is to figure out what God wants me to do with the things he's given to me. None of it belongs to me." Second, "I came away with a fear of wealth, of business success." Citing Matthew 19:23, Alan says, "It's hard for a rich man to enter the kingdom of heaven." Barnhart leadership see themselves to be part of the *missio Dei* in our times.

Hobby Lobby is a national chain of hobby and craft stores founded by David and Barbara Green, who expanded a picture frame company in their garage in 1972 into the company that it is today. Green is the privately held company's chief executive officer and his son Steve is its president. In 1981, another son, Mart, founded the Mardel bookstore chain, which concentrates on religious material.

Hobby Lobby and Mardel include mission statements on their corporate websites that outline their dedication to Christian principles: "Hobby Lobby aims to honor the Lord by following biblical principles; establish a work environment that builds character, strengthens individuals and nurtures families and provides a return on its owner's investment so he can share the Lord's blessings with its 13,000 employees."

Mardel was established "for the equipping of the saints for the work of service, to the building up of the body of Christ," quoting St. Paul's letter to the Ephesians. No Hobby Lobby store is open on Sunday "in order to allow our employees and customers more time for worship and family."[4]

In 2017, *Forbes* magazine contributor Jerry Bowyer interviewed founder David Green. In response to Bowyer's question relative to Hobby Lobby being called a "Christian" company, Green responded:

> You know I think prayer could come in there really well. The Bible says, "You have not because you ask not." And I think as we ask Him for His advice and His Holy Spirit leading and directing us, I think

He will do that; I know He will. As we are serious about wanting to do things God's way, then I think He will start dealing with us. He dealt with us about closing on Sundays, and He's dealt with us in different areas in our spirit, in different areas—He dealt with us when we didn't have people around here that were helping our people with anger management and all the different issues in marriages. So I think God will definitely lead and guide them in areas that they're falling short.[5]

Bowyer then asked Green about his favorite Bible verses for learning how to run a business and overall business wisdom:

Well, I guess it might be Proverbs 3, verse 5 and 6. It says, "Trust in the Lord with all thine heart, lean not unto thine own understanding, in all thy ways acknowledge Him, and He shall direct thy path." It is to be serious about trying to follow after God. And we have to start by believing this is His word and I'm going to stand on it.[6]

In 2019, a Chick-fil-A restaurant finally opened in north Seattle, not far from my home. It was a long time coming to a city that prides itself for its progressive character. I have enjoyed talking with others of how the restaurant is "different." The Chick-fil-A corporation has shown consistent growth throughout the years, and it is now the most profitable fast-food chain in the United States on a per-location basis. It has grown to twenty-three hundred restaurants in forty-seven states; but contrary to most other businesses, money is not the end goal of Chick-fil-A: it is the sharing of God's love for people.

Trudy Cathy White says it all began when her father, S. Truett Cathy, the founder of Chick-fil-A, committed himself to the principle that while they loved selling chicken, they were really more in the people business.

Dad helped me understand this concept that we can look at others and see what their needs are and help them to accomplish what they want to accomplish, and we'll find some great reward out of that. Jesus said it is real simple. He said, "It's better to give than to receive."[7]

In her book *Climb Every Mountain*, Trudy explains:

> My dad built this business based on biblical principles. He felt like his business decisions kind of go hand in hand with biblical principles. That's no secret. There's a lot of things that we are taught in God's Word and we've been able to put it into practice in our business. We're in business to glorify God by being a faithful steward of all that's been trusted to us and to have a positive influence on all who come in contact with Chick-fil-A.[8]

Chick-fil-A's consistently high rating for excellence, quality, efficiency, care for employees, customer service, and overall value are well known. But for the family members in this giant family-owned business, it is rooted in the mission of God. He is at work in the world, and they as stewards are partners in his work, demonstrating his love for all people. And they do it well.

Michael Cardone is the founder of the world's largest after-market auto parts manufacturer, Cardone Industries in Pennsylvania. In reference to his calling and part in the mission of God, he states, "I am not called to be a pastor; I am not called to be a missionary. I am called to be a businessman . . . and I see no difference. Work is worship."[9] That's it! God is at work everywhere and in every workplace and in every situation. We join him in that work for the greater glory of God.

There are many other North American examples of business owners and managers who understand God's mission in the world and want to do their part as stewards of his ownership of their business or endeavor. They demonstrate a gospel that is credible, integrous, and authentic. They are at the front edge of the bell curve, and they are innovators disrupting the mission industry. Although none of these business owners would call themselves "missionaries," they are on a mission for God by operating missional kingdom businesses for the glory of God.

CHAPTER 5

Missio Dei in Action around the World

*We must serve our customers, staff and suppliers
with professionalism, excellence and integrity,
and trust God for the kairos moment.*

—Mats Tunehag

When people see the gospel, they will then listen to the gospel.

—Patrick Lai

If we combine the definition of the *missio Dei* with Disruptive Innovation Theory, a biblical theology of work, historical studies of
missions, a theology of the mission of the church, and a hope for
the future based on a fresh understanding of God at work in the
world, where does it leave us? The hope is that we arrive at a place
where we become less aligned with our evolved Western theology
and more aligned with a better understanding of God. This requires all believers to use their faith and assets to bless their neighbors, across the street and to the ends of the earth.

This is not a tweaking of mission strategy. It is not adjusting
for the migration of peoples or a renewed understanding of inter-
racial justice or preaching missions in every seminary. No, it is an
innovative disruption. It is what Losch calls "A Better Way" because
it is the way of Jesus from the first century. With a lapse of nearly
two thousand years since Jesus taught and lived a perfect example,
this can be truly considered an innovation. It is new to the people
of God today.

We have shared examples of *missio Dei* being lived out in the
marketplace in North America. If the mission of God can work
through the marketplace in the Western world, then why not to
the ends of the earth? As we have seen, this is sometimes called

Business as Mission, marketplace mission, kingdom business, tent-making, and so on. All of these can bring the mission of God to people of other cultures, ethnicities, and languages through business and the everyday marketplace.

Dan and Jodi loved Jesus and wanted to serve him, and so after graduating from university, they headed off to Asia for two years as missionaries. They had a good experience, learned a fair amount of the national language, and returned to the States, praying that God would clearly lead them to their next steps. But God had touched their heart for the people they had already been living among, so he led them back to a large city in a more unreached area. By this time, Dan realized that God had gifted him with entrepreneurial skills, and so they started a business—one of the hardest ones—manufacturing.

God led them to investors in their adopted country and in the US, and the business grew to nearly thirty employees and relationships developed in the community. Dan joined the local chamber of commerce as the only American member, and he gained a vision for extending his kingdom business beyond this city to more unreached areas.

The business was clearly set up for success. With nearly $500,000 a year in sales, they had created jobs, and their product was being sold internationally. But Dan knew enough to know he needed help. Although he was trained in evangelism and missions, he had no background in business and had experienced his first bad account. He needed to modernize his financial record keeping with updated software, and he needed capital to expand. Thankfully, God's people serving as consultants provided necessary training and support, allowing the business to grow. Dan and Jodi have found their niche in making disciples among the unreached. They seek to hire people in need, and they contribute time and funds to a local orphanage as a part of this plan.

Making disciples of Jesus has been an integral part of the project from the beginning. Dan and Jodi continue to live out kingdom values in their business and community. They offer fair wages, pay their bills and taxes, and produce a quality product (a variety of textiles and sports equipment). They are respected as different in a positive way in their city. They live out the gospel.

They also seek opportunities to give spoken testimony of the hope that is within them. They share that they are "Jesus followers," how he makes a personal difference as well as helps their business be different and respected. This has led to several people coming to faith, being discipled by Jodi and Dan, and then joining micro churches in the area. Certainly, Jodi and Dan are not missionaries as we have thought more traditionally of them over the years, but this is *missio Dei* for them and it is most certainly disruptive when compared to traditional missionary efforts.

What Is "Business as Mission"?

While the term "Business as Mission" originated in the 1990s, the concept goes back to the Old and New Testament history. We have already acknowledged the Creation account and the role played by God as the first Creator, and how he gave unfinished business to humanity to transform the world, thus co-creating with God. And we have already discussed the Hebrew word *avodah* and how it combines our English words *work*, *worship*, and *service* into one. In Deuteronomy 8:18, Moses acknowledges that God gives the ability to create wealth; and in Exodus 35:30–35, craftsmen Bezalel and Oholiab were filled with the Spirit of God to do their work. Since then, Judeo-Christian thought has been infused with an integration of work with faith.

In his helpful article, "Deeply Rooted in the Future," one of the leaders of the global BAM movement Mats Tunehag briefly traces two millennium of the integration of faith and work:

> Judaism values work, wealth creation and a framework of freedom which accommodates dignified work and the creation of wealth through business. They do not struggle with the sacred-secular divide which so often is prevalent among Christians. In Old Testament times work was the way in which one worshipped God.[1]

In "The Difference Christianity Made," George Weigel argues for the strength of Christianity in the development of the West with the purposeful integration of faith and work.[2] In keeping in line with the Benedictine *ora et labora*, which gave self-respect and dignity to manual labor, monk Gregor Mendel is credited with the discovery of modern genetic theory. Various other Roman Catholic orders, as well as Christian missionaries such as the Moravians, have maintained a strong praxis of work as important to Christian orthodoxy.

It would thus be grossly unfair to imply that the idea of faith-work integration as the theological basis of Business as Mission is a recent concept of our times. Its roots are found in God and throughout the historical traditions of both Judaism and Christianity.

While there are many variations of the term "Business as Mission," perhaps J. D. Greear of Summit Church in Raleigh-Durham, North Carolina, expresses it best when he says: "Christians in the marketplace today are able to gain access more easily to strategic, unreached places. Globalization, great advancements in technology, and urbanization have given the business community nearly universal access."[3]

Greear reminds us that God has placed in his church everything necessary to penetrate the most unreached parts of our world, business skills along with related skills that create value such as engineering, teaching, information technology, agriculture, and financial services. Businesspeople, says Greear, should focus on a twofold vision: "Whatever you are good at, (a) do it well for the Glory of God; (b) do it somewhere strategic for the mission of God."[4] Mats Tunehag suggests that it is simply a legitimate economic activity by a workplace professional that serves as a vehicle for sharing the love of Christ.

What I've learned is that it is also through the product and the process of our work that we honor God. BAM takes place in every workplace in the world where God's people in business are faithfully living like Jesus and looking for ways to bring people to know him. Christians in business see their work as a testimony and a mission. Michael Cardone, CEO of Cardone Industries, says that service and excellence create a platform to talk about who God is and Jesus Christ. Similarly, David Green, CEO of Hobby Lobby, notes,

"We try in all decisions to ask what God would have us do. . . . We don't put our Christian faith on the shelf when we come to work."[5]

Three propositions developed by John Warton may help to justify and explain the Business as Mission movement:

1. *The Sanctity of Work.* It is important that we all have clarity on the biblical divine understanding that God is a God of work, and he intends his people to be workers (Gen. 1). We should not feel guilty or like second-class Christians when we succeed in business; God expects us to drive for excellence, to be ambitious and to do "all for the glory of God" (1 Cor 10:31). While business and work can tempt us to sin, they are fundamentally good and provide many opportunities to glorify God.[6]

2. *The Christian at Work.* This proposition suggests that Christians should engage in work like anyone else but live differently from everyone else. Christians work ethically, view their customers differently, love and serve others, seek justice, and use their work to serve their communities. In so doing, believers become a testimony and draw others to become followers of our Savior.

3. *Work and the Kingdom of God.* The book of Matthew suggests that the kingdom of God is "not yet" (heaven) but also "here and now." As we create jobs and wealth, we are advancing the kingdom of God, which essentially is obedience to the Second Commandment (i.e., to love our neighbors). The Great Commission enjoins us to make disciples of "all peoples." So, the Christian businesses that we develop here in our home neighborhoods represent a transferrable model. We can participate in business start-ups, franchises, or multinational business efforts abroad in the developing world and all the while live like Jesus. That is Business as Mission.

A friend of mine, who is a kingdom-business entrepreneur in an Asian country, recently sent me an email that demonstrates this:

Upon entering a local office where local authorities facilitate some aspects of our company, I saw my national friend who manages the office. Amidst the hubbub we greeted one another and caught up on personal news. Suddenly my friend asked, "Do you have a divine connection? I'm sensing a positive energy emanating from you and I don't know what it is." Stunned, I replied, "Well as a matter of fact, I do have a divine connection to Jesus!" I then went on to explain who Jesus is and His presence in my life. He listened intently. Something is going on in this man's heart.

Business as Mission is not "business as normal." Neither is it "missions as normal." It is living out the commands of Jesus in the workplace: to love our neighbor and make disciples so individuals and communities are transformed—spiritually, economically, and socially—for the greater glory of God and the establishment of his church.

A BAM Business Will Be Profitable and Sustainable

Tunehag and the Lausanne Committee on BAM insist that BAM activities must (1) be profitable and sustainable, (2) create jobs and local wealth, (3) produce spiritual capital (disciples of Jesus), and (4) be good stewards of the resources in the earth. This quadruple bottom line is a guiding force for the BAM movement.

The first is the importance of a business that is profitable and sustainable. For most of the twentieth century, businesses and MBA programs would answer the question, "What is the goal of your business?" with a simple response: "To maximize share-holder value" or "To make a profit." However, the real goal of business is more importantly to serve others and bring glory to God. God's original purposes are evidenced in the Creation Mandate, which demonstrates that he is a God of enterprise, creativity, and production for his glory. From the first human couple until now, God intended creation to grow and expand as humanity began to produce and distribute food, and build, manufacture, and trade goods.

The fundamental function of creating wealth is that it is intended to be a "high and holy calling." Jeff Van Duzer expresses the purpose of business as twofold: (1) "to provide the community with goods and services that will enable it to flourish," and (2) "to provide opportunities for meaningful work that will allow employees to express their God-given creativity."[7] Clearly, the nobleman's command in the parable of the ten minas to "engage in business until I come" (Luke 19:13 ESV) carried with it the expectation of a profit. Business is the only human institution that actually creates wealth. Education, the church, and government all consume wealth. Business creates it! "But remember the LORD your God, for it is he who gives you the ability to produce wealth" (Deut. 8:18).

While it is true that profit can be abused like any good thing, profit is a necessary and important component in adding value, providing good stewardship, and multiplying resources as a way of helping people. "Profit is a sign that others are being served effectively, not that advantage is being taken of them."[8] Profit is a necessary condition if we are able to continue to provide value to customers. Profit, however, is not the goal. As Kenneth Mason, CEO of Quaker Oats, states, "Making a profit is no more the purpose of a corporation than getting enough to eat is the purpose of life. Getting enough to eat is a requirement of life; life's purpose, one would hope, is somewhat broader and more challenging."[9]

In recent years, many businesspeople have concluded that there is a wider purpose of business. John Mackey, CEO of Whole Foods Market, puts it this way: "The purpose of business is to create sustainable value for all stakeholders."[10] Mackey and others are focusing on the dignity of all their stakeholders, not just the shareholders. They want to make a difference, seek a common good, and make the world a better place. This idea is incorporated in the modern trend toward CSR, Corporate Social Responsibility.

Traditionally, development agencies, churches, and governments have focused on providing aid to poor countries. While there is a place for aid and disaster relief, aid will never alleviate poverty, and these are rarely self-sustaining projects. When funding dries up or interest declines, the "false market" that created this dependency is exposed and more problems develop than are solved. Only investing in sustainable profitable businesses creates employment and true economic development for poor countries. As theologian Wayne Grudem states,

> I believe the only long-term solution to world poverty is business. That is because businesses produce goods, and businesses produce jobs. And businesses continue producing goods year after year and continue providing jobs and paying wages year after year. . . . If we are ever going to see long-term solutions to world poverty, I believe it will come through starting and maintaining productive, profitable businesses.[11]

A BAM Business Creates Jobs

The second bottom line is the creation of value, particularly jobs. Since the kingdom of God is also "here and now," kingdom living is about living out the principles of Jesus in every sector of life, including the workplace. It demonstrates the integration of our faith with our work.

We bring the kingdom of God "on earth as it is in heaven" (Matt. 6:10) via business transactions because business creates value and we have the opportunity to create holistic value based on the fruit of the spirit: love, joy, peace, patience, kindness, goodness, faithfulness, gentleness, and self-control (Gal. 5:22–23). Pete, a business owner in Asia, says it succinctly: "Everyday on the factory floor is an opportunity for discipleship."

One of the key values created by business is jobs. When we think of Jesus being aware of the social condition of his day and doing something about physical realities such as hunger, danger, illness, and death, we can easily transpose his practical concerns to the concerns of today.

Gallup, Inc. surveyed over 150 nations in their renowned World Poll of the major issues of life. They wanted to "discover the single most dominant thought on most people's minds," says CEO Jim Clifton. "Six years into our global data collection effort, we may have already found the single most searing, clarifying, helpful, world-altering fact. What the whole world wants is a good job."[12]

Consider the world conditions of today: extreme poverty (15 percent of the world lives on less than $2 a day), unemployment (in some countries over 50 percent), victimization and exploitation, disease, wars on several fronts, and persecution.[13] Job creation will not heal all of this, but growing economies that create good jobs bring dignity and opportunity for positive relationships, and it is vital in the ultimate transformation of individuals and communities. God created humans to work and be productive (Gen. 1:28), to work heartily "as for the Lord and not men" (Col. 3:23) and to "shine before others, so that they may see your good works and give glory to your Father" (Matt. 5:16). This all takes place in the marketplace of work.

Here are a few affirmations from the 2004 "Lausanne Business as Mission Issue Manifesto":

- We believe in following in the footsteps of Jesus, who constantly and consistently met the needs of the people He encountered, thus demonstrating the love of God and the rule of His kingdom.

- We believe the Holy Spirit empowers all members of the Body of Christ to serve, to meet the real spiritual and physical needs of others, demonstrating the kingdom of God.

- We believe that God has called and equipped businesspeople to make a Kingdom difference in and through their businesses.

- We believe the Gospel has the power to transform individuals, communities, and societies. Christians in business should therefore be a part of this holistic transformation through business.

- We recognize both the dire need for and the importance of business development. However, it is more than just business per se. Business as Mission is about business with a Kingdom of God perspective, purpose, and impact.

- We recognize that there is a need for job creation and for multiplication of businesses all over the world.

- The real bottom line of Business as Mission is "for the greater glory of God."[14]

A BAM Business Makes Disciples of Jesus

The third bottom line is the development of spiritual capital: making followers of Jesus. Most writers and practitioners of kingdom businesses recognize that the spiritual (or missional) bottom line is the raison d'être for any activity, and certainly a BAM company. This bottom line requires an intentional living of kingdom values in every element of the company, as well as a continual striving to honor God in every aspect of corporate life. A kingdom company is specific, conscious, clear, and intentional in establishing Jesus' kingdom in the world.[15]

Ken Eldred describes this as spiritual capital that includes a corporate culture of integrity, accountability, honesty, hope, loyalty, trust, servanthood, fairness, and love. Incarnational living is observed every day in a kingdom business and becomes the basis for proclamation of faith. BAM businesses have a vision, mission, and strategy evidenced in their policies, procedures, and culture that encourages godly values.[16] They do what is right from God's perspective. For several decades, the ServiceMaster Company was known for its four objectives: Honor God in all we do, help people develop, pursue excellence, and grow profitably. But these were not inert platitudes on the wall. They "needed to be shared, experienced, taught and discussed to keep them alive."[17] Every decision was fundamentally rooted in those objectives.

The end of such integration of faith and work, a truly biblical concept, creates an optimum climate for people to decide to follow Jesus. The business provides the context for discipleship. One such Asian business that benefited from IBEC consultants is noted by Dale Losch:

> For Andrew, the answer lay in living out the gospel every day by being fair with employees, paying his taxes, paying a fair wage, placing

verses from the book of Proverbs on the office door and starting the day in prayer for everyone (all employees were non-Jesus followers). It involved building relationships, caring for families, and even weekend camping trips with employees. It meant talking about the real issues of life and showing them who Jesus is and how a follower really lives. Some call it discipling people into the kingdom.[18]

Recently, a woman who had been an intern in my office in Pennsylvania many years ago wrote to me from her home in a large country in East Asia. She and her husband are now employed in an engineering firm in the country. I had asked her to comment on how their lives and business have resulted in disciples of Jesus, even though the country is antagonistic to the Christian faith.

She spoke of how they live as people of integrity, invest in the lives of the employees, and seek excellence in all they do. This has resulted in many of the workers becoming interested in sharing their personal lives with them in a deep way, opening up to them about issues of personal crisis, depression, and marital struggles. In addition to "on the job" relationships, it has been important for them to get involved with community programs, have their children attend local schools, and help start a new business in the city. While there have been times of discouragement, there have also been several people come to faith and be discipled. There is now a community of believers.

A BAM Business Is a Good Steward of God's Creation

The 2017 BAM Global paper, "Wealth Creation and the Stewardship of Creation," speaks to the issue of God's creation, stating:

> Each business run by wealth creators has a specialty, a God-gift, and points of excellence that can be applied to a pressing environmental issue. A transportation company can work on innovative fuel efficiency and improve transportation of needed medicines. A restaurant can source its food stocks with care and reduce food waste by supporting the food bank with excess, then composting the rest. An office can install passive cooling, energy efficient lighting and provide incentives

to reduce commuting or increase the use of less polluting transport for their employees. Companies have the advantage of scale and resources to do much good quickly. Environmental discipline is financial discipline (conservation of resources), social discipline (respect of local communities and the resources under their stewardship), and spiritual discipline (obeying God's commandment to steward the earth).[19]

The eleventh affirmation of the BAM "Wealth Creation Manifesto" states that "creation care is not optional. Stewardship of creation and business solutions to environmental challenges should be an integral part of wealth creation through business."[20] As environmentalist and biologist Mark Polet reminds us,

> We acknowledge God as Creator. His creative work gave us the resources "to work it and keep it" (Gen 1:15). We are stewards. It has been given to us as a good gift to use and care for. A creation steward sees business as a web of relationships, not a linear progression. The premise of this web comes from an ecological understanding of everything being related to everything else.[21]

In his role as coordinator of the BAM Global Creation Care Consultation, Polet calls all Christians to action: to lead the charge in creation care, and to bring back hope to the debate on environmental stewardship. He calls everyone—certainly, kingdom business leaders—to collaborate with all people of goodwill to take care of our common home, and to work together to provide solutions for environmental problems.

Reconciling and integrating all four bottom lines is a key issue for a BAM business, as well as for all believers in the marketplace. It is not an easy task, however, and involves more than just a business plan. It necessitates an integrated plan that brings together all four bottom lines. In so doing, we will be able to respond positively to the 1949 query of British author and philosopher, Dorothy Sayers:

> In nothing has the church so lost her hold on reality as in her failure to understand and respect the secular workplace. She has allowed work and religion to become separate compartments, and is astonished to find that, as a result, the secular work of the world is turned

to purely selfish and destructive ends, and that the greater part of the world's intelligent workers have become irreligious, or at least uninterested in religion. But is it astonishing? How can anyone remain interested in a religion which seems to have no concern with nine-tenths of life?[22]

In summary, a kingdom business has a quadruple bottom line that includes *profit* because this is what sustains an authentic economic life; it includes *job creation* because this helps fulfill the Great Commandment to love our neighbor (Mark 12:31); and it includes the *making of disciples of Jesus* so we can obey the Great Commission (Matt. 28:18–19) while caring for the creation in every respect. As Patrice Tsague of the Nehemiah Project states:

> Simply put, a Kingdom business is God's business, managed God's way, by God's steward, for God's purposes in the world. . . . The business operations must be managed by the guidelines of the King which are found in the Bible. Moreover, the products and services must be approved by the King; thus, there should be no sin products. The business must be . . . where we demonstrate our salt and light to a dark and dying world. And of course, it must be profitable since the King is concerned about the proper stewardship of His resources. However, the profit is not for us, the operators of a Kingdom business, but for the King, the owner of the business, so we must use the profits as He directs.[23]

The following three chapters contain stories of businesses that meet the criteria we have developed thus far. These businesses have: (1) successfully achieved the quadruple bottom line (profitability, creating jobs, making disciples, and being good stewards of God's resources); (2) been in operation or involved in the business for ten years or longer; and (3) become sustainable in the sense of being profitable and developed a well-crafted model of disciple-making.

CHAPTER 6

Missional Professionals in the International Marketplace

My work is my ministry.

—Mark Roche, Physician in the Middle East

Data Terminal Group
A Global Company with Kingdom Workers

"My job is to point people to Jesus," stated Emily, a Data Terminal Group (DTG) manager in Central Asia. Emily knew at an early age that she wanted to enter the workplace with the goal of integrating work and faith in a God-glorifying way. By God's grace, Tim Keller's book *Every Good Endeavor* became influential and pivotal in her adult decision-making. Keller writes, "Work of all kinds, whether with the hands or the mind, evidences our dignity as human beings—because it reflects the image of God the Creator in us."[1] This book, along with her employment in a refugee settlement in the Carolinas, showed her the value that God placed on work. She learned that every job has dignity and can be powerfully transformative.

More than half of the world lives on less than $10.00 a day, and a major problem facing the world is an inadequate supply of good jobs. In his landmark book The *Coming Jobs War*, Jim Clifton asserts that "what the whole world wants is a good job."[2] He goes on to affirm the importance of both innovation and entrepreneurship and credits the problem-solving capacity of those who can bring jobs quickly and magically to the unemployed in poverty. One such solution is impact sourcing, which brings the type of digital work traditionally performed by outsourcing providers to people living in economically depressed areas. It becomes a win-win: business clients cut costs and communities thrive.

Data Terminal Group (DTG) is a multinational, high-quality digital service provider with core offices in Asia, Africa, and Europe. They use a combination of the latest technology and an on-demand, global workforce for web applications, big data, machine learning, artificial intelligence, data entry and processing, transcription, and much more. The decade-old company uses technology to connect workers to the global economy and to raise up leaders to fight poverty and change their communities. They believe that while talent is widespread in the world, opportunity is not. The goal of positively impacting the lives of workers and their families drives every facet of their business.

For their many clients, from Fortune 500 companies to small start-ups, tedious back-office work is now completed faster, at a lower cost, and to a higher degree of accuracy. As an impact sourcing company, it makes businesses more efficient while creating thousands of new jobs and transforming the lives of millions.

All of this was attractive to Emily, who had a degree in economics from the University of North Carolina and a heart to live with and for God. She saw DTG as a social-enterprise business committed to helping people in the developing world leave poverty, while allowing her an opportunity to live out her faith in practical ways on the job. She applied to DTG and was hired as a project manager in 2015.

I asked Emily what has sustained her for more than five years in an impoverished country in central Asia, helping to build DTG into the largest employer in the country. She credited God with sustaining her and giving her a love for the culture and the people whom she describes as "talented people without jobs." She explained that many workers begin with the more tedious jobs that DTG provides, but after two or three years, most of them move on to other, more advanced jobs. Immediate on-the-job training is therefore an important component in company life.

She had the opportunity to transfer to a post in HR leading a team of thirty, where she was responsible for helping employees learn lessons on values, leadership, character, and community service. This allowed her to interact with most of the more than two thousand employees on issues of poverty, relational brokenness, heartbreaks, and a personal relationship with the Creator, along with the technical aspects of the job. She now is a project manager, again running experiments to test ways of improving their product and processes.

Although the country prohibits conversion to Christianity, Emily confidently lives out her faith in such a way that people want to ask her questions. People respect her for loving them and working to learn their language. She has many friends, and together they experience the rich cultural traditions and the natural beauty of the country. Because spirituality is part of the cultural fabric, she told me, "It is easy to talk about spiritual things and easy to pray." Some even want to read the Bible with her. Her job is to point people to God.

True, there have been challenges and discouragements. The pollution can be grievous to her health and loneliness can be difficult. But God is constantly teaching her new lessons. She says she is learning "to live with him and not just for him." She wants to receive from God and live in communion with him in order to be sure that people see Jesus in her. The ultimate aim of her life with Jesus is to show others with her actions who Jesus is. It reminded me of the old adage that sometimes actions speak louder than words.

Reflecting on her years growing up in the church, Emily says she had missed the idea that her profession could be a vehicle for living and sharing faith. With so many people in the impoverished world without jobs and with little exposure to God, she feels privileged to be able to point people to Jesus while on the job as a project manager at DTG.

Miles away in an East African country, Andy is also a manager for DTG. After a year in their Asia office, he transferred to Africa, where he has served the company and the people of the country for nearly four years now.

As I listened to his story and learned more about DTG, I realized how well the corporate values of the company are embedded in the leadership. He reminded me that they are all about empowering local employees, creating opportunity among the talented unemployed, and allowing Jesus-followers to make the best of everyday moments for the kingdom of God. As of this writing, he is the agreement operations specialist in East Africa, a facility with about twenty-six hundred employees and contractors.

Andy graduated from a university in Texas with a BBA in management and took his first job at Apple Inc. in Austin. He was living the American dream, but one day the Spirit of God asked him, "Is there not something more to life than this?"

So, although he loved working at Apple, he left the company to serve with Adventures in Missions for two years: one as a team leader in India, and one as start-up project manager for Kingdom Journeys, a Business as Mission consulting group working specifically with international businesses and social entrepreneurs around the world. It was a great time of evaluating his strengths, especially as he began to see kingdom-minded businesspeople who had figured out how to be a professional with God's kingdom purposes. He was intrigued and began to wonder what was next for him.

While growing up in his Christian family and in a local Baptist church, he came to believe, like most Christians, that the highest form of spirituality and service was to be a professional minister or missionary. He also saw how revered his grandparents had been as missionaries in India and Africa, as well as his parents, who were involved in missionary work. But he began to realize that the perspective of a hierarchy among Christians was not taught in the Bible, and the idea of living off donations did not sit right with him. He lamented the times he had observed churches pushing people to go into ministry-related professions when God had really given them the skills to be in business. When he returned to work back in the States, he began processing all he had learned.

In early 2016, Andy served in management at DTG before transferring to East Africa. The work strategy in East Africa is a mirror image of that in Asia, with both entities responsible for managing employees and contractors while procuring and serving clients. When he arrived in Africa, DTG had ten employees. That first year, they hired about one hundred employees and over two thousand contractors. The philosophy of finding talent and providing an opportunity for training and work experience is the same in both countries.

My keen interest in the integration of faith with professional work was also important to Andy, who readily affirmed how God created us as relational beings. In his own work, he has found that "everyday moments have the greatest impact." DTG follows the same MO in Africa, with the company being a transitional stepping-stone toward greater things for most contractors and many employees, since there is high turnover in business process outsourcing companies like DTG. This is an opportunity for DTG to teach how to interview, transition and how to deal with cultural differences, entrepreneurship, and leadership.

It gives Andy great satisfaction to see employees like Ben, who worked at DTG for two years, move on to a degree in electrical engineering and land a job managing a team at a large East Africa engineering firm. He also told me about a staunch Hindu employee in his first DTG country with whom he had many faith conversations. Although this Hindu friend asked plenty of questions on his journey toward the Christian faith, Andy's friend finds it hard to understand the religious and cultural differences. They now continue their friendship and conversations over video conferencing.

As with Emily, it is natural for Andy to integrate his faith with his role as a manager at DTG. He has found his calling to be a missional professional as an alternative to becoming a professional missionary like his parents and grandparents. God wired him for technology and management and gave him a passion for people and their needs—economic, social, and religious. He represents the heart of the quadruple bottom line of Business as Mission: a sustainable business, creation of jobs, disciples of Jesus, and stewardship of all of creation.

Engineering Spreadsheets
Relevant to God's Purposes

When I turned sixteen, I got my driver's license as soon as I could and bought my first car. Working for only 65 cents an hour, I quickly learned how to do light maintenance on the car—like changing oil, replacing the alternator and spark plugs, flushing the radiator and brake fluid, replacing headlights, cleaning the carb, tracing down electrical problems, and such. These days, I don't dare try many of those things on my late model SUV!

The auto industry is not only much more specialized today, but most of the technical work is outsourced in our highly globalized world. No longer does it all come out of Detroit or the greater Toronto area. Sure, I have nostalgia when I think of my 1956 Ford Fairlane, but I would not exchange it for the wonderful innovations of today. Designers now use spreadsheets, applied mathematics, mechanical engineering software, and industrial design techniques. Sound boring or over your head? Not to Brandon, who works full time to improve automobiles for his employer in the US while living and working in Asia.

Brandon and Ashley have lived abroad for twelve years and have been married for eight. When Brandon stated in the first five minutes of our conversation that "God created each person with unique skills," and that he had found a professional niche in an engineering firm in Asia, I was intrigued. How did this happen? What did the journey of this mid-thirties couple look like? How did this relate to God's purposes in the world?

Ashley came to faith while in college and soon joined a short-term mission team to Asia, where she experienced traditional missionary activity: serving was closely aligned with teaching, preaching, and overt evangelistic activities.

Growing up in a Christian home, Brandon likewise was taught that the epitome of cross-cultural spiritual service was to teach English, work in linguistics, or preach. Like Ashley, he joined a mission trip to Asia, and it was there that God "blew up his worldview" as he learned to appreciate other cultures through the lens of his own skills and experiences.

He wondered, though, how he could use engineering for the kingdom of God. This is when Brandon was introduced to the BAM concept. As a kingdom-business owner I know in China says, "BAM is most simply walking with God at work."

This resonated with Brandon, so he took a part-time job in Asia and began to learn the local language in university. There he met Ashley. After their marriage, they continued to work in the country, using their skills and basing their lives on the principle that everything one does is sacred; there is no sacred/secular divide; there is no divide between work and faith; no divide between word and deed.

Today, he works for an American company that produces automotive parts in their Asian country. This country does not grant visas to religious workers, but they do respect foreigners who live out godly values, produce excellent products, and create jobs and value for the community. Brandon sees the role of engineering manager as a sacred commission, a fulfillment of God's will in his life and his "work as worship."

During their eight years in this city, Brandon and Ashley have seen the departure of more than twenty family units who had come as disguised missionaries. They had an average stay of three years. After time, they realized that these departures were the result of an incomplete understanding of missions.

And so for Brandon, spreadsheets are not irrelevant. As he creates them with excellence, presents them with integrity, and pursues a product with joy, colleagues and associates come to see a higher purpose. For him, spreadsheets are the vehicle for working closely with many people and providing ways to grow in influence with others. As trust is built through these day-to-day relationships, unique opportunities inevitably arise to both show (deed) and tell (word) these friends and colleagues of a God who loves them dearly and has an amazing story of salvation with them in mind.

Likewise, Ashley applies the same principle as a wife and mother. She sees herself as working for a common cause together with Brandon, whether she encounters business associates in the firm or fellow mothers in the community. All is for God's glory.

They both seek to live missionally using the strengths God has given them, which means being faithful in all the small things of everyday life. Soon after they moved to their current city, they met several local Christians who had also recently moved there. None of these young, professional believers were active in local churches, mostly because they found it difficult to relate to the traditional church structure. Knowing the importance of meeting together, Brandon and Ashley started a small Bible study with these young believers. What began as a small Bible study soon grew into a small church.

Without a background in formal Bible college or seminary training, Brandon and Ashley relied on the Holy Spirit and elder Christians in the community to provide guidance, accountability, and training for the local believers who lead preaching and teaching each week. They served in whatever supportive role they could, leading music, hosting small groups, babysitting toddlers, or coordinating leadership training. Church members began to pray for God to provide a shepherd for their church; and as they continued to meet faithfully over a period of several years, God provided a young, passionate pastor to lead the young church full time. This amazing church grew out of small, repeated moments of daily life that were a testament to faith in a big God.

None of it came about because of a "church planting strategy." It was because of faithful, righteous, and obedient living in the context of life that trust was gained among the "seekers" who later became core members of the church.

When I asked about his life on the job, Brandon spoke of his role as department manager with twenty engineers reporting to him. The national culture is one of high "power distance" and low individuality. Power distance refers to the way in which power is distributed and the extent to which the less powerful accept that power is distributed unequally. In their country, people accept a higher degree of unequal power distribution. People at the low end of the corporate totem pole see themselves as having less value than the top leaders, but it is readily accepted.

This came into debate one day during a discussion of how one can disagree appropriately. People wanted to know how the honorable foreigner would respond to this question in their high-power distance culture. Brandon saw an opportunity to take advantage of the power distance (with him at the top) and explain that he valued people with less power because he believed that God created all people with equal value and worth. He determined that he would show the same respect to everyone, whether they were a junior janitor or the CEO. He explained, "These roles have very different responsibilities, but our value as individuals is equal and precious, as image-bearers of an all-creating Father God who loves us. The practical result of this in everyday office life is that everyone must treat each other with respect." This was living out kingdom values in a counter-cultural manner. But it is what Jesus would do.

Ashley also has practical examples of how faith intersects with her everyday life. As a leader in a house church group with six to eight new mothers, and with three children under six years old herself, it was obvious to others that she served with joy as she demonstrated what a Christian home is all about. Because she knew the language and culture so well, she could take a biblical principle and ask what that would be like for them. What does Proverbs 22:6 mean when it says that one should "train up a child in the way he should go"? What does it look like to love their husbands, to be self-controlled and temperate in their culture (Titus 2:3–5)? What does "sowing discord" with neighbors look like and how does one avoid it (Prov. 6:19)? How could they practice the fruit of the spirit—love, joy, peace, patience, kindness, goodness, faithfulness, gentleness, self-control (Gal. 5:22–23)?

Brandon and Ashley are in Asia for the long term with a kingdom mentality. They have decided to turn from a typical upward mobility perspective. After much prayer, they have turned down career advancement with its lure of more money, travel opportunities, and an easier life for the sake of optimizing the chance to integrate faith with their work. Their career decisions are based on a clear understanding of how God has wired them with a biblical theology of work and the goal of pursuing the growth of God's kingdom in their city.

That does not mean life is easy, but they know that their work is ministry and that their spiritual life is integrated with their work. They are pioneers in an age where most Christians still think that the best way to serve God is in a professional ministry role. Brandon and Ashley have found otherwise. They have discovered how to live with and for Jesus with integrity in the automotive industry while living in a foreign community—all for the greater glory of God.

Bethel Avodah Foundation
A Ministry of Eurofragance Philippines Inc.

Our God is a Creator God, and he gave humanity the ability and responsibility to create. Deuteronomy 8:18 specifically states that God gives us the ability to create wealth. As creators in the image of God, we create all kinds of things: a colorful flower bouquet, a crab cake, a historical novel, the latest software, an overture, the COVID-19 vaccine, a Boeing jet, a space vehicle, a drone, and something I've recently discovered—creative fragrances!

Did you know that out of our five senses, the sense of smell is most closely linked to our memories and emotions? It has the ability to bring to the surface our deepest memories, which is why the art of fragrances has been celebrated across time and around the world, with one of the most recent being the annual Olfaction Week in Barcelona, Spain. It is complete with webinars of perfume and fragrances, an international perfumery contest, and presentations on olfactory science and culture. Eurofragance S.L.,[3] an event sponsor, is an international designer and manufacturer of creative fragrances with locations worldwide including a partner in Manila.

Eurofragance Philippines Inc. (EPI) forged a partnership with Eurofragance S.L. over twenty-two years ago and has been steadily growing every year since. It was a privilege to talk to Catherine Tan, who owns the business along with her husband Richard Tan, who is from Singapore.

You guessed it: EPI is a BAM Company. I would never have guessed that a fragrance and flavor company could be 100 percent committed to the quadruple bottom line. Here is what I learned.

Our entire conversation centered on the importance of God as the owner of the business with Richard and Catherine as the stewards of his resources, and their journey with him in terms of spiritual growth and making Christ-centered decisions in the world of business. She reminded me of the challenges of doing business in a developing economy with processes and expectations that counter the values of a kingdom business. But through it all, God has honored their commitment to integrity in bookkeeping, excellence in product and service, honesty, fairness, and devotion to the ways of the Lord in all things.

Seven years ago, it dawned on them that EPI was really a kingdom company when they learned about Business as Mission. Catherine recalls her discussion with Richard regarding a vision they both received from the Lord. It all came together and the "lights came on" when the Lord impressed upon them to construct a new building for the company, with the topmost floor dedicated as a worship hall for his glory to shine. Although this was something unexpected, they heeded the call and obeyed whole-heartedly, despite the many challenges they had to face.

Today, the Christ Our Redeemer We Trust (CRT) Building stands as a testament of God's redeeming grace and mercy in the lives of those who obey him and remain faithful to his word. At the highest portion of the structure is the Bethel Avodah Foundation, which signifies "Our work is our worship to the Lord." Through the CRT Building, EPI serves as a lighthouse in the community. Catherine describes this as "Purpose, Profit, People, and Planet."

Purpose

If you click on the "About Us" icon of the Eurofragance.com.ph website, the first thing you read is *To God be the Glory* and their theme verse for the year. In my case, it read, "You are the light of the world. A city set on a hill cannot be hidden" (Matt. 5:14). Elsewhere, their core values are listed with God-fearing being first and foremost, followed by integrity, dedication, loyalty, teamwork, and excellence.[4]

Catherine was eager to talk about how the Hebrew word *avodah* literally combines three English words into one: *work*, *service*, and *worship*. It is important for her therefore that all three function together in their new five-story building where they work, serve, and worship together in one place and at one time. It is an integrated whole. Since their company is a blessing and a gift from God, they worship him through their work, which springs from hearts of immense gratefulness and joy for God's faithfulness in their lives.

In short, their priority of purpose is to live out the whole gospel, making Jesus known from within the company first and then to the community, and together, glorifying him in everything—which led to the founding of Bethel Avodah Foundation, Inc. in 2021.

People

People are a priority, so they focus on continuous learning, both in terms of career development and personal growth. Through various programs and trainings, they promote the overall well-being of each company member. Every person who is part of the EPI team is uniquely valued—as management models the message that the success of one is the success of all. Everyone is aligned together to look ahead and focus on their common goal.

But what makes work more rewarding and meaningful for all EPI employees is knowing that they have a Christ-centered purpose complemented by their God-given gifts and abilities. Since the completion of the new building, the entire staff of more than fifty employees gathers weekly at the Bethel Avodah Worship Hall for a service led by the company pastor, with praise and worship led by their very own (in-house) music team.

"At the heart of it all is the heart," Richard is often heard saying at home and at work. At EPI, everyone's spiritual growth and maturity takes precedence. This is nurtured through short devotions Catherine sends out every morning by phone, daily Bible study fellowships with different groups, regular sharing of testimonies, daily company-wide prayers of thanksgiving and concerns from employees, home visitation Bible study to reach out to entire families (house churches), and the newly established EPI couples ministry.

It is obvious that EPI's definition of development and growth is a matter of the heart and mind—a heart that continuously draws closer to God and a mind transformed in Christ.

Profit

Along with other true BAM businesses, EPI achieved profitability some years ago. For this, Catherine gives all the glory to God, as she witnessed how he sustained them from their humble beginning. As market demand increased, profits followed, which were then plowed back into the business to promote continual growth. Their annual strategic plans are structured on a theme verse that God impresses on their hearts, which they then include in their marketing materials for clients and partners, such as paper bags and calendars.

In 2016, their annual theme verse was Isaiah 40:31:

> But those who hope in the Lord
>   will renew their strength.
> They will soar on wings like eagles;
>   they will run and not grow weary,
>   they will walk and not be faint.

Catherine said it gave her the strength and courage to soar above the challenging obstacles the business faced at the time. Year after year, with the leading of the Holy Spirit, EPI sets into motion plans of further heightening the business, which is also driven by their desire to be used by God as a vessel of blessing for their clients and partners.

Planet

When I asked Catherine how EPI demonstrated creation care in the Philippines, she pointed to their new eco-friendly building run by solar power. EPI's ISO certification also includes certain environment-friendly initiatives they incorporate into their facilities, such as water system care and maintenance. In terms of their role in the manufacturing industry, EPI together with Eurofragance S.L. endeavors to promote fragrances that have long-term benefits to consumer health and the environment.

Much more could be said of Eurofragance Philippines Inc. and its ministry, the Bethel Avodah Foundation, but for Catherine and

Richard, it is all summed up in the phrase, "As for me and for my company, we will serve the Lord."

Faith with Education, Business, and Medicine
An Integrated Model in Indonesia

I had never experienced anything of this scale before and I was nervous, to say the least.

Our small group had been invited to the Riady mansion in the Karawaci section of Jakarta, Indonesia. I looked down at the dining table and noticed that I was assigned to sit right next to our host, who had just entered the room. I—a poor country boy from Alberta, Canada—was about to meet one of the richest men in Asia: James Riady, who was worth multiple billions of dollars. I was more than nervous. I was terrified.

Just months earlier, after I retired from a management position in Pennsylvania and moved to Oregon, I was invited to join faculty and donors of Corban University on a trip to one of their overseas opportunities in Indonesia. Corban is a Christian liberal arts college in the rolling hills east of Salem, Oregon, with a vision for quality education, the character development of its students, and meeting the needs of the world through missional professionals. When we boarded our plane, I had no idea what the next ten days would entail.

Our small group visited a well-developed program that integrated teachers from the States with educators in schools developed by the Lippo Group in Indonesia. This included rural primary schools for the poor, city secondary schools, schools for the well-to-do, and Sekolah Pelita Harapan University (SPH), a Christian university in Jakarta with thirteen thousand students. We came to learn and explore opportunities.

We experienced a model of education that was Christ-centered, missional in focus, and financially sustainable. From a Business as Mission perspective, it was profitable, it created hundreds of jobs, and it had an identifiable social and missional purpose. SPH schools have a clear vision and mission statement posted publicly on their website:

> Our vision of *True Knowledge*, *Faith in Christ*, and *Godly Character* sets out our goals for our students—that they may come to understand that all *Truth* emanates from God the Creator and Sustainer and is to be found ultimately in a relationship with Jesus Christ, His Son, and our Savior. The end result of the acceptance of these truths is the development of godly character as one made in the image of God.
>
> We aim to achieve this goal by focusing on Christ as the preeminent One in God's plan of redemption in the world's restoration from its brokenness. We want our students to be people of influence and action in the world, well-equipped to engage positively wherever they may serve.
>
> We are grounded in an Evangelical, Reformed theology that seeks truth wherever it may be found and recognizes that all truth is God's. The International Baccalaureate and Cambridge programs—within a biblical worldview—allow us to develop mature, thinking students who are committed to life-long learning, able to utilize inquiry to search out the truth.[5]

This is not merely the vision of a small idealistic start-up. It reflects more than twenty-five years of growth and development that includes five flagship international schools in the Jakarta area, each with hundreds of students, with a total of sixty schools throughout the country. It also includes SPH University, which offers study programs as diverse as biotechnology, information systems, medicine, law, music conservatory, design, and engineering.

All Harapan schools were founded by two Indonesian businessmen: Johannes Oentoro and James Riady. They envisioned a network of schools in Indonesia that would transform the nation by raising educational standards at every level of society through Christian educators, which God could then use to impact Indonesia for his glory. SPH schools work in partnership with dozens of partner schools to serve families across the Indonesian archipelago.

The first SPH school was built in Lippo Village in 1993 and now serves as the directing school for the group of schools located in the

Jakarta metropolitan area. They offer Indonesian citizens and expatriate families top-quality education based on international standards with instruction in both English and Indonesian. The campuses are modern, well-resourced, and attractive. Resources include spacious classrooms, science laboratories, libraries, internet access, gymnasiums, music facilities, dance studios, swimming pools, and so on.

The faculty is a blend of expatriate and national teachers who are recruited internationally and locally. All teachers are highly qualified and relational, while also committing to grow in their own personal relationships with Jesus Christ. All seek to be used of the Lord as they serve their students in the classroom and beyond.

This is where Corban University students from Oregon come into the picture. Each year, several education students spend a minimum of one semester in an Indonesian classroom where they work alongside local teachers, overcoming cultural and language differences with their own academic experiences and spiritual journey. The impact on the students is immense.

The vision of Oentoro and Riady extends its work in education to SPH and its graduate and doctoral studies, a teachers college, an international teachers college, and a medical college. Beyond the world of education, the partnership extends to medical hospitals throughout Indonesia, providing world-class health care. In remote regions, the group establishes schools alongside clinics that serve the health needs of people in the name of Christ.

The Harapan Foundation (created by Oentoro and Riady) is doing interesting work in the remote state of Papua, serving eight villages with schools and clinics. The foundation's goal is to follow the work of pioneering missionaries of decades ago who built trust and churches among the Dani people, as well as scores of other ethnic groups.[6]

I survived that dinner engagement at the Riady mansion, even though I had not been oriented in Indonesian manners or culinary arts! I had little in common with this man of wealth, spiritual maturity, and vision for the impoverished and spiritually unreached among his country's more than three hundred ethnic groups, but our love for Christ and our life goals and values were clearly aligned.

Indonesia, with seven thousand islands spread over three thousand miles from east to west, is the fourth-largest country in the world by population and the largest Muslim nation. How is it that one man and his friend can make such a colossal difference?

In 1990, James's father, Mochtar Riady, founder of the Lippo group, sent him to the United States to set up banking interests there. It was during this time that James came to faith in Christ. He says his experience was real and produced a visible change in him as he returned home with a vision to share his faith in the ways God had gifted him: through business, hospitals, banking, retail, and education. Today, the Riady family enterprises are a wonderful example of how many sectors of society can be integrally connected with *missio Dei* in penetrating the many-layered culture and religious milieu of Indonesia. James credits God with his success in business ventures, which has given him a respected platform for missional purposes.

In addition to the Riady education vision, Siloam Hospitals are first-class facilities that provide mass health care. The foundation established a medical school by recruiting a top physician from India to lead it. Today, Siloam is the largest hospital chain in the country. As of July 2019, the chain operates thirty-six hospitals, seventeen clinics, and twenty *medikas* (medical technology centers). Here, people of all religions and walks of life are treated. We visited several of the schools, sat in classrooms, interviewed students and teachers, and marveled at what God has done as faith is integrated with business, education, and medicine to achieve his grand purposes.

On that Thursday evening, we attended a dinner with about forty high net-worth businesspeople who were all friends of Mr. Riady. What I thought was a dinner party turned out to be a prayer meeting for their trip the next day to lead discipleship groups in various distant places. Early the next morning, they headed to the airport and flew in private jets to major cities all over Muslim Indonesia to lead Bible studies. While some discipleship groups comprised only a handful of people, some had more than two hundred in attendance. This is what I call high-end Business as Mission. Because of their business success, recognition, and decision to make a difference, these businesspeople are able to help the poor and disenfranchised receive needed medical treatment as well as attend school, which then enables college students to learn a profession that brings glory to God.

James Riady would be the first to tell you that he's made mistakes along the way, but he will be most remembered as an example of the principle that when God changes the heart, the hands should respond as well. As another James of long ago reminds us, "What good is it, my brothers and sisters, if someone claims to have faith but has no deeds? . . . Faith by itself, if it is not accompanied by action, is dead" (James 2:14–17).

I was blessed to observe how an American university administration and professors, committed students, a wealthy businessman, professional people, and the Christian faith could all come together to bring change. Certainly, it is a model of what could be done many times over—in other places in the world. The system of businesses, schools, and hospitals connected to the Harapan name took seriously the Great Commandment of Jesus to love their neighbor and his Great Commission to make disciples. I had the privilege of experiencing with my own eyes how this could be integrated into one missional enterprise.

The Story of *Kerusso*: A Steel Pan Band in Brazil
From Musical Entrepreneur to Sustainable Ministry

I answered the phone on the second ring. It was Rick in the Amazon city of Belem, a rain forest jungle location where I had lived for twenty-one years. I knew the area well as I had cared for many personnel, legal, and strategic affairs as president of the mission there. I was now vice president of operations in the Philadelphia suburb of Bala Cynwyd, Pennsylvania.

"You won't believe this," Rick mused halfway through the conversation. "Chris wants to import a dozen steel pans into Brazil from Trinidad so he can start a steel drum band. What should I do?" Without hesitation, I told Rick it was a bad idea and that he should tell Chris he couldn't do it. I thought that would be the end of it, but I was wrong!

Chris was an energetic young Trinidadian missionary who had been educated in Jamaica and the United States. In 1996, I had taken him with me from the States to Brazil for his first trip to that country, but I soon discovered he didn't need me. On our first night, we stayed at the seminary in Sao Luiz. I was awake before the tropical sun rose about 5:30 a.m., but there was no Chris. He soon wandered in, and I asked him where he had been. "Oh," he replied, "I was in the dining hall all night singing songs and talking with the students." It didn't matter that he had never studied Portuguese or that he had never met anyone in Brazil before, or that the dining hall was supposed to be closed and the students sleeping. That was Chris! Gifted with languages, a musical genius, and a winner of hearts everywhere he went.

After that visit, Chris went back to the States to prepare to return to Brazil the next year as a full-time missionary with Crossworld. Soon, his entrepreneurial mind came up with the innovative idea that he could teach Brazilian young people an instrument they had never seen or heard of before: the steel pan from Trinidad. Keep in mind that this is not a small instrument like a flute or a clarinet. The steel pan is a large drum, and he needed twelve of them from an island in the Caribbean twelve hundred miles away! Not only that, but customs officials in Brazil didn't take kindly to importing such things. It was an easy no from me.

The steel pan its origin in Trinidad, where it emerged in the 1930s from industrial waste such as car parts, paint pots, dustbins, oil drums, and biscuit tins. These items are hammered into a shiny surface with a series of dents, and each dent creates a different note according to its position and size. The result is a unique percussion instrument that took time to evolve and musical skill to learn to tune.

After initial experimentation, old fifty-five-gallon oil drums came to be preferred because the bottom of the drum could be pounded into a concave bowl, and then shaped and tuned to form distinct resonating surfaces. The musical tunes for the pans came from the bowels of impoverished lower classes who merged the lyrics of their slave history with the steel pan born out of a local ban on drums by the British authorities. Although rhythmic structure closely resembles calypso music, pannists pride themselves in being able to adapt all kinds of music—Latin, jazz, pop, classical, and even music soundtracks.

Today, manufacturing steel drums is a highly specialized skill as pans are not standardized and depend on innovation and creativity in the tuning, designed to meet the demands of the customers, who often compete with other bands. There are bass pans, rhythm pans, and tenor pans. Today, the instrument's origins in folk music and rusty drums on the streets played by rebellious teenagers is often forgotten, as the music of a steel band is respectable and recognized as the national instrument of Trinidad. Similarly, Calypso music plays an important role in carnivals and concerts, as it often documents the stories of yesteryear and provides social and political expression.[7]

Despite my opposition, Chris and Rick did import the drums, which experienced a miraculous clearance in customs and survived the literally rocky road to the city of Sao Luiz. On August 9, 1997, Chris and more than twenty teenagers and twenty-somethings, who were eagerly waiting to see their first drums, become the first pannists in Brazil. The following January, I arrived in Brazil for a visit. I was picked up by friends at the airport who took me to the mission base where I once again enjoyed a Brazilian meal and then made my way to the first conference meeting. My British friend Joe Rowley met me at the door. "You won't believe what you are going to hear," he said. "The great English hymn 'Holy, Holy, Holy' is being played by the new steel drum band led by Chris; they are called *Kerusso*" (meaning "I proclaim the gospel"). While I'm not considered a music aficionado and have a serious lack of skills in comprehending musical styles, I could tell that I was about to hear something special.

It turns out that Chris, a son of the islands, was true to his heritage. Not only could he play the drums but he could also compose. That night we all heard "Holy, Holy, Holy" arranged with a mix of English hymnology, Trinidadian calypso and reggae, Brazilian *sertanejo*, and a flare of American country. And so began the journey of the twenty-member Brazilian steel pan band *Kerusso*, which continues after more than twenty years. They have now played for the Brazilian president and performed at sold-out concerts on five continents.

Music is an important component of every culture. It has the ability to preserve cultural nuances, tell stories, encourage emotion in the soul, share ideas between age groups, connect to others, teach, encourage dance and celebration, communicate theology, and provide identity. As Henry Wadsworth Longfellow once observed, "Music is the universal language of mankind."

Kerusso makes music, and its music speaks across cultures. There is something for everybody. Even as I have listened to them numerous times, my thoughts have traveled in the direction of a Christian hymn, or the pain of the enslaved, or the history of my own culture.

Besides being a first-rate musician, Chris was also committed to making disciples of Jesus, beginning with his band members. One of them, Marcia Lima, says, "Chris was our conductor and our pastor, and he always ministered to our heart, reminding us of how important it is to have an intimate relationship with God and recognize our identity in him who is God above all things." I have talked to several others, and they all credit Chris with not trying to make them missionaries or pastors; instead, he continually encouraged them to develop their profession for the greater glory of God.

Even though they all came from the humble beginnings of poverty in the *bairros* of northeast Brazil, they began to see what God is doing in the world, and their engagement with *Kerusso* inspired them to move toward professional studies. Marcia remembers their trip to Germany in 2015, where *Kerusso* played and spoke to the various audiences, while also helping Syrian refugees. She relates how she listened to their stories of pain, loss, and fear, and how she was changed herself, so that today she is more sensitive to Muslim people. Since then, she has begun to take steps toward opening a school for victims of persecution.

Band members became engineers, medical doctors, teachers, tech professionals, architects, designers, and therapists, among other professions, but their passion for music and Jesus began with many hours a week spent in disciplined practice. In their first year as a group, they traveled to other Brazilian states, having added some other complementary instrumentalists, and learned to share their testimonies during the concerts. In their second year, they launched their first CD. Two years after their start, the group wanted to take their first international trip to the United States and Canada, and Chris wanted me to make the arrangements in North America. By this time, I had come to realize that sometimes leaders don't have all the answers; sometimes leaders need to listen; sometimes they need to break the rules. And so it was that I learned from Chris, who listened to God, and I learned I needed to listen to Chris as well as God. I coordinated that first two-week trip to Washington, DC, Philadelphia, Los Angeles, San Diego, Chicago, and Miami, among other cities, small and large.

I will never forget the sight of fourteen young people coming out from a concert in Chicago and experiencing snow for the first time. Who taught them to lie on their backs and make snow angels? Who taught them to take wet snow and make snowballs and throw them at each other? Who taught them to make snowmen? They learned it all in one day in Chicago! Everywhere they went they made friends, and everywhere they went they saw their mission fulfilled: people drew closer to God, others came to faith for the first time, and many determined to follow Jesus with their whole lives. The group was a novelty wherever they went; but more than that, they drew attention to God and to the Savior of the world, Jesus Christ.

In 2000, *Kerusso* returned to the United States where missionary Glenn Kurka coordinated their trip, and then on they journeyed to Switzerland. Chris remembers their two weeks in Europe among people with behaviors and mannerisms totally opposite from the relational culture of Brazil. "Imagine the idea of *being on time* having a higher priority than *talking with people*," he said. But they adapted quickly and used these differences as an opportunity for spiritual growth and developing flexibility.

Chris remembers their first trip to Canada. After playing at a Christian college, a student came up and confessed he was planning to commit suicide; but because of the *Kerusso* testimonies, his life was changed. Similar stories can be told of their trips to England, the Philippines, Italy, France, Egypt, Peru, Germany, Trinidad and Tobago, and three trips to the United States.

Now, many years later, Chris has married and moved to Europe, all the while discipling others and serving his community. But what about *Kerusso*? The steel drum band continues with Junior Viera, who began as a teenager and is now the leader. More than twenty years later, he plays with his son, who is a university student and a *Kerusso* drummer. Today's band of fifteen members consists of seven original members.

The band is financially independent and sustainable. They have presented concerts on Brazilian national television and regularly travel within the country with one or two concerts per month. In 2020, their planned trip to Spain was postponed due to the coronavirus, but they are not deterred. At this writing, Junior assured me that the original passion for all people to hear the good news continues, which "takes dedication, hard work, commitment, responsibility and love for the gospel."

Marcos, who was thirteen when he first played in the band, says that he credits this experience with his spiritual formation. This is because Chris required everyone to be able to share a short testimony. This not only contributed to their spiritual growth, but God used it to touch other lives as well. Marcos remembers the time in Egypt when they met persecuted Sudanese Christian refugees in Egypt who were totally destitute. As they played, danced, and worshiped God with them, God spoke to him. Marcos took the money he had set aside for souvenirs and gave it to them. He told me, "Today, I can say that was the best memory I could have."

I remember Luciana, who joined the band at the age of eighteen. She had prayed when she was seven years old that God would change the color of her skin because she only ever saw Black people as raw material for jokes and disdain; she wanted to be white. But when she met Chris, who is also Black, she realized that her identity as a Black woman was a gift from God, and that she would serve the Lord the way he had made her. God began to heal her childhood race-related traumas, and she saw that she was not only accepted by him but also important to him.

Luciana has told her story many times. One she remembers well also took place in Egypt, when she spoke to members of the Sudanese refugee church. "That night while talking, I saw eyes shining, impacted, and identifying with me. Refugees saw themselves as subservient to whites and saw themselves less valuable and wished they had fair skin. They were seeing right then that their identity was important to God and others, and some came up to me afterwards with thanks and enormous joy."

Band members like Junior, Marcos, and Marcia—along with Lucianne, Nadalia, Luciana, Allen, and so many more—have learned that their profession, their love for music, and their identity in and love for Christ all join in an integrated whole. Sunday is not different from the other six days of the week. Chris says that they are comfortable speaking before five to ten thousand people or living and sharing their faith one on one. They truly represent the spirit and the intent of this book: integrating faith with work and faith with sustainable activity. "Whatever you do, work at it with all your heart, as working for the Lord" (Col. 3:23).

Matt's Story
"It May Be More about the Journey Than the Destination"

Matt lives in a crowded city in Asia where his business demands a driver take him from place to place. Naturally he has become close friends with the driver, Wang Wei, who had plenty of opportunities to observe Matt's family. As he did so, he saw something quite different from what he was used to—something he wanted for his family too. He kept watching and then began talking to Matt about what he was seeing. There were plenty of conversations before Wang Wei became a true follower of Jesus. Matt now is privileged to disciple him in his new life in Christ.

There he was—as big as life on my computer screen. Thanks to video conferencing, I was able to "visit" with Matt in his living room in East Asia.

I had not seen him since Albuquerque, New Mexico, in 2012 when we had shared teaching roles in a seminar. We now talked about his completion of an MBA in Texas, his marriage and subsequent children, and his business endeavors in the real estate sector in Asia.

Before I met Matt, he had graduated with a degree in computer programming and worked for a multinational IT service company in Europe. Then it was off to manage a leather factory in Asia for seven years. It was all pretty impressive for someone to accomplish while still in his twenties and early thirties. But I was curious about the condition of his soul, his passion, how he viewed the world, and what his driving force consisted of beyond technology, real estate, and business success.

I couldn't help thinking about various questions: What makes for good choices? How does one find good mentors? How does one balance faith and work? What really makes one happy? Here is what I learned from Matt.

Spend Time with God-Fearing People in Church, Family, and Community

Matt found himself at a point of decision after college and again after graduate school. By then, he knew that he wanted to listen to God and obey any direction God might have for him. Even though the exact opportunity was not obvious, he started with what he knew for sure. He knew God had given him technical skills. He also had passions for art, his family's real estate business, and he wanted to be available to serve God cross-culturally. These clues made him think about the tech world, about how art speaks to the soul, and about how he could program computers. Concerned that there were too many options, he prayed and asked others to pray. He also talked with his family and friends. It wasn't long until an opportunity presented itself for him to work overseas using his management and technical abilities.

Look for People to Be Your Mentors

The Greeks used the word *mentor* to mean a wise advisor, counselor, or teacher. In Homer's *Odyssey*, Mentor was a friend of Odysseus who advised his son Telemachus and whom Odysseus put in charge of his household when he left for Troy. A mentor encourages a person toward desired ends and provides a model, stretching that person toward a higher level and empowering them by providing positive influence.

Matt knew that everyone needs a mentor, but finding one isn't always easy. The first step is to remind yourself that you need one and not resist the idea. Then be on the lookout, praying all the while that you'll know it when the timing is right. Sometimes a mentor comes about through hanging out with the person or just paying attention to what you can learn from someone who has been down the trail before you.

Matt remembered a mentor after college who advised him to use the skill set from his BS degree in computer programming and learn what it means to depend on God as a programmer. He knew he could handle the programming job but had no clue what it meant to depend on God through his work. The mentor knew that he needed to learn that.

Matt also cited two mentors he had in Asia on his first stint over there. These mentors were in two different businesses but had the same heart and desire to mentor him. From them, he learned the importance of listening. One of them taught him how to pray about how his business could meet human needs by providing a job in the factory. Matt learned that God wanted him to work *with* God in all he did, not just *for* him. That meant "walking with God at work." He learned that the key factor of success is his relationship with God, which affects his relationships with political authorities, bosses, employees, suppliers, customers—everyone!

Matt mentioned how important it is to be salt and light in all we do. His mentors taught him to have that intuitive response, and now it comes naturally to him. He has learned to go beyond creating value in the company product and now seeks values such as love, trust, grace, joy, forgiveness, respect, and truth.

Find Ways to Serve and Even Mentor Others

Matt told an interesting story of a two-month internship trip he took to Ukraine after college. The leader there sent the interns into an unfamiliar city to observe and discover what they should do for their two-month assignment. Although this host person knew what they should be doing, he designed a Socratic exercise to help them discover it for themselves. Matt never forgot that learning experience, as the next two months were amazingly profitable as the group found Ukrainian youth to mentor in English and in faith.

While working for the IT company years later, Matt decided to get involved with unreached people in the metropolis where he resided. He would take the subway to the section of the city with emigrants from the Middle East. There he joined the "Speakers Corner" and talked about religion and heart issues with them, learning about Islam while sharing his Christian faith. The day I talked to Matt via video conferencing, he was studying the book of Genesis with Wang Wei, who is only one of those he was mentoring.

Keep Flexible and Be Willing to Learn

Matt reflected on the various jobs he has had in relationship to his commitment to live out his faith in the marketplace. He has worked as a "job taker" while with the multinational tech company in Europe and in the real estate business in the United States and in Asia. That meant he was under authority like everyone else and could demonstrate kingdom values such as faithfulness, timeliness, respect, excellence, community, hospitality, encouragement, and giving.

He has also been a "job maker." For seven years, he managed more than a hundred people, hiring, supervising, and caring for those who were disadvantaged and disenfranchised. He did so with a servant's heart, by empowering them, and providing familial

help, care, love, generosity, encouragement, and many more kingdom values.

He also has experienced being his own boss and working pretty
much alone with infrequent contact with only a few people. This
caused him to consider different strategies but still be intentional
in integrating faith with business dealings. Once on a business trip,
he and his partner found themselves in an open conversation about
spiritual things. One doesn't usually ask others what they would do
if they died today. But it seemed appropriate that day. As a result,
his business client said he wanted to believe in Jesus. Amazingly,
so did his whole family. This story reminded me of Crispus, the
synagogue leader, who became a believer, along with his entire
household (Acts 18:8).

Due to his networks in other cities, Matt was able to recommend some pastors from local house churches to disciple the family.

Open Your Eyes to Human Need and Do Something About It

We know that not all of life centers in the business or marketplace. What about the community? What about connections unrelated to business? For these areas, Matt developed a perspective of
keeping an open mind and heart.

One time on a business trip to a larger city farther north, he
learned about a ministry to help victims of human trafficking,
which takes place in three phases: (1) Reach those entrapped in
slavery; (2) rescue them by bringing down barriers and providing
a safe place; and (3) restore them through counseling, therapy, and
by providing vocational training for a new career. As an entrepreneur, Matt knew what he needed to do, and he set about addressing the third phase: starting a business as a means to restore these
survivors and help them find hope with a job. Today, this ministry
thrives with others in leadership roles.

His income and flexibility in the commercial real estate industry provided an even greater vision, such as constructing an office
high-rise building. From his office rental profits, Matt helps fight

trafficking by aiding victims. In his church where he is an elder, he helps others to get involved.

I came away from my discussion with Matt dreaming of the same involvement for all young people entering their careers in the marketplace. While some are called to church or parachurch ministries, which they should pursue, most will enter the marketplace seeking to integrate their faith with their work.

A Philadelphia Lawyer
At Work at Home and in Asia

In 2005, when I was living in the Philadelphia area, I attended a prayer meeting at my church that focused on Business as Mission, particularly in the unreached areas of the world. The meeting was coordinated by Tony, a Philadelphia lawyer. Our group met after church a couple of times a month, so I got to know and appreciate Tony's passion of how his profession could connect with God's mission in the world.

I had heard the term "Philadelphia Lawyer" before, but I had never met a Philadelphia lawyer and didn't know the history of the term. The first known published use of it dates back to 1788, when many noted attorneys hailed from early Philadelphia. Some speculation credits Benjamin Franklin with inspiring the expression. Others suggest the Scottish-American Philadelphia attorney Andrew Hamilton, who famously helped acquit newspaper publisher John Peter Zenger of libel charges in 1735, paving the way for freedom of the press. In any case, the term describes a lawyer who either knows the minute points of the law or is an exceptionally competent lawyer.

Tony is a member of the Philadelphia Bar Association and has his own law practice, concentrating on civil rights and personal injury as well as corporate, nonprofit, and international business law. I wondered how his faith and his work intersected in Philadelphia as well as with his interest in the world, particularly those regions with social injustice records and those unreached with the good news of the gospel.

Tony was raised in a loving, churchgoing family in Pennsylvania, but he never understood the gospel when he was young. He was musical, so he joined rock and roll bands and the party scene. While in university, he joined a top academic fraternity, but it was full of drinking, drugs, immorality, and plenty of parties. He remembers thinking, "Is this all there is?" By God's grace, in his senior year he was drawn to the "I've Found It" program sponsored by Campus Crusade for Christ, which is where he finally really heard the gospel. He didn't begin to follow Jesus until he was in law school when he realized how God kept putting Christians into his life: a roommate, members of a Bible study, and invitations to attend a Bible-preaching church. It was then that he realized he needed a savior and prayed to receive Christ.

Today, Tony heads up the local mission outreach at his church. Together with other churches, he serves the community and disciples those he meets, such as a foreign student who attends university and a high school student who is now in ministry as a career. Tony is currently mentoring a student he met overseas. In his work, many of his clients have become friends. They all have heard the good news by observing it in his life and hearing his verbal witness to them. He also works hard to share Jesus with the unbelieving members of his family.

Tony likes to remind people that God is a God of love and a God of justice. The conversation reminded me of Scripture verses such as Psalm 140:12: "I know that the LORD will maintain the cause of the afflicted and will execute justice for the needy" (ESV). Tony fights for the victims of injustice both in America and in Asia, trying to make a difference. His overseas efforts have led him to nine different countries, including one that he visited twenty-five times over a twelve-year period. He teaches classes in English and in law with a focus on justice, litigation, international business, and ethics.

His country of preference (the one he visits so often) prohibits proselytism and most people fear the secret police. But a foreigner like Tony can live out his Christian faith in all aspects of a typical day. Such a day for Tony includes formal class lectures and discussions, but also living in a hotel, eating breakfast while getting to know the local staff, interacting with the students, getting together after hours to play the guitar and teach English songs, going to the gym, and then having dinner with more students. Everywhere he taught law, English, and life lessons; and everywhere, he made friends and encouraged people.

For a while he worked with Global Scholars, a group "called to equip missional Christian academics to have a redemptive influence among their students, colleagues, universities, and academic disciplines." Their vision "is that one day every student, colleague, university, and discipline will have Christian professors who communicate the truth, goodness, and beauty of Christ in the power of the Spirit for the flourishing (*shalom*) of society as they serve Christ in global higher education." Their mantra is: "To change a nation, teach its leaders. To teach its leaders, influence its universities."

Tony represents well the testimony of the group as stated on the website:

> Our academics also have had unprecedented influence beyond their universities. Afghan universities invited Global Scholars to provide leadership training for top-level university employees. They carried with them Jesus's message of servant leadership. The Nigerian government once tasked our professors to develop an AIDS awareness program. They targeted the pupils in public elementary and secondary schools. Teachers taught biblical values to hundreds of thousands of children using this program. A Global Scholar in Central Asia served on a presidential commission. Leaders asked him to improve and "humanize" criminal law procedures in that country. He was able to introduce a biblical view of law and justice to a nation closed to the gospel.[8]

Tony's story reminds me of another attorney friend of mine who traveled to the newly formed country of Slovakia in the early 1990s during a time of turmoil in Eastern Europe. Because of the network my friend created, God opened the door for him to use his law experience and knowledge of the US Constitution to help this new country write its very first constitution. It is my hope that through stories like Tony's, many Jesus-followers will understand their unique role in integrating faith and work. Thank God Tony did—and still does!

Super Gifts Inc.
Valuable Gifts Made by Valuable People

Just about everyone loves to receive a gift, but we also have the privilege of giving to others. We may browse a department store, or more likely surf the internet for something that might be appropriate, thinking about the recipient's tastes, the quality of the product, how soon it can arrive, and so on. But have you ever thought about the people who make your gifts?

For the owners of Super Gifts, the quality of the product is important, but they put even more emphasis on the people who make the product: how they are treated, the needs of their family, fair wages, and a loving community. In short, Super Gifts is a business that cares for people first and then the product.

In 2012, I met Gary Sanders, founding partner and president of Super Gifts, at a conference in Atlanta. Since I expressed interest in how their factory functioned in Asia around their principles, he invited me to visit their US office and then their factory in Asia. When I visited their office and warehouse about a year later, I met with Gary to learn more about this company. Here is their mission statement:

> For twenty-five years, Super Gifts has been dedicated to the art of giving. We understand that at the intersection of what a gift means and how it makes the recipient feel is just a little bit of magic. Gifts are often at the center of the most important relationships in our lives. Combining our craftsmanship, luxury materials, innovative design and personalization on every product, Super Gifts customers can make a significant impact for a reasonable price. We care as much about people as we do about our products. We believe work should be more than just a place to earn a living.

As we walked around the building, I noted dozens of large boxes along one wall. "These are T-shirts and towels for a cruise company," Gary explained. "They order thousands of such items." I then learned that universities of the Southeastern Conference (SEC) are also clients of Super Gifts—and even one US president!

Although Super Gifts began in 1991, it wasn't until 2004 that they decided to stop sourcing their product from various independent suppliers and open their own factory in Asia. By product offshoring, which became popular after China joined the World Trade Organization in 2001, they were able to implement the principles at the core of the company. Gary and cofounder Jake Wilson decided to make this change after they learned about Business as Mission and decided that their business also had a core purpose beyond profit to the shareholders. Their product is quality gifts; their mission is people.

My guide as I visited their factory in Asia was the manager Kelly, who arrived in Asia in 1985 but then returned in 1992 when someone encouraged him to "go back to the East, love people, and see what you can do." He was mentored by George, who owned another factory nearby and lived what he taught. George's principles soon provided the light for Super Gift's future, such as "Business as Mission is simply walking with God at work," and "Find out where people are and meet them there." In fact, as we observed more than one hundred workers that day, quotes emerged everywhere, representative of a much deeper reality.

"All day long on the factory floor," Kelly stated, "is an opportunity for discipleship." He then told my tour group about an event earlier that week when two line foremen were having an argument, with one blaming the other for holding up his production line. Kelly was called and he treated them both respectfully, asking questions and providing insight. After things had calmed down and a couple of days had passed, one of them asked, "Where did that response of the boss come from? We don't do it that way in our culture." The answer, of course, is rooted in the principles of Jesus. In that event, Kelly had discipled the two employees, even though they were not yet Jesus-followers.

As we observed production lines at work, we heard the story of two production teams of deaf-mute workers, supervised by Lilly. It is best told by Kelly himself:

> Lilly was quite shy when she first joined Super Gifts in 2004, in part because of her deafness. Soon after her first day of work, several Super Gifts co-workers made a commitment to learn sign language and befriended Lilly. Today, Lilly has blossomed into a confident, outgoing, and popular member of the Super Gifts family at our factory. She now seeks out new employees and gives of herself to make them feel comfortable and respected as integral members of the team. She loves the nurturing, supportive atmosphere at the factory, where value is placed on friendship, encouragement, and excellence.

How is it that in a country where the handicapped and disenfranchised have limited opportunities, they are treated so differently at Super Gifts? Kelly explains:

- It starts with who God is: "Lord, our Lord, how majestic is your name in all the earth" (Ps. 8:1).

- Sacrifices (religious activities) are meaningless unless we have a repentant heart and do justice. "Learn to do right; seek justice. Defend the oppressed. Take up the cause of the fatherless; plead the case of the widow" (Isa. 1:17–18).

- Building the kingdom of God starts in the relationships with colleagues, as in John 15:12: "My command is this: Love each other as I have loved you."

- Take time to build relationships, so people will see authenticity; we ask ourselves continually what relationships look like.

- We look at truth like the two rails of a railroad—one is demonstration, and one is proclamation; one does not work without the other. We live out truth and we speak truth.

- People see God by the way we live out our life; the way we treat others is a reflection of who God is.

- Love builds trust, which creates opportunity.

- We love the employees, not because we want them to be Christians; we love them because we are Christians. That is why we pay above market and provide medical benefits, even though we don't have to.

- People matter as people; not because they are a project.

- Work is ministry; work is worship.

- Every part of life is to bring glory to God.

Kelly told the story of a university freshman, whom he had saved from desperate conditions in an orphanage when she was a baby. And he told another story about a girl now graduating from college who had been rescued as an abandoned toddler.

We learned more stories about how this company cares for their employees. They cared for Will enough to provide him with a low-interest loan to build a house for his family. When May had cancer and feared she would lose her job while she was off during treatment, they assured her that wouldn't happen. Not only that, but the company even helped pay her medical bills. They figured out a job for Shelle, a woman with Down's Syndrome, as well as Shadrach, an amputee.

Although there was a small elevator, I'll never forget hiking up six flights of stairs to a floor completely dedicated to handicapped children, a social project of the company. Appropriately named "Giving Hope," this program provides medical treatment and even surgery by a team of twenty professionals who work within the state system. This community development arm not only works with special needs children but also manages a care room for infants at risk, provides a day camp for employees' children in the summer, and teaches skills to the kids.

Super Gifts is a successful business with many well-known companies and organizations as clients, plus a hundred and fifty boutique retail stores across the United States. But it is more than that: it is a ministry; it is a place where owners and managers live and work *with* Jesus, not just *for* him. They have all learned to integrate their faith and work, for God's glory. The factory exists for kingdom activity, and in the words of owner Gary Sanders, "All we have to do is listen to the Lord, obey, and watch him work."

Kijabe Hospital and MyungSung Christian Medical Center
Sustainable Missional Medicine

In the world of missions, one does not normally think of medical ministry as meeting the BAM "financial stability" criteria, or even considering it a priority. God's people have traditionally supported medical efforts in the name of Christian altruism and concern for the human condition. And so most efforts to this day that address disease, emergency medicine, modern surgery, pediatrics, and routine health-care diagnosis are provided as something that Christians should do.

However, using the assumption that charity will not always be there to solve the world's medical needs, it is admirable to find examples of medical facilities that champion sustainable medicine. Two examples are highlighted here.

Kijabe Hospital is a faith-based hospital forty miles north of Nairobi, Kenya. It was started by African Inland Mission and is sponsored today by the African Inland Church (AIC). Originally named Theodora Hospital, it was established in 1915 as an outpatient clinic at the Rift Valley Academy. Today it is a multi-specialty facility with a bed capacity of 363, serving patients from all over Kenya and other African countries. The hospital's mission is to "glorify God through compassionate health care provision, excellent training and spiritual ministry in Christ Jesus."[9]

They have experienced continual growth such that today there are nine operating rooms, a modern ICU, dental and ENT clinics, and laboratory/pathology units, among other services. The Comprehensive Care Clinic provides free outpatient HIV/AIDS care in partnership with the Christian Health Association of Kenya (CHAK). The hospital also runs three satellite clinics in Nairobi, Marira, and Naivasha. The Kijabe School of Nursing (now Kijabe

College of Health Sciences) was registered with the Nursing Council of Kenya in 1980 and officially commenced training as the Kenya Enrolled Community Health Nurses program (KECHN). The Kenya Registered Community Health Nurse (KRNA) and Emergency and Critical Care Clinical Officers (ECCCO) programs have since been introduced as the college continues to grow.

The nine hundred staff facility is as modern as any hospital in the West, with inpatient facilities for internal medicine, ICU, oncology, pediatrics, maternity, nutrition, and physiotherapy. Outpatient care includes audiology, emergency medicine, chemotherapy, dentistry, maternal/child health, OB/GYN, HIV/AIDS, physiotherapy, and more. Surgeries include cataract, caesarean section, ear/nose/throat, general surgery, orthopedic/joint replacement, pediatric, plastic and reconstructive, and urology.

My original interest piqued when my wife's cousin Steve and his wife Melinda joined the staff. Melinda is a physical therapist, while Steve serves the local Maasai community with technical skills. Steve and his five brothers were born and raised in Africa and speak Swahili and Lingala fluently. While studying in the States, their hearts remained in Africa, and three brothers returned to the continent to serve the African people.

While living in the Philadelphia area, I met a Dr. Bob Snyder, who taught emergency medicine at Thomas Jefferson Hospital. He introduced me to *The Saline Solution: Sharing Christ in a Busy Practice*[10] and to his own stories of making disciples as a physician and medical professor. He had learned practical ways to integrate faith in the hospital, which included spiritual conversations initially rooted in the patient's experience. He showed me that all Christian medical professionals realize that their knowledge and skill may be God's way of fulfilling the promises in Jeremiah 30:17: "'But I will restore you to health and heal your wounds,' declares the LORD." He spent four years in Eastern Europe teaching integrative principles to medical professionals in Hungary, where he started IHS Global, which helps to "equip Christian healthcare workers who are already caring for the physical needs of their patients to also care for their spiritual needs."[11]

The link between physical and spiritual health is well established in Scripture, and hospitals like Kijabe have an advantage in drawing those connections together in time of suffering. The doctor's office or the surgeon's table may be where the body is healed, but it also is where patients draw near to Jesus. As the prophet Isaiah said, "You restored me to health and let me live. Surely it was for my benefit that I suffered such anguish" (Isa. 38:16–17).

Mary survived emergency surgery in the Kijabe Hospital, giving birth to a twenty-six-week-old premature baby at less than two pounds. She and the baby are healthy today, and she has grown spiritually. Looking back, she thanks the staff: "God bless you all as you serve mankind and to God be all the glory. It is all about God."

Regarding financial and management sustainability, although historically a mission hospital, Kijabe today is 100 percent operated by Kenyan administrative staff, leaving only a few international medical professionals who volunteer to provide specialized services. As they say in one of their value statements, "We are a national hospital that is socially and environmentally responsible, that is focused on financial stewardship to ensure ability to meet our financial commitments and reward our employees appropriately." The hospital's major source of funding is patient revenue, which funds operational costs, and it does source development funds for capital projects from local and international donors.

There are many medical facilities in the developing world today that provide a needed service, though they rely on expertise and funding from abroad. But the sustainability story of Kijabe is welcome in today's world; it is a function of a mature national church and a country with political and economic stability.

Ethiopia is the more populous country to the north of Kenya, which has experienced strong economic growth in recent years. However, the country is still one of the poorest in Africa, with 45 percent below the poverty line, ethnic tensions, violence, a large displacement and refugee population, and acute cases of HIV/AIDS, tuberculosis, maternal mortality, and malnutrition.[12] Needless to say, medical care is at a premium, and many places are dependent on foreign-funded hospitals and clinics.

One such hospital, MyungSung Christian Medical Center (MCM), is located in Addis Ababa, Ethiopia. Founded in 2004 by MyungSung Presbyterian Church of South Korea, its goal is to provide quality health care to Ethiopians and others. As the first state-of-the-art hospital in the country, it strives for enrichment over profits as it looks to make a positive long-term impact on Ethiopia's health-care infrastructure. All profits remain in the country for growth and development.

Our interest here relates to a small start-up facility operating under a revenue sharing MOU (Memorandum of Understanding) with MCM. Sight for Souls has three ophthalmologists committed to addressing a serious eye disease in the country, trachoma. My good friend Ken Leahy is the treasurer of this for-profit organization.

Trachoma is the leading infectious cause of blindness worldwide, affecting 41 million people, most of them in the world's poorest countries. Children are the most frequently infected by trachoma. If untreated, it causes a painful and irreversible blindness between the ages of thirty to forty. Ethiopia is severely affected and makes up 30 percent of trachoma cases in all of Africa. In fact, trachoma is the second leading cause of blindness in the country. Trachoma is a completely preventable cause of blindness that can be treated through a safe, affordable surgical procedure that costs only $40 per patient. Ken provided much of the financial planning and work for what now is a clinic with nine staff members plus doctors.

Sight for Souls is inspired by the self-sustaining Aravind Eye Care model, developed in India by Dr. Venkataswamy, who wished to establish an alternate eye care model that could supplement the efforts of the government and also be self-supporting. Aravind, with its mission to "eliminate needless blindness," provides large-volume, high-quality, and affordable care. Fifty percent of its patients receive services either free of cost or at a steeply subsidized rate, yet the organization remains financially self-sustainable. Much importance is given to equity—ensuring that all patients are accorded the same high-quality care and service, regardless of their economic status. A critical component of Aravind's model is the

high patient volume, which brings with it the benefits of economies of scale. Aravind's unique assembly-line approach increases
productivity tenfold. Over 4.5 lakh (one hundred thousand) eye
surgeries or procedures are performed a year at Aravind, making
it one of the largest eye care providers in the world. Since its inception, Aravind has handled more than 5.6 crore (fifty-six million)
outpatient visits and performed more than 60 lakh (six million)
surgeries. The Aravind Eye Care System now serves as a model for
India and the rest of the world.[13]

The Aravind approach is not only unique for its competent
eye care and financial sustainability, but also because in India it is
linked with the spiritual Hindu component of life. It was an easy
transfer for the American organization Sight for Souls to design
a Christian integration of spiritual insight to improved physical
sight. Now a modern eye clinic facility in a high-risk country
like Ethiopia is proving the ability to bring sustainable eye care,
financial stability, and the making of disciples of Jesus into one
integrated whole. Sight for Souls has a myriad of standard medical values, but this one stands out for the spiritual component of
the work:

> Sight for Souls is committed to caring for the spiritual and emotional
> needs of patients and their families affected by blindness in the de-
> veloping world. In all our endeavors, we aim to demonstrate the love
> of Jesus Christ through our words and actions and conduct all as-
> pects of our organization with honesty and integrity. We will partner
> with local churches and ministries and all communities who invite
> us to serve, in order to build the Church strategically where we work,
> maintaining a special focus on the urban and rural poor.[14]

As of mid-2021, Sight for Souls in Ethiopia had arrived at the
financial break-even point and was looking to expand by starting
vision centers separate from the hospital to provide more accessible
and convenient treatment. Ken reports that a grant has provided
funds for equipment for retina treatment. Funds have been made
available for outreach in rural communities, and the project is experiencing encouraging results.

Surely, modern medicine is one more example of professional expertise becoming the catalyst for *missio Dei*, which thus disrupts the status quo. Although it may take a long time, as in the case of the Kijabe Hospital, it is attainable. It may need to start off with strong capital, such as with MCM, or the expertise required as in the case of Sight for Souls following the Aravind model. Both cases provide evidence for sustainable medical careers as kingdom work—for the greater glory of God and the extending of his kingdom in all the earth.

Transnational Missional Executives as Disciple-Makers
Witness as a Noun, not a Verb

It is the proposition of this book that the making of disciples is the task of every Jesus-follower and that the assumption of the past two hundred years that the task is best out-sourced to the professional "missionary" should be challenged and perhaps even rejected. Without a doubt, the words *missionary* and *missions* are (at minimum) being subjected to varied and contradictory nuances and (at worst) even being distorted. What is a missionary? Who are missionaries? Are all believers missionaries? Are missionaries needed today? Should we not focus on our own country first? If the Bible doesn't use the word *missionary*, then why do we use it today? With the missionary enterprise changing so rapidly, does it mean God is changing his mission as well?

In a 2018 *Atlantic* article titled "A New Generation Redefines What It Means to Be a Missionary," Sarah Imtiaz writes,

> In 1970, according to the Center for the Study of Global Christianity, there were 240,000 foreign Christian missionaries worldwide. By 2000, that number had grown to 440,000. And by 2013, the center was discussing in a report the trend of "reverse mission, where younger churches in the Global South are sending missionaries to Europe," even as the numbers being sent from the Global North were "declining significantly." The report noted that nearly half of the top 20 mission-sending countries in 2010 were in the Global South, including Brazil, India, the Philippines, and Mexico.[15]

There is an increasing propensity today to attempt a demys-
tification of the meaning of the term "missions" and attempt to
redefine and recalibrate the Great Commission. Certainly, the first
disciples and their apostolic leaders were not encumbered with institutional bureaucracy, pay scales, and spiritual metrics. Missional
business leader Jim Lapinski risks a charge of reductionistic thinking when he asks missional business leaders in the international
marketplace, "What is God asking you to do?" The question begs
the simplest of responses: "To introduce people to Jesus."

Lapinski tells the story of an exchange he had with Noreen, an
executive of a global industrial design company assigned to a strategic Asian division. She had been recruited because of her strong
record of corporate turn-arounds, and her faith was recognized as
a positive thing. Noreen wanted to make a difference in her new
company, so she set about changing policy and procedures to reflect her Christian values. It was her way of trying to be a witness,
but the company atmosphere remained as toxic as ever and without
the desired sales results.

At a weekend seminar, Noreen asked Jim for his counsel. He
soon made the assessment that as a believer, Noreen was wrestling
with the question of how to lead the "spiritually dead," expecting
employees to respond to godly things as Jesus-followers would. She
failed to realize that the spiritually dead could not be expected to
pretend they were alive. Jim then asked her the question, "What
is God asking you to do?" After some time of reflection, she responded, "To introduce people to Jesus."

But what did it all mean? Was she not trying her best to witness
to her employees? After several stimulating questions and multiple
sessions at the seminar, alternate conclusions began to emerge. She
could introduce people to Jesus by caring for them, spending time
learning more about them and their families, helping them with
issues, or just caring (without trying to change them!). She began
to look at each person individually and build a relationship with
them committed to their personal good, helping them flourish in
their position in the company. She began to see biblical "witness" as

a noun rather than a verb. She was to be a witness (Acts 1:8) before she was to do witnessing.

So, she stopped demanding improved behavior from her employees and started to live like Jesus would live. The results were amazing, and employees began to ask about the change in her. She stopped demanding that they follow her Christian values, and she began to serve and develop them as people, caring for them in holistic ways. Before long, the operation that had been hemorrhaging began to heal and the atmosphere improved.

What does this have to do with missionary work? After all, Noreen was not a missionary. She did, however, become a missional professional, living the values of Jesus in a way that gospel principles were "caught" by the members of her team. She began to experience what Billy Graham described as the missional world of the twenty-first century: living out the gospel of Jesus in the marketplace.

Jim tells story after story of Christians who had given up on the idea of linking their faith with their work. They gave up witnessing. It just didn't seem to work. One such American executive, Ryan, was working in Asia with a difficult anti-Christian boss. Though he loved his work, Ryan hated the job because of this problematic relationship. Would he ever see a change in the situation? Would he ever see this man come to faith in Jesus? Would his attempts to witness ever pay off?

Jim pointed out that the adverse relationship was never going to change until God did a work in Ryan himself—until he was so connected to Jesus (the vine) that he could hear what God was teaching him and honestly ask God what he wanted him to do. In this case, God wanted Ryan to live like Jesus by reaching out to his boss and by showing God's love. Jim explains it this way: "Everyone is trying to figure out how to tell someone about Jesus; but they never hear you because they are experiencing you as something different." He says that only as people experience you living as Christ will they climb to the next step of experiencing Jesus himself. This is different from bringing a little more Jesus-speak into the workplace. Currently, Ryan's atheist boss has begun asking questions and is watching him closely. As Ryan learns to live more and more like Jesus—with kindness, love, care, and compassion— his boss likewise begins to experience Ryan and thereby experience Jesus.

All of this is meant to remind us of what we already know: God gives us gifts and validates them with the fruit of the Spirit, which is the sum of attributes of a person or community living in accord with the Holy Spirit. "The fruit of the Spirit is love, joy, peace, forbearance, kindness, goodness, faithfulness, gentleness and self-control" (Gal. 5:22). When we as branches are connected to the true vine, Jesus, we can bring forth real fruit (John 15:1–17).

It is then that people can experience our good works as a prerequisite to hearing the good news (Matt. 5:15), and godly businesspeople will begin to make a difference on the job, both in North America and abroad. It is then that we will obey the commands of Jesus and make disciples as missional professionals. Seeing the Christian life in action will be more impactful than hearing the good news without seeing the fruits of the Spirit in action.

What would it be like if the tens of thousands of North Americans and Europeans living abroad in non-Christian environments, who are truly followers of Jesus, were actually living like him every moment of every day on the job at work? They would be witnesses rather than witnessing. Now *that* would be missional!

CHAPTER 7

Missional Professionals in International Large-Scale Business Start-Ups

*Making a profit is no more the purpose of a corporation
than getting enough to eat is the purpose of life. Getting
enough to eat is a requirement of life; life's purpose, one
would hope, is somewhat broader and more challenging.*

—Kenneth Mason, CEO Quaker Oats, 1979

Asia Engineering and Manufacturing

*The world has yet to see what God will do
with a man fully consecrated to him.*

—Henry Varley, British Revivalist, to
Dwight L. Moody in 1873

"Be sure to be home for dinner," shouted Randy's mother as he dribbled his basketball out the door, headed for the community basketball court. Randy was often the only white boy in this crowd, representative of his ethnically diverse community in south Chicago. But Randy was also different in another way: he grew up in a loving Christian home where he learned to love God and family—and to be home for a family dinner! On the basketball court, he learned to love his African American neighbors; and at church, he learned to love God's grand purposes in the world.

At age six, he gave his heart to Jesus and began reading missionary biographies; as a teenager, he led evangelistic Bible studies and was "on fire" to spread the good news to those around him. And he was the only one of fourteen hundred graduates in his high school to say he wanted to be a career missionary, not exactly a popular career choice in the mid-1970s. At age nineteen, he had determined that God was calling him to assist the Chinese Christians, but business was not on his mind. By the time he graduated from college, he was a pretty good basketball player and followed his dream of playing professional basketball in Taiwan. There he soon observed how businesspeople in Asia are well respected and gain wide-open doors because of this—more so than teachers, government people, researchers, and even athletes.

Fast-forward nearly five decades and imagine one of the most respected and unique BAM companies in the world: Asia Engineering and Manufacturing (AEM). AEM fits all the necessary characteristics of a BAM company: they strive to operate a profitable business, while intentionally operating in way that seeks to support and participate in creating disciples and planting churches. Randy boils this down succinctly to two components: profitability and making followers of Jesus with a focus on starting Bible studies and churches.

For AEM, profitability means wealth creation through the creation of jobs and equity return to investors. This means dividend growth and increase in valuations, as well as increased service to partners, customers, and suppliers in each cluster of world-class companies they own. Making disciples of Jesus means creating aggressive Great Commission goals, each with an intentional plan and a measurable objective. It means focusing on the unreached, seeking people of peace, and followers of Jesus worshiping in small fellowships of believers.

As with all kingdom business owners, Randy is often asked to respond to questions related to the value of Business as Mission. In such conversations, he likes to cite a scientific study reported by Steve Rundle of the Crowell School of Business at Biola University.[1] Rundle and his team were interested in comparing "missionaries" as members of a sending agency, who raise financial support, with missional business professionals, who earn their salary from their business work. The 119 respondents were controlled for business size, business location, and business type.

Here is Dr. Rundle's "Business as Mission Comparison":

Missionary-Sending Organizations	**Businesspeople**
• Donor supported	• Self-supporting
• Spiritual fruit is all that matters	• Mission is more than "just" evangelism
• Business can distract from "ministry"	• Business itself can be pleasing to God

After three years, Rundle and his team posited the following two hypotheses:

Hypothesis #1: BAM practitioners who draw a salary entirely from the business will have a greater (more beneficial) economic impact than their donor-supported peers.

Hypothesis #2: Donor-supported BAM practitioners will be more "effective" in producing spiritual fruit than their business-supported peers.

The results of the survey indicated that Hypothesis #1 was strongly supported while Hypothesis #2 was not supported. In other words, the study found that practitioners who are fully supported by the business tend to outperform—sometimes significantly—donor-supported BAM practitioners in economic impact and are no less fruitful in terms of spiritual impact. Although this was only one of the study findings, it has become an interesting factoid in establishing the value of Business as Mission companies in serving to fulfill the Great Commandment of Jesus (economic and social impact) and the Great Commission (spiritual impact of making disciples).

The magnitude of all of this for AEM's thirty-year history is that over twenty-five technology-based companies have been started in cities of more than one million people, each with between thirty and five hundred employees and an evangelistic, discipleship, and church-planting plan with accompanying results by the grace of God. None of this happened overnight—nor did it happen without cost, sacrifice, failure, worldwide partners, or, most importantly, without God at the center.

Today, AEM is a premier management and consulting company in Asia. They are an American privately held holding company, which has held equity in and managed almost thirty mid-sized manufacturing and media companies in Asia, and which has successfully provided turnkey solutions to help over forty international start-up operations. They have hired over three thousand employees in Asia and managed operations in more than thirteen cities. From aerospace and automotive industries to telecommunications and medical devices, AEM is an organization with proven expertise in building businesses in Asia and surrounding regions.

AEM is headed up by a team of individuals from the United States, New Zealand, South Africa, and Malaysia, and is focused on building best-practice business operations. They are an organic group still growing in strength, with a network of entrepreneurs, both expatriate and indigenous. AEM's connections enable them to draw personnel from all backgrounds and areas of expertise needed for successful business operations in Asia and around the world. They have experience in marketing, joint ventures, and wholly foreign-owned enterprises, and have worked with companies ranging in valuation from $3 million to $1.2 billion, starting factories with average initial investment of $5 million.

Randy is an expert in sourcing team build-out, technology transfer analysis for carbon-based crucibles, writing national specs for pressure-vessel manufacturing, and performance evaluations for suppliers, and he has built local Chinese engineer-to-engineer sales teams and made equipment decision buys for multiple factories.

It is not the purpose here to trace Randy's colorful thirty-year story of life and business in Asia. That has been told elsewhere. In all of it, Randy is the first to give glory to God and give him all the honor and credit. The story is informative and interesting, but our primary interest here is to focus on the lessons he has learned along the way.

Many years ago, I learned a key question to ask after a major business initiative. While consulting with business start-ups in Asia, team leader Ken Leahy would always insist on having a session where he asked the question, "What did we learn?" He taught me to do the same, as well as ask the question of others.

After listening to Randy in person and reading elements of his story, I was most intrigued to personally hear him talk about the lessons he has learned. I dream of others starting in kingdom business getting a head start because they benefit from his pioneering experiences. The wise will certainly take advantage of Randy's wisdom gained from some sad, painful, and lonely experiences, and from difficult work as well as wonderful successes.

Randy suggests that his two biggest struggles are the drive toward profitability and keeping a kingdom focus. You can't gain the right to be consistently heard over the long term without proving that your business is successful; nor can you succeed in God's eyes if there isn't a clear kingdom focus and disciples of Jesus as a result. Here are some lessons from Randy I hope others will heed.

Lessons Learned from Thirty Years of Doing Kingdom Business

1. *The business you choose is important to disciple-making and business growth.* This means there must be an incarnational presence with a bandwidth for opportunities with employees, customers, and suppliers. It is with them that conversations take place and Bible studies begin. It is important that there is an ecosystem to support disciple-making.

2. *Focus early on where and to whom you are called.* AEM set their focus on unreached cities in Asia, so they committed themselves to starting businesses in cities of a million people or more that were less than 2 percent Christian.

3. *Business needs mission agencies and agencies need business.* Missionaries bring a lot to the table: evangelistic training, spiritual accountability, contextualization with culture, and missional fervor, to name a few. Business leaders bring job creation, respect in the community, and important relationships. It is mandatory to have a healthy relationship between missionaries and businesspeople.

4. *Think big.* Randy learned the importance of dreaming of all that God could do in a kingdom business. He suggests seeking investors early on, as they can help with company business plans and other missing resources. Just as missionaries can help with spiritual and Great Commission accountability, fellow businesspeople can hold start-up owners accountable for business goals.

5. *Pray for great partners.* This is especially true when you have a minority control (his aim is to own 15 to 35 percent of the company). While he seeks to control the people and capital sectors, he also seeks partners with market and technology expertise. In other words, he wants to do what he does best and let a partner fill in other key areas of markets and technology. In all cases, he realizes that while not every leader will be a believer, he seeks those who are "people of peace" for leadership positions.

6. *Think technology-leading and world class.* It is important even in lesser-developed countries to stay current with the technology curve. There is always a newer technology that your company should acquire and utilize.

7. *Be a leader using industry standards.* Always do a best-practices analysis and strive toward it with regular benchmarks. This holds true for the product of the business as well as spiritual values and transformation standards.

8. *Expect spiritual opposition.* Randy's story includes business failures, a family tragedy, and other domains Satan will definitely exploit. You need to recognize that you're operating in enemy territory and that spiritual accountability is a must.

9. *Long term is better than short term.* You need to acknowledge that short-term individuals, owners, and top-level managers need to be at home in the area, learn the language and culture, commit to the call, and stay the course for five years or longer.

10. *Never underestimate the need for incarnational presence.* In Asia, as for most places in the world, people are flocking to the cities. As first-generational urbanites, they are open to change. Quality and excellence in business will serve as a magnet. Having a robust internet model in the business and community is important as it provides exposure to people. You need to have face time.[2]

Clearly, AEM is a successful profitable business with the components of strategy consulting, turnkey solutions, human resources, supply chain contacts, merger and acquisition experience, sales, and marketing. They have succeeded in the drive toward profitability and all that it provides. Certainly, God has given Randy and his team the ability to create wealth.

Business success provides visibility, credibility, and desirability. While there are plenty of obstacles along the way, local residents generally want businesses, and the government wants you there. For example, AEM has found an open door for owning a legitimate, legal Christian media company. As of 2020, hundreds of Christmas boxes were being prepared with Christian books and other holiday items, which Christians would then distribute to those who had never heard the good news.

In the current international business milieu, Asian economies are vying for market prominence and are thus in competition with many world economies. Randy has contributed to the value structure of not only his company but any company seeking to understand Judeo-Christian values. Randy and his team have many stories of people coming to faith through the relationships developed with kingdom people in business. Likewise, over the past thirty years, many house churches have been established. This result can be attributed to excellence and success in business along with focused Great Commission intentionality.

One of those intentional decisions is to hire nonbelievers who are people of peace and who are not resistant to the faith of the owners. Jia Li started working in the HR sector of an electronics factory owned by AEM but was later promoted to general manager when the position became vacant. Jia was in her third year in this role when she said to Randy, "Boss, I am feeling too much pressure from you to become a Christian." Randy was confused by the comment and asked her for specifics, but she could not provide any. He then knew it was the Holy Spirit at work in her conscience because she knew what was right, despite not having a Christian "competitive advantage" nor a community in a local church. After six years of working in the company, Jia Li came to faith in Jesus and is responsible for one of AEM's most strategic divisions.

There are hundreds of people all over the world who grew up in Christian homes. Sometimes they have come to believe the lie of the sacred-secular divide, so they think that if they pursue a profession—like business, engineering, teaching, medicine, or sports—they're second-class Christians because they're not pastors, church leaders, or missionaries. Nothing could be farther from the truth. Any believer can serve God's kingdom purpose while working in their chosen profession.

Randy would never have seen thousands of people come to follow Jesus and start or join house churches if he had come to Asia as a professional missionary. Today, all doors are open if one comes to a country providing value to that country, while doing that in the name of Jesus and for his glory. You can choose to follow Jesus like Randy; study God's word, be mentored by godly men and women, and grow in your faith. During this time, you can work on a marketable profession and skill and look for opportunities where you are. As you do everything with excellence, your world will expand, and you will serve your generation.

First Step English Institute
"To Know Jesus and Make Him Known"

A few years ago, I was contracted to provide crisis preparation training for the leadership and staff of an English school in East Asia. I arrived thinking this was just another typical English language school, subsidized by foreign money and staffed by overworked, underpaid expatriate teachers. I came prepared to analyze the risks of living in this country, help them prepare a contingency plan and then see a few tourist sites before I left. Although I did what I set out to do, this particular experience has stayed with me. In fact, the memory of my time there is what gets me up in the morning. It is what my organization and I live for.

But first a little context.

Learning English can have a huge benefit in low- and middle-income countries, both for individuals and whole societies. A study by the British Council concluded that knowing English can increase the earning power of individuals by 25 percent and that English, as a global language, is needed for developing countries to position themselves in the global economy.[3] As a consequence, there is huge demand for English teachers in rapidly developing countries.

The Euromonitor Report interviewed companies in several countries and found that on average about 50 percent of people need English in the workplace, and about 65 percent said that employees would advance more quickly if they had a high level of English.[4] In rapidly developing, middle-income countries—such as China, Russia, Indonesia, and Mexico—English is especially important as trade links increase. In fact, the TEFL (Teaching English as a Foreign Language) industry is booming in most countries. Indonesia and Mexico are in the so-called MINT group, a group of four countries expected to become economic giants, following the BRIC group, which includes Brazil, Russia, India, and China.

This means that if present trends are to continue, the demand for English is likely to keep increasing exponentially. Even in smaller countries with less international exposure, individual demand is at every level. Young children, students, adults, and businesses all have a desire to improve their English skills.

The First Step English Institute (FSEI) is located downtown in a city of about 1.5 million. When I arrived, I was greeted by a young citizen of the country, no more than twenty-some years old. "Welcome," she said in flawless English. As she led me to the office, other young people greeted me in English. This was not a journey down the long, dark, dingy hallway I expected from other similar visits elsewhere. On the contrary: everything was bright and colorful with appropriate learning materials everywhere. It seemed like I was back in a Montessori school in America.

FSEI was started more than fifteen years before my visit by Jack and Sue, a couple from the Upper Midwest of the United States. Jack had taken early retirement and considered living comfortably on his savings from an engineering career, and Sue had retired as an English teacher. Why reject a nice retirement in Florida and head to a polluted city in Asia? The answer lies in their developing personal discipleship: understanding what it means to love Jesus, obey him, and follow him where the need is the greatest. They did not want to be missionaries, but they wanted to be "missional" with their professions. What could that look like in Asia?

God gives all of us gifts, experiences, abilities, and talents with the expectation we will use them for his glory. While some might give up their professions to go to the ends of the earth, this wasn't Jack and Sue. They knew God wanted them to use those professional skills; and as they made their way to East Asia, they prayed earnestly for direction.

Jack is the administrative, organized budget man, and general fixer of everything. Sue, as a master teacher, put her skills to work to produce an environment of quality English education. This truly was a school with excellence, character, and efficiency with a marketable product (English).

During those days, I saw more than six hundred students, over sixty fully trained teachers, and a mentored national administrator prepared to assume Jack's duties. The school operates on fees from the students without foreign monies and has a vision for changed lives in their city and in similar schools expanding elsewhere. In my conversation with him, Jack stated it this way:

> We call the purpose of what we do as being a workplace discipleship company that intentionally focuses on the disciple-making of our staff and students, which results in people and their families being

transformed by the love and grace of Jesus Christ. So, what are we? We are both a profitable business and a missional presence in our city. We call ourselves a "transformational workplace discipleship form of Business as Mission." On the business side, we are professionals who train our staff to operate in all areas of the company, whose goal is teaching English in our city. On the ministry side, we focus, in an intentional way, on our staff and students to introduce them to Jesus. The staff is with us forty hours a week, and we take advantage of that time to impart kingdom values while training them in their work.

Our method of training them is for them to do their jobs well with the method we saw Jesus carry out as he trained his disciples: spend a lot of time with them and show them how he did his work. After some time, he gave them the opportunity to try it themselves as he sent them out. Then he processed their experiences with them and continued to build into them as he raised them to the next level. Everything he did with them had meaning. He was looking to have them transformed by being with him. That's our goal for our staff.

Our company is a place where biblical concepts can be made practical. As Colossians 3:17 says, "And whatever you do, whether in word or deed, do it all in the name of the Lord Jesus, giving thanks to God the Father through him." This should include our daily work, whatever it is.

In the work environment, we can demonstrate that biblical principles make work and life better, even before people become Christians. Workers "catch" the ideas of working faithfully, harmoniously, diligently, and with integrity more easily when we show them how to do it and they see that it makes the work go better and the company profitable. At the same time, when the company demonstrates real care for workers and their families, they begin to realize that we are a different kind of company because we have different values. It's not long before people are asking where these concepts come from and how these principles might work in other areas of their lives. Much fruit eventually comes from this.

Promotions to higher levels of responsibility help to build into the teachers the people skills necessary to prepare them for a supervisor position. Each new level or position requires more of the model/assist/watch process from the one training them—very much like discipling does, for the ones that want to be able to help others.

As I walked around, conducted my crisis training, and talked with teachers and students, I wondered: How does something like this get started, how is it maintained, and is it real? One answer hung on a sign on the wall that read "Team Core Values," followed by these lines:

1. An obvious Christian mentoring community

2. Being excellent professionals

3. Culturally appropriate in our discipleship

This was then followed by their vision statement:

> To know Jesus and make Him known by supporting and developing locally run, viable, intentional Christ-centered business models where we are actively discipling individuals and families in and out of the workplace.

Sounds good, I mused, but how can this exist in a country the missiological pundits back in my homeland call "closed"? One cannot proselytize here, and foreigners with expertise are just tolerated by the government authorities.

We can't ignore that God is in it all and has cared for them and given them supernatural wisdom and key people in their journey, which at this writing is almost twenty years ago. One key factor is an unwavering commitment to excellence. All the national teachers we met spoke as if they were citizens of an English-speaking country. Teaching didn't just include grammar and culture; it also included robust professional enunciation training in voice and diction, articulation, use of diphthongs, the palate, and tongue. The outcome: excellence! Not only did the school not need foreign English speakers as teachers; but when these trained teachers were ready to move on, several national schools and training centers in the country were ready to hire them. They were creating value in their city and country.

Sue was the real architect of such high-level excellence. She wrote all of the original lesson plans and has been the primary trainer of the teachers. She also trained managers and supervisors in running meetings, evaluating the staff, and conflict management. Jack affirmed her contribution to the company by saying, "She creates training for whatever is needed, and she really has amazing administrative skills."

Since I still had more questions, I was given permission to talk to small groups of teachers by myself. Sometimes I interviewed them in a classroom and sometimes as a group, even in a restaurant and in their homes.

I learned that everyone is grateful for the skills they have learned, but they also told us of hurdles they faced in coming to FSEI, sometimes as students, sometimes as trainees. Most of their parents had high aspirations for their sons and daughters—engineers, doctors, lawyers, diplomats, and so on—and they considered teaching English inferior. But these teachers loved their jobs because of the culture—a culture of love, care, passion, mentoring, character, and family. One teacher said, "I have learned how to love others, and if you love someone you can help that person to grow." Another said, "We know that Sue loves us, and we are learning to love others also." Jack is a father and grandfather figure who provides examples of what it looks like to spend time with people doing life together!

Although not all the teachers are Jesus-followers, many are and it is obvious how the Lord has transformed them. One can see how God is directing them to spread that transformation in the widening circles of their family, neighborhood, and throughout the city.

Before I left the FSEI community, Jack shared a new vision with me. He encouraged me to help find potential interns and apprentices to come from abroad and join them in Asia. He wondered if the success they had experienced at FSEI could be transferrable to other similar businesses in their country and elsewhere in Asia. These goals for interns and apprentices include:

1. Learning to live cross-culturally in a mentoring community of professional missional workers.

2. Learning the business side of an English language school, including management, accounting, principles of HR, and marketing, as done in the local culture, while gaining TEFL certification.

3. Learning how to use culturally appropriate discipleship skills in a community that demonstrates intentional building of transparent relationships with others.

4. Learning some of the local language with study and practice while living in the community.

5. Growing personally in cross-cultural, professional, and missional components of life.

6. Completing the FSEI teacher training plan and then successfully teaching in a classroom setting; facilitating group discussions using directed topics and structured methods.

After a week, I left FSEI with new friends, with a vision of what "excellence really can be" and a model of what a missional business is as a full integration of faith and work. I wish every aspiring businessperson and teacher could be mentored by Jack and Sue, and even some of their proteges in Asia.

NightLight
A Journey with a Freedom Business

International BAM spokesperson Mats Tunehag was an integral part of the first Freedom Business Forum in Chiang Mai, Thailand, along with freedom business specialist, Jennifer Roemhildt Tunehag. Mats captured the concluding keynote address by Annie Dieselberg, who is the founder and CEO of NightLight Design, a freedom business in Bangkok.

Freedom businesses endeavor to bring freedom, dignity, and restoration to victims of human slavery and injustice. Mats quotes

Pope Francis's statement on the important role business plays: "Business is a noble vocation, directed to producing wealth and improving the world. It can be a fruitful source of prosperity for the area in which it operates, especially if it sees the creation of jobs as an essential part of its service to the common good."[5]

Annie's address gives important insights into her journey with BAM and her unique business in Thailand. I was granted her permission to use it here.

"Hold Fast to Your Dream" By Annie Dieselberg

My children recently decided they needed to make some money. Secretly they began creating products and then they laid them out on the table and announced their store was open. They invited Mom and Dad to come and to make purchases. What they had created was paper bookmarks, origami, and drawings, which they had priced at around 10–20 baht each. My husband and I each chose a couple of their products, and my kids proudly pocketed their income with plans for an outing to the nearest 7/11. They had figured out that earning money was purchasing power and the ability to make choices.

Most of us, if not all of us, at young ages, became aware of the power that money has to give us choices in life. Most of us probably came up with innovative ideas of how to make some money to gain choices that our parents were not providing for us. From lemonade stands, to car washes, to babysitting, or mowing peoples' lawns, there was in us a desire to create money, because money is purchasing power and gives the ability to make choices. The ability to choose is not something to be taken for granted. It is something that comes with freedom. Freedom allows for choice, which can be used for good or for evil, for self entirely or for the good of others.

My older daughter Kristina was a nanny for a very wealthy and prominent business family. One day my daughter and the three-year-old were discussing friends. The wealthy family traveled so much that she didn't have any friends to play with. The three-year-old announced, "That's okay, I will buy friends."

This three-year-old already understood that money was power. From her worldview she could get anything she wanted with money. She was too young to understand the negative consequences of misuse of money and power, especially when it comes to relationships.

The business of prostitution and sex trafficking makes billions of dollars of profit for people with evil and selfish goals. It preys on vulnerabilities of people who have few choices in life and turns them into slaves and commodities. It is an obscene abuse of power and of wealth. The dreams of the victims to gain income for their families and improve the quality of life quickly turn into terrorizing nightmares that scare away their dreams.

Prior to working with women in prostitution, I mostly viewed the business world as the other side: where greedy and selfish people used money for privilege and exclusivity while ignoring or exploiting the vulnerabilities of the poor. I made the mistake of dismissing business as a whole.

Somewhere around 2003, however, I was introduced to Business as Mission and I began to see the strength of business and the opportunity for individual, community, and global impact. I realized that it wasn't business or making money that was evil and self-serving, but the misuse of that privilege. I realized that the creation of business is a key to sustaining freedom by providing survivors life-giving choices.

I am a survivor. I have survived being a pioneer in the freedom business movement. In 2005, my team and I began NightLight Design Co. Ltd. The story I have told many times over is of a humble beginning with one girl learning to make a necklace over a coke at McDonalds. She needed a job and I promised her one, so with a prayer and a leap of faith we began. Though I had five years of experience working with survivors, I did not have any professional business experience. Being a pioneer in the field, I had no mentors who could guide me in creating or operating a freedom business.

Initially, visiting businesspeople provided advice, but they lacked awareness of the challenges of working with survivors. Mission groups came through with advice on addressing their spiritual or emotional needs, but their advice lacked the understanding of the business side. I quickly discovered that we were pioneers with a big machete in hand, hacking through the jungle vines. We would encounter valleys and mountains; we would get hit in the face with branches, bit by spiders and snakes, trip and fall on our way to find the path. It was messy, and it was and is an adventure.

Nevertheless, the business took off quickly with a lot of excitement. By the third year we had eighty-eight women employed. I made a hasty and foolish promise to God that I would not reject anyone who came our way for help. It was a promise I couldn't keep. As other organizations began to emerge with similar businesses and the market quickly became saturated, we began to realize that our model was not sustainable.

We came to a crisis point a few years ago. The negative voices thundered in my head, and I began to cave in and doubt the vision that I had believed came from God. I almost quit. I almost gave in to shutting down the business. At about that time, Jennifer Roemhildt Tunehag came through with encouraging news about the launching of the Freedom Business Alliance and instilled some hope back in me.

Around the same time, God gave me a vivid dream that was a clear warning against giving up the vision. I decided to take a stand, and rather than give up, we did some restructuring to save a failing business. That restructuring began to turn things around.

Freedom Businesses Are Hard

Recently, my family was returning from vacation at the beach when my six-year-old daughter asked, "How do you get a hotel?" Wow, what a loaded question. Now that I have been in business, I began to list many of the steps from planning to investment, to design, to construction, interior decorating, restaurant set up, menu, guest services, staffing, and marketing.

By the time I was done listing, I concluded that it is a huge project that involves a lot of work. My daughter was not anywhere near as overwhelmed as I was and announced: "I am going to have a hotel." What was it that made her decide she wanted a hotel? It was her positive experience. She had made the connection, albeit naive, that having a hotel could give people, including herself, a positive experience. She had a dream.

I had a dream of a business that would employ survivors and give them a positive experience. I really had no idea what I was really getting into, but I had a dream and in spite of the challenges I was not going to give up.

Since 2005, we have seen 175 women come through the holistic employment program of NLD and NLF. The women are employed in an environment of faith, hope, and love that they have never experienced before.

One of my heart stories that drives me is that of a woman I met when she was still in prostitution. She told me that sometimes she did not know if she was still a human being, so she cut herself. She said if she saw blood and felt pain, she knew she was still alive—still human. When she started making jewelry at NightLight she said to me, "Annie, I used to catch myself with my head low because I was so ashamed of who I was and what I was doing. Now I catch myself with my head up high because I am proud of what I am doing."

Today that same woman is on staff managing the materials department. She teaches new women and expat groups how to make jewelry. She now has power of choice in her life, and she is choosing to make an impact in her community.

Freedom businesses are about the business of restoring that hope, of restoring the power to choose, of redeeming the value of life, and the ability to make money for good and positive impact. Freedom businesses give people the chance to dream again, to believe in a future that has quality of life.

I believe many of you are starting out or in a stage of the dream where it feels hard, and honestly when we hear the presentations of some of the very successful businesses it can feel overwhelming. We wonder how we will ever get to that measure of success. We wonder sometimes if we can legitimately call ourselves a business in comparison. We resonate with that woman's description of heart-driven decisions. But honestly, none of us here are only heart people. We all have a brain also, and the brainy people also have some heart.

The Freedom Business Alliance is in fact an intersection of the two. If we were all heart, we would be content just working at a soup kitchen or a relief agency. If we were all brain, we would probably be doing business completely oblivious to the crying demands of survivors. All of us are here because we either have big hearts with growing business brains, or big business brains with growing or enlightened hearts. We all dream of a world where business has a great social impact and provides jobs, freedom, choice, and quality of life to survivors, their families, and their communities.

Langston Hughes wrote, "Hold fast to your dreams, for if dreams die, life is a broken-winged bird that cannot fly." The women we encounter in the sex industry are broken-winged birds who cannot fly, birds caught in cages, bought and sold, and with each sell they lose sight of themselves and their dreams.

Freedom businesses open up the cage doors and bring the broken-winged into a place of security, of love, of healing, and of hope. Freedom businesses give women back their dreams, and through freedom businesses women are given back their ability to fly. Hold fast to your dreams!

Freedom business founders and leaders, hold fast to your dreams! I cannot promise it will be easy, but with each bird, each woman, who flies again, we forget the costs, the labor, the sacrifice, and we celebrate life and freedom.

HM Manufacturing United
The Jesus Way in Hyderabad, India

*No, he will not compromise on quality
because he is a Christian.*

—Hindu corporate officer

I have always been fascinated by India with its vibrancy of colors, languages, tastes, smells, impressions, history, and innovations. It is truly a mecca of diversity. One time when I was adjusting to the food in India, a friend of mine who was a resident there lovingly described the food as "exploding in his mouth." Truly, the entire India experience is one that explodes all of one's senses.

Although I did not meet Henry Moses when I visited India's Gujarat state in 2012, I was privileged to meet him in an online BAM workshop during the COVID-19 pandemic. Later, my good friend Mark Polet made the personal introduction. Henry lives in the state capital of Telangana, Hyderabad.

Henry Moses's journey includes all four aspects of the quadruple bottom line. My favorite part of an interview is always when I ask for a story about impact in a person's life because of the kingdom business. Henry shared this with me:

> One of our key managers once cheated us with wrong bills without purchasing the materials. In his absence, we found out that he colluded with the supplier and submitted a fake bill for payment. Everyone in the company wanted me to fire that person, but I did not fire him. They asked why I was not removing him from the job in spite of proving him guilty of theft. I told them, "If I cannot forgive that person, I cannot ask my Father in Heaven to forgive my sins." As I forgave that person, he repented but could not stay in the company and left by resignation. But he tasted the love of Christ and continued to seek my counsel in the events of crisis in his life.

Henry graduated from Andhra University with a degree in electrical engineering and began working in the government sector. His expertise led him to merge into mechanical engineering, and with lots of study and hard work eventually the management of a department. He quotes Romans 8:28, "All things work together to be the best for those who love the Lord," as he realizes that the strain of those days provided the professional confidence for starting his own company in the field of mechanical design and structures using composite materials. He was set to become a classic entrepreneur.

He shared openly that his faith never wavered from those days of his youth, even though his human weakness caused him to sometimes disobey the truth he knew. However, God never forsook him and always brought him back to the fold. He knew God had a purpose for him, and he continues to be flexible for new challenges that God might provide.

After working for the government for fifteen years, he took voluntary retirement at age thirty-seven and used his small retirement fund as start-up capital for a new business, manufacturing fiberglass-reinforced plastic products. Here is more of what Henry told me:

> My first product was a cooling tower, which was followed by other chemical process vessels. Although I created employment for people, I always encouraged them to be entrepreneurs, so that they in turn can provide jobs to others and can lead independent lives. I would rather invite my employees to be my sub-contractors and even my competitors. I would teach and support them to see that they are successful in their businesses. I do not see that I am creating my own competitors since I treat it as a win-win game. We all should be winners—and glorify God together!

Henry became a serial entrepreneur as he learned to nurture people to help him diversify into many unrelated areas of manufacturing and contracting. Whenever a new opportunity knocked at his door, he immediately grabbed it without much thought about the consequences, all the while trusting God. He had, as one entrepreneur explained it to me, "the ability to see around corners."

He went from manufacturing highly corrosion-resistant chemical process equipment, to the manufacture of fishing boats to support tsunami victims, to telecom network products, and underground manhole chambers and shelters during the telecom boom in India. He then diversified again to prefabricated buildings using panels and structures for fast-track construction of offices, cabins, shelters, and quarters for temporary laborers.

All the while, Henry thought about human need, seeing each person as a creation of God living in his created space. One such project was a response to the Clean India Campaign promoted by the prime minster of India to stop the poor of India from openly defecating in public places, something quite normal in rural poor India.

As he became aware of this problem, he diverted resources toward prefabricated bio toilets and sewage treatment plants. He promoted this in some places in cooperation with World Vision, addressing the need in rural and urban slum communities with the bio toilets and cluster toilets. These have been distributed widely in order to stop open defecation and to care for women, particularly those who had been walking longer distances to the jungles to attend to nature's call, sometimes in the dark of night at high risk.

His emphasis on the care of God's people as well as his creation includes water treatment plants and gas scrubbing systems to mitigate air pollution from harmful chemical gases. In all such diversifications, he claims to not have the personal skill to execute; however, God has given him the skill to find the right people and then ensure their skill development so they can complete the assigned task. He monitors and provides for the success of the project, all the while praying and trusting God for wisdom. Henry says, "God has never let me down, and we are all at peace."

> We at HM United are trying our best to control air pollution coming out of chemical and pharma industries and water pollution through sewage treatment plants and effluent treatment plants and bio toilets. Thus we are playing our part in caring for the creation. We should not spoil the good creation of God with our selfish motives. When the underprivileged people cannot afford to maintain a clean environment, the privileged people should join hands to support them to build toilets, so that everyone enjoys a clean and healthy environment. Wherever there is inevitable air pollution, everyone should use his God-given ability to help the helpless so everyone can breathe clean air.

Henry has been the managing director of HM United since 1997, where he has focused on Fiber Reinforced Plastics and other composite-molded products. He has operated from the state of Andhra Pradesh and now operates from Hyderabad in Telangana, though he serves all of India with his products.

While considered a success, he has not been immune to challenges. Like any business, there are the unforeseen difficulties. For example, abnormally delayed payments from government contracts and private clients causes financial problems that inhibit the ability to grow new projects. Sometimes, however, adversity creates new open doors. When COVID resulted in India's lockdown, Henry shifted his focus to manufacturing protective gear as well as disinfectant tunnels and prefabricated isolation rooms for hospitals.

Hyderabad is the eighth-largest state economy in India and Telangana is the fourth-most populous state and is considered a hub for pharmaceuticals and biotechnology. The population is 85 percent Hindu with only 1.3 percent Christian. Technologically, it is a great center of operation, and obviously filled with plenty of spiritual opportunities.

Henry is not only an opportunist when it comes to business, but he is also one when it comes to sharing and living his faith. Here is another story that Henry told me:

> Our clients trust us based on our value system. For example, we developed an underground FRP Manhole chamber for OFC network that can take a vehicular load of 25 tons, replacing conventional problematic RCC manholes. We did this for a major government Telecom company (BSNL). After many tests, the first product proved to be successful. Then BSNL wanted to place an order from us for the entire state and called all the heads of divisions for a meeting with me. Then one of the officers expressed a doubt that I may not maintain the same quality while supplying larger quantities. Spontaneously, the director who was chairing the meeting said, "No, he will not compromise on quality because he is a Christian" (all persons in the meeting except myself were Hindus).

By maintaining strong character values like this, Henry and his HM United see doors open for giving "an answer to everyone who asks you to give the reason for the hope that you have within you" (1 Pet.3:15).

In summation, the HM United is a great example of the quadruple bottom line (QBL).

1. It is a profitable and sustainable business for the greater glory of God.

2. Jobs are created as a key factor to community and family transformation.

3. People are hearing the good news of Jesus and disciples are following him.

4. HM United sees the importance of caring for God's creation.

Henry summarizes it best: "The journey of HM United doesn't stop. We keep innovating and rising to the need."

Three Guys and a Dream
Jurassic Valley Tourism

Although the setting description and names have been changed to protect the best interests of the protagonists, this amazing story is true. It is a story of faith, love, hope, work, grace, miracles, and ultimately transformation. The narrative is written to provide you with a glimpse of the process from start to finish as three couples partnered with God to develop an international kingdom business for the glory of God. Such a story is a prototype for young people today to replicate as they follow God and their dreams. At the very least, the story suggests on-ramp ideas for others.

Step 1: Faith and Friends

It all started at a small Christian college in the Midwest with two buddies, Barry and Max, who had a passion for Jesus, along with their girlfriends, Jane and Teri, and another young woman named Lindsay. They had all developed their passion through regular communion with Jesus and fellowship with likeminded others. They trusted God for spouses with a similar passion, vision, and commitment, and for his guidance for the steps ahead.

Another fellow, Evan, asked Lindsay out on a date. Afterward, she made it clear to him that she wouldn't continue to date him if he wasn't willing to go overseas, that her heart was committed to what God was calling her to do. Although Evan was indeed open to going overseas, it was her strength of character that impressed him. "That really attracted me to her," Evan said. "What a blessing it was!"

By graduation time, God had gripped the hearts of all three couples for the nations, specifically for unreached people groups.[6] Knowing God had brought them all together, the three couples began to dream and ask themselves and God what it would look like to live out their passions overseas together.

Step 2: Problem-Solving and Trust

The glory college days came to an end, and the couples married and found jobs in the United States to gain work experience, pay off loans, and look for opportunities overseas. The questions were constant. How do we get there? Do we need more training? How can we have authentic identity in an unreached country? Who can help us? How do we pay for it? How do we keep the passion alive?

Not long into this time of searching, they came across the idea to take a survey trip to Central Asia, India, and East Asia. They prayed all the while that this trip would be fruitful and that God would bring them to the right place. Indeed, God did lead them to a place where the people were 99 percent non-Christian. "This is it!" they exclaimed as they returned to the States. Now they needed to figure out their next steps.

Step 3: Preparation to Go

As they sought counsel from others, it seemed best to join an organization with people who resonated with their passion—one that would allow for some creativity and innovation as they followed their dream. That meant some training and orientation at the agency's campus. They knew that God had brought them together as a team and given them a group doing the kind of work they envisioned—work that would bless the people group in physical, social, economic, and spiritual ways. The agency agreed with the passion of the couples and the target geographical location.

Although they sometimes felt impatient with all this preparation and fund raising, their commitment to trust God for everything eventually brought answers to their questions along with a key realization. They knew the country denied visas to missionaries, but as with all countries there were profound needs. As they studied and sought counsel, they discovered business as something that would create jobs and bring income to the underprivileged community.

There was, however, a problem. They had all studied Bible and culture in college, and they had absolutely no preparation in business—certainly not for starting a business. But they were committed to an authentic identity. If they were going to have a business, then it would be a real business. They all agreed, and out the window went the idea of a part-time job to gain a visa and then spend most of the time in evangelism. They would now be full time in business. This was when they first heard the term "Business as Mission."

Step 4: Arrival and the Start

They arrived on location in 2002 and settled into their beautiful valley of dreams. The mountains towered above the scattered communities along the river. What a place to raft, hike, explore; and what a place to bring tourists to enjoy some adventure as well as the culture of the people: their customs, food, and colorful lifestyle.

The agency insisted that they learn the language first, a wise principle for all such endeavors. As they learned more and more of the language, they began to pray and work toward a tourism business.

With the help of friends back in America, they developed a business plan that included components of a market analysis, management team, and product development, along with operations, marketing, and financial plans. Advisors helped them test the plans with questions like: What is the problem you are trying to solve? Who will be your customers? What will be of value to the customer (sometimes called the value proposition)? What start-up capital will be necessary? How can we develop a hypothesis, test it, and pivot toward a viable model? It was all something every team member had to learn from scratch.

As it happened, the group had a wonderful mix of skills for the task. One of them had begun to build strong leadership skills, which proved critical in helping to set the vision and align the movements of the group. God grew strong entrepreneurial giftings in another, as well as the ability to sell to even the most stubborn of clients. A third discovered amazing relationship-building skills and competency in developing local staff and workers. The way in which they complemented each other was something only God could have orchestrated.

It was a steep learning curve—working to develop capital (mainly from friends who believed in them and their passion) and learning every aspect of the supply chain, how to build appropriate HR policies and practices in the local culture, how to be profitable, how to integrate life transformation into the business, and much more.

They started with activities that integrated the interests and skills of the team members, which allowed for an inexpensive start. Activities included trail rides with mules, yak camping safaris, and hiking to key viewing points that took advantage of breathtaking views of towering mountains and pristine countryside with some of the best air quality in the world. Since these trips passed through villages where the team had developed friendships, they helped some locals to develop their native artisan activities for sale and unique cuisine for the tired hikers.

It took two years of language learning, making friends with the villagers, exploring the options for adventure tourism, and building their first simple hotel. The first international paying customer arrived in late 2004. They well remember the commitment to a quality experience and the satisfaction of that first customer. When the week was over, they stopped to thank God and acknowledge his grace in it all.

It truly was God's grace and answer to prayers that the capital came just when needed and the wisdom of good counselors and coaches met the need for each business challenge. The team was always open to help and opportunities to learn.

Five years into the project, there still were naysayers. Some said they were too focused on "ministry"; others doubted their ability to crack the local religion, which seemed to be a mix of karma, animism, and meditation on cultic spirits. There was the ever-present tension between business and the ministry. They strove to diffuse the sacred-secular dichotomy and to integrate their faith fully into the business. They felt that in that culture, the gospel should first be seen and then heard. It should be lived out and then explained.

Step 5: Taking off—by God's Grace

As they achieved moderate success, they added a second, larger hotel, which meant more than doubling their employees. They soon came to a critical point when they felt the flywheel[7] beginning to gather significant momentum and breakthrough results seemed imminent. The villages provided huge opportunities for training and employment. As they prayed, God reinforced Jesus' parable of the minas (Luke 19:11–27). God had given them something to grow. They were seeing some financial success, they had created jobs for unemployed villagers, and there were several Bible study groups in process. As they asked God what was next, they heard him say, "There are more villages to bless, more economic needs to meet, and more people to hear the good news." They knew that "to everyone who has, more will be given," and they wanted God to ultimately say, "Well done, my good servant."

And so, their vision continued to adapt as they focused on an adventure company that took advantage of natural phenomena. The river the locals navigated with native canoes was determined to have Level 3 rapids with occasional Level 4 sections. They set to work to develop white water rafting certifications for Level 3 rapids and purchase the necessary equipment to test the idea. On the property site which they purchased from the local chief, they developed a ropes course and climbing wall. They also led tours to remote villages, focusing on ancient embroidery and pottery art. It was amazing how many quilting artisans in the UK and US took an interest in these historic arts.

When they discovered a remote valley with several hundred acres available for purchase, they expanded beyond the two hotels.

This became the center for a rustic cabin experience that focused on amazing vistas, constellation viewing, creek fishing, quiet reading, and evening discussions on topics ranging from local ecology, mountain wildlife, the purpose of life, native religions, and the faith of the foreigners.

All of these events opened doors for relationships—hiring tour guides, artisan contracts, helping to develop small proprietorships for local cuisine and art, animal experts for the rides, and hotel managers and workers. As people came to faith, some were trained and hired for roles that helped them develop skills. Many employees, however, were not believers and this gave them an opportunity to see believers live out their faith. As the company grew to a worth of over $5 million, they brought in other Westerners, mainly English speakers so that the monolingual tourists could be well cared for.

The transformational impact spread to more remote communities up and down the valley. With God's help, these communities began to see Christ lived out in the foreigners and in the nationals, who came to follow Jesus. The scaling of the business meant more residences, some of them in the form of remote cabins, all of which needed staff and created increased presence in the community.

Step 6: Continual Hurdles and Continued Learning

Their adventurous success was not, of course, without hurdles and challenges. It seemed that there were continual government issues as they learned of ever-changing regulations and taxes. Even natural disasters like wildfires or mud slides after heavy rains were cause for discouragement.

As people turned to Jesus, the native priests became agitated, accusing them of proselytism and making converts to Christianity. There were even threats of poisoning the foreigners. The team calmly maintained that they were there to do business as they had been invited to do and that their commitment was to help the people. This was demonstrated by the jobs created and their community projects, such as irrigation using the river water. They also made it clear they were Jesus-followers and simply answered questions and entered conversations as employees and others saw their lifestyle.

The team avoided traveling down the valley to distant churches or associating with the little house churches that grew up and down the valley. This avoided the impression that they were bringing division into the community. The team saw their role as kingdom sowing and encouraging small groups meeting for fellowship in the spirit of "not forsaking the assembling of ourselves together" (Heb. 10:25 KJV).

Business hurdles included the sourcing of capital for the expansion, something that is always a challenge in small and mid-size business development. Sometimes it was difficult to explain to investors how they were able to integrate faith and the making of disciples with a profitable business.

Another challenge as the company grew was finding senior leaders who were both kingdom-minded and skilled in management. It was expensive to find and bring proven leaders from elsewhere in the country or from abroad. It required adjustments in team responsibilities and waiting on God as they made inquiries and prayed for who might be available.

A spirit of humility and a strong team of coaches and prayer warriors added to the reasons that allowed them to grow and remain viable. As of this writing in 2020, Jurassic Valley Tourism has received the Certificate of Excellence on Trip Advisor for five straight years. They have become a go-to destination for mountain and cultural tourism. And through it all, to this day, they give God the glory!

PhotoUp
Photo Editing Outsourcing in the Philippines

Have you ever wondered how real estate agents acquire those interesting 3-D, 360-degree photos of the homes they're selling? Have you ever wondered how your photos come back from a photo editor looking better than you remembered? How about the fast turnaround on a major photo editing project? Enter PhotoUp.

PhotoUp is a leading photo editing outsourcing service that provides all their customers with sales and support from their offices in Grand Rapids, Michigan. They are the #1 platform for real estate marketing, which includes photo editing, virtual staging, property websites, and virtual assistants. They provide professional photo editing services for any type of photographer or online business. And it all takes place in the Republic of the Philippines, on the other side of the world from Grand Rapids.

Risk, Ambition, and Many Unknowns

Founded in 2011 with a team of four, PhotoUp now employs hundreds of the best photo editors and has the technical expertise to handle any size of photo editing job. Kristian Pettyjohn graduated from the University of Alaska with a degree in finance and marketing. While working in the real estate sector, he realized his talent for design and landed a job at Sundog Media in Anchorage, Alaska. After one experience led to another, he decided to start his own business and advertised online for a web developer. Only one person answered: Godwin. But Godwin lived on the island of Mindanao in the Philippines.

He decided he needed to meet his new employee, so he bought a one-way ticket to Mindanao and stayed nine months. They hit it off and began to work in the area of software development and design. In 2012, Kristian returned to the States and met Devon, a real estate photographer who helped provide vision. When Devon joined as a partner, they registered as an Alaska LLC and officially started in January 2013. By then, there were four employees in the Philippines and Kristian had returned to the country—this time to Cebu City, the oldest city in the Philippines, where the team is still located.

A Slow and Steady Beginning

As Kristian talked about the first six years of PhotoUp, I thought of the concept of patient or long-term capital. Obvious from the name, patient capital generally refers to long-term investment that is prepared to wait a considerable amount of time before seeing financial returns—about five years minimum. Indeed, it took more than five years of faithfully reinvesting everything back into the company before they reached the break-even point. They were grateful for two investors who understood the need for real estate photographers and had the means to invest more than $500,000.

During this time, Kristian began to learn about social entrepreneurship. Over time, he developed a middle-class wage for the new company. He understood the importance of developing employees professionally and as individuals. This included micro loans, communication tools, and leadership training.

Kristian's father had grown up overseas as a missionary kid, and Kristian subsequently grew up with an understanding of the Great Commission. He understood and cared about God's heart for the world. But as a business owner, he didn't realize that a States-based business could effectively serve the spiritually unreached and economically impoverished areas of the world. His team began to build a strategy to create jobs and live out their faith both in North America and the Philippines.

As a result, lives are being changed and communities are being positively impacted today. Their strategy is simple: Revenue is achieved by their customer base in the United States and Canada, while a significant portion of their new jobs are being created in an area of the world where hope and encouragement are often just words without meaning.

Over a six-year period, PhotoUp grew from just a handful of employees to about two hundred and fifty. One of the primary reasons for this growth is the company's commitment to their people. PhotoUp's ability to integrate employee development programs into the culture of the organization has allowed for vertical growth for many of the employees.

As an example, one individual was selling candy on the street when the organization brought her on board in a minimum wage position. After this, her life began to change in every way. She is now in charge of custodial services and is the primary breadwinner in her family. Not only did the company change her life, but it has had a significant impact on her family as well.

By fiscal 2019, the company realized $2 million in revenue and $162,000 in profit on sales. And then came the coronavirus.

COVID-19

Like most companies, PhotoUp felt the pressure, stress, and uncertainty of COVID-19. From a record sales month in March 2020 to a record sales low in April 2020 and the ensuing need to move their entire staff to work remotely with four days' notice, 2020 was a monumental challenge for the team. While there was extreme uncertainty and layers upon layers of contingency plans, often re-written weekly, PhotoUp found new focus and forged a path to profitability while still placing priority on their social mission: to put people, planet, profit, and purpose on equal footing in business and beyond. Kristian shared with me:

> I think the biggest benefit of COVID has been the incentive to re-think our business from the ground up and focus back in on our core business. We have big, bold, long-horizon ideas, but we had to pivot quickly to reign in expenses. For example, we're still investing in future R&D projects, but we've now linked expenditures to revenues and become more focused on expanding what we're best at, photo editing and real estate marketing.

This new-found discipline helped PhotoUp strike a better balance between growth and profitability.

> We looked at the numbers and were like *wow*, we are flat on the top line for 2020, but we've improved our free cash flow significantly. I'd be lying if I said we weren't pulling out our hair for a few months, working twelve-hour days and calling our board members frantically every few days. We had to make some hard calls. We put many staff on forced leave for several months, myself included, and permanently dismissed our seasonal employees early in 2020.

When the dust settled, however, PhotoUp brought 100 percent of its core staff back to full-time work by August and still remained cash flow positive.

The company was also able to pivot their business, which is heavily based on the real estate industry's summer boom and winter lull, to a more flexible model that now includes seventy socially distanced employees in-office, one hundred employees reporting from home, and over one hundred new flexible freelancers.

> The idea to build a freelancer program was born out of necessity; we typically run three shifts per day to meet tight industry deadlines, but when work-from-home was required, we didn't have enough workstations. Amazingly, we built and launched a freelancer editing program within a matter of days and now we don't know how we ever operated without it. It was the missing key for how to tackle our seasonality problem. Once we were able to reopen the office at a limited capacity, we realized many of our staff members didn't own personal transportation and much of the public transit system was still largely shut down. COVID forced our hand at another wonderful innovation: micro-lending.

To help with this issue of transportation, PhotoUp piloted their first micro-lending program by purchasing six motorcycles for managers. The program offers a three-year repayment term with low interest and a partial forgiveness grant if the employee remains on staff for three years. "Employees have been really excited and thankful about the program. In a very literal sense, it allows us to be the hands of the church, meeting the community at their time of need and providing them upward mobility. It's what business should be, business for good."

PhotoUp ended 2020 on a high note, with sales projections growing, new product and service launches, and a new website to help the company position itself to sell directly to realtors (they previously only sold directly to real estate photographers), greatly expanding the company's addressable market.

"In a year that has been so hard for our team and humanity at large," Kristian said, "we're filled with gratitude and contentment for the blessings we've discovered in this challenging season." PhotoUp is a comforting reminder that in turbulent times, there is also opportunity to embrace change and be a blessing to those around us.

Lessons Learned

Kristian learned how to work with investors during some rocky times, determining their motivations and their needs. As the company grew to millions of dollars in revenue, issues of risk became much more pronounced. They learned to have local management teams develop cost-based structures. They learned in times of stress that they were bloated with too much overhead. Tough times forced change and consequent growth.

Most importantly, however, Kristian and others in management learned that the employees are the vital component in the company—something that is now in their corporate DNA. Leadership has made it clear that they are in the business to change lives, both in the company and in the community. Focus on sustainability, job creation, being disciples for Jesus, and reflecting good stewardship represent the daily activities of the PhotoUp team.

They also learned the value of coaching when coaches from IBEC Ventures teamed up with PhotoUp.[8] They observed the team becoming united in passion and their desire to see changed lives, especially those who were hurting the most. They focused on building a sales model that would not only drive revenue and enhance profitability but also create new jobs and help employees to develop. Monthly calls between the coach and team members focused on the tactical objectives that are critical to this ramp-up, plus the constant reminder of the strategic plan that also needed to remain visible. Kristian advises others: "The earlier you can get a mentor the better. . . . Bob Bush has been that for Devon and me."

Kristian and others have learned that in terms of the biblical metaphor of planting and harvesting, business is about planting. The business leaders model character, godly principles, and the loving Christian life. Although investors look forward to a sale and capital gain, a kingdom business like PhotoUp is not just about profits, and they have no plans to sell the company. They are there to see changed and growing lives.

There will always be challenges such as COVID restrictions, endemic corruption, environmental disasters, sales dips, and so on. But they learned they can always learn and do *something*—like the beach parties where company teams clean up trash.

Kristian reminded me that when it comes to social impact and meeting people in their time of need, it isn't always what you expect. In 2018, PhotoUp's team in the Philippines was deeply shaken when a good friend from a company located in the same building was held up at gunpoint on his commute home by two men on a motorcycle. He was waiting for a bus after a late evening shift, just two blocks away from the office. Even though the victim complied and handed over his wallet, he was shot and later died. Since he had been the primary breadwinner for his family, PhotoUp ran donation drives for the medical and funeral costs, and they helped advise the other company's foreign CEO on how to best support this team.

> I pray to God we never have another experience like this again, but it's a reminder that in developing countries, economics isn't the only thing developing. Often the legal, justice and medical systems are weak. It was a huge testimony and blessing to the victim's family to have the support of their community.

Kristian continues to realize the power of prayer in helping the Philippines recover from COVID and his dependence on God as the company continues to grow their impact and be a model of sustainable social enterprise and a model to other BAM entrepreneurs who are watching and learning from the PhotoUp experience.

Sinapis

Faith-Driven Entrepreneurs Growing Companies That Change the World

The taxi shook violently and sputtered to a halt in downtown Nairobi, Kenya.[9] It was January 2009. For the next several hours, Courtney Rountree sweltered in the noonday sun while the cab was being repaired. She was in the country as a graduate student at Harvard University, completing research on how to ease bottle-necks in the private sector.

That day, she was determined to buy her own car, so she asked a wise Christian Kenyan friend where she should look. His response framed her career for more than the next decade: "Courtney, the one piece of advice I can give you is that if someone tells you he is a 'born again' Christian, do not buy your car from him. He is almost certainly a con artist." She laughed at the apparent joke.

But it turned out to be no joke. Marketplace Christians seemed to have prostituted the name of Jesus for economic gain to such a degree that to claim to be a Christian had a negative connotation. If this was true, it was a tragedy of epic proportions.

She was surprised to hear this since this country had more churches than the state of Texas with 85 percent of the people claiming to be Jesus-followers. She saw potential everywhere in Kenya, but as she researched, she realized that it ranked in the top forty most corrupt countries in the world.

Courtney knew about endemic poverty in Kenya; from the endless sea of tin roofs in the Kibera slums, she saw economic and social inequities all around her. But now she knew there was also a spiritual poverty—one of Christian leaders not reflecting the light of Jesus in the marketplace. There was a dichotomy between life on Sunday and life on Monday. Today, we call that an integration issue.

Courtney returned to Harvard, finished her master's thesis, and declared that she had discovered two things in Kenya. First, the biggest bottleneck to solving the poverty problem is the lack of growth in the small to medium sector. This is the "forgotten middle" with weak infrastructure and difficulty finding capital. However, this is the sector that creates jobs, provides opportunities for young people to develop and grow, and develops a true middle class in a community. Educated middle-class entrepreneurs were missing out in the growth of Kenya's economy, and the country and its people were suffering for it. The solution was to stimulate the potential of the small- to medium-enterprise sector.

Second, as she continued to develop her understanding of the profound cultural influence of successful entrepreneurs worldwide, she started to catalyze a strategy for addressing the challenge of helping Christians live as Christ-followers in the world of business. With success, their influence would provide an undeniable resource to God's kingdom.

And so, the seeds of a business accelerator began, and the story of Sinapis can be woven into ten lessons learned in the joys and sorrows Courtney experienced over the next decade and more. Here, she tells it in her own words.

Ten Lessons Learned

Lesson 1: Entrepreneurs have the potential to solve economic poverty as well as a poverty of Christ-like leadership.

Entrepreneurs create jobs and economic wealth for their country through their ingenuity and perseverance. If these entrepreneurs are Christ-like leaders themselves, they can lead their communities as good and sacrificial examples for others around them. Thus, Sinapis was born with this mission: to make disciples and alleviate poverty through the power of entrepreneurship. Like the Latin meaning of our name, "mustard seed," our goal is to help entrepreneurs take seeds of ideas and grow them into God-glorifying enterprises.

We do this by providing them with advanced business training that also teaches them how to integrate their faith with the business. This is paired with consulting, mentorship, and access to capital. To date, we have accelerated over two thousand early-stage companies in our program in cities across Kenya, as well as in nine other countries in Africa and Latin America. Our goal is to empower ten thousand kingdom entrepreneurs around the world, in every country where economic poverty and a poverty of Christlike leadership exists. By doing so, we want to play a major role in taking back the marketplace for the kingdom of God.

Things were not always easy, and our beginnings were certainly humble. After developing the concept for Sinapis in graduate school, I moved to Nairobi in August 2010. My cofounder, an amazing Kenyan I met at Harvard named Karibu, and I submitted the paperwork for our company and then we waited . . . and waited . . . and waited. Finally, with our first cohort of entrepreneurs starting in only a few weeks, we went to the NGO [non-governmental organization] board to understand the delay. They could *smell* our desperation. It was the moment they had been waiting for. The "friendly" case officer said that he would meet us at the coffee shop right next door the next morning. I was hopeful, but Karibu looked worried. He told me to let him do most of the talking and handed me a hand-held recorder to put in my purse.

The case officer wanted a minimum of $1,000 "facilitation fee" to get the NGO permit expedited. Karibu expertly managed to get the case officer to tell us each of the seven different beneficiaries of this money, one of whom was the head of the NGO Board, as well as the case officer's "target" number of facilitation fees for the month from his supervisor. *This is the definition of systemic corruption*. Karibu then informed the case officer that due to strict anti-corruption rules, we were actually required to report this bribe. The panic on his face was evident! Our permit was signed on the spot that day.

We then realized that systemic corruption is not just something that we face; it's what our entrepreneurs face *all of the time*. They have factored in the bribes, delays, and poor government services as just a cost of doing business. And we knew that it would take real intentionality to give them the courage to stand against it. So, this is the second lesson:

Lesson 2: We must equip local leaders to fight systemic corruption, but this change must first happen from the inside out.

We use a fantastic biblical ethics model called Holiness-Justice-Love created by Alexander Hill in the book *Just Business*[10] combined with realistic case studies and very lively debate to help our entrepreneurs understand the righteousness that God requires of us, even in the marketplace, and the faith that it takes to trust God even when doing the right thing costs you everything. And we do see real transformation as a result. In our impact studies, 72 percent say that they have refrained from paying bribes in the last year as a direct result of what they learned at Sinapis.

So onward with our story. In late 2010, after receiving our NGO permit, we finally launched our program with our first seven companies! Hooray! To raise support, we then produced our first video. When I started showing the video with entrepreneurs talking on the screen, some people were shocked to see them dressed well in their business clothes, smartphone in hand, and speaking perfect English. Some wondered why support was needed when the entrepreneurs appeared to be middle class and not poor.

I want to answer that question for you by telling you about a man I met when I first moved to Nairobi named Robert. I found myself so super-busy with the business that I lost control of my garden. One day a young man, wearing tattered clothes and old tires for shoes asked me for a job, and I hired him to tend to my garden and cut the grass. He had a wife and a young baby.

But in 2011 I married, and we moved to a smaller house that came with a gardener as part of the rent. I did not want Robert to be out of a job, so I decided to help him start his own micro-business. I was sure I could help him succeed.

I tried setting him up selling lamps, but one evening I got a call from Robert—from jail! He had violated some city code about selling lamps on the street. We got him out of jail and since that effort failed, I then tried linking him up with some friends in a computer business by giving Robert my old computer and teaching him some basic tasks. The friend decided not to pursue the business, and we were back to square one again. When I tried to connect with Robert, I couldn't reach him because he had sold his phone for $10 to pay for critical medicine for his sick baby. I finally found him, and he announced he was returning to his rural village and would like to buy some cows and try selling the milk in his town of Kitale. My husband and I loaned him $1,000 and helped him write a business plan. Things seemed to be going well with his cows and their milk.

Early one morning, Robert called from the hospital. His wife was pregnant and had tried to abort the baby. Without a car, Robert was not able to get her to the hospital to save either his wife or the baby. Things got worse. Because Robert had never paid the dowry to his wife's parents and he had no money, they seized the cows as payment and took his living child.

At this point, I realized that I had utterly and completely failed to help Robert and his wife and his unborn baby, despite my good intentions. I felt that I had failed in the eyes of God. So, why am I telling you this sad story? Because the lessons I learned on this journey with Robert have been very influential in how I think about helping the poor today:

1. The simple fact is that there aren't enough jobs in poor countries, so we must create new companies and new jobs.

2. Foreign companies are not as sustainable as local ones. We must develop homegrown entrepreneurs.

3. The very poor are sometimes not able to be successful entrepreneurs themselves. Their life situation is too fragile to take on the lack of security that goes hand in hand with entrepreneurship.

What follows from this logic is my third lesson.

Lesson 3: Sometimes helping the poor can mean not working directly with the poor.

While it's true that I had failed Robert, I was succeeding in helping others like him through the work I was doing with Sinapis with local middle-class, educated entrepreneurs. New businesses were being created out of our program. Over 50 percent of our participants who start with no business go on to create businesses after the program. These businesses are creating about two to three jobs on average per year, and they are growing. On average, they are growing their revenues by between 35 to 50 percent in the year following the program. And in fact, nearly 76 percent survive three years or more, which is significantly higher than average start-up survival rate.

When I saw the first set of businesses start to grow and employ more people, I saw Robert's face in each one. But, unlike Robert, they were earning an income, feeding their families, and sending kids to school. Today, Sinapis entrepreneurs have created over 4,500 new jobs that are supporting over 22,000 people economically. Every time I see that number grow, I feel that I am helping one more Robert. Let's get back to our story. In the first few years of Sinapis, Karibu and I worked with Acton School of Business in Texas to create a super rigorous curriculum and then spent years customizing it for the local context. We thought we had nailed it! But then came the real world where we saw the inadequacy of focusing on brilliant business training alone. In 2012, the second cohort contained fifteen new companies, and one of the strongest was owned by Daniel Mwaura, an architect who had developed an interlocking concrete block that allowed for homes to be built much faster and cheaper. He brought on Naomi as his cofounder and the company, Buildmart, showed great potential as they raised $85,000 in angel investing. It was not long before there was contention between Daniel and his wife over Naomi's part ownership. She was fearful of giving up ownership, and it turned out to be reflective of the historical fears and sensitivity related to colonialism. I was able to finally help her understand that a bigger pie that continued to grow was a benefit to everyone, and Naomi was important to that growth. This story is just one example of the challenges of culture and mindsets, and we needed to address such things. That leads to my fourth lesson.

Lesson 4: Business training is easy, but mindset shifts are hard.

It's the mindset shifts in combination with the business training that makes the difference. We were challenged to address these mindsets just like Jesus did: through story. Our stories are a set of case studies we developed about a husband-wife team (named

Joseph and Mary) who started a milk processing business that developed in our program in 2011.

As the entrepreneurs go through the program, they watch Joseph and Mary transform from short-term hustlers doing a copycat venture to being long-term strategic visionaries with an innovative business model, operating with excellence, standing up to corruption, inspiring and developing their employees, and giving their company to God with humility and obedience.

Of course, the biggest mindset change we hope to achieve with our entrepreneurs is how they view faith in terms of their business. In the beginning of the program, most entrepreneurs have no idea what faith has to do with their business. We were extremely fortunate to be able to use the Kingdom Business Framework from Gateway Church.[11] As the entrepreneurs go through the course, they dive deep into each part of the framework, and they also watch Joseph and Mary wrestle with it through the cases. We see our entrepreneurs experience their faith in a totally different way, because now it is something they can engage with every day of the week, not just on Sunday. Now 70 percent of our entrepreneurs say that their faith was significantly strengthened, and around 70 percent say that they completely changed their mindset as to how their faith relates to their business.

While we were excited about these results, there was, however, still something missing in our program. We realized that while internal transformation is fantastic, without external action it doesn't produce many results. This leads me to our fifth lesson.

Lesson 5: A spiritual integration plan is as important as a business plan.

We started having each entrepreneur write a detailed spiritual integration plan and commit to putting their faith into action. Even more exciting for us is that around 70 percent of our alumni today, even the alumni going all the way back to 2011, report that they are still actively following a spiritual integration plan for their business. These spiritual integration plans help our entrepreneurs stay accountable for producing external actions to reflect their internal transformation.

Some people wonder why we are working in the "Christian" nation of Kenya. I always tell people that Kenya is one of the most reached and simultaneously unreached places I have seen. It's still a frontier for missions, just one focused on discipleship instead of conversions. In addition, in my opinion, the greatest frontier left in missions is the marketplace. The marketplace exists in every country around the world, and it is highly influential. This leads me to my sixth lesson.

Lesson 6: One of the places we need missionaries the most is in the boardroom.

To prove this point, our impact data actually shows that 38 percent of our alumni reported that at least one person came to know Jesus as a result of their efforts in their businesses as kingdom entrepreneurs. With over two thousand alumni, it goes to show that if you want to do missions effectively, the marketplace is a fantastic place to start.

Back to our story. After the first few years, I felt that we had really come a long way with our program, but we had accelerated only twenty-two companies. While I was proud of that, I also wanted to reach exponentially more. I started to recognize that job growth comes from two sources demonstrated by two of our alumni.

Frank is a macadamia nut processor and exporter, with a business called Ten Senses Africa. Frank went through the program in 2013. After the program, through a combination of learning key business principles that helped him unlock operational bottlenecks and being a naturally gifted businessman, Frank grew by 10 times, from $250,000 in revenues to $2.5 million in only a few years, and now provides income for thousands of small-holder farmers and hundreds of employees.

Sharon is the owner of a lovely small-shop photography business who also went through the program in 2013. Within a little over a year after the program, she doubled her revenues from $60,000 to $150,000 and tripled her employees from three to nine.

Who has the bigger impact? Most people would probably say Frank, but Frank is actually pretty rare. There are many more "Sharons" operating small businesses across Kenya, all making a tremendous amount of impact. I wanted to meet the needs of both groups, but I couldn't offer all of our services to everyone. So, in 2013, I decided to take the business and faith integration training and scale it to as many businesses as possible.

Then we took the consulting, mentorship, and access to capital—the parts of our model that are much harder to scale—and reserved it for only the highest performers and called it the Fast Track Fellows Program. That separation of services helped us reach many more businesses, while still keeping our Fast Track Fellows Program small to provide customized support to entrepreneurs like Frank who have the potential to scale. As a result, we went from fifteen companies in 2012 to over two thousand today across ten countries.

Lesson 7: We must figure out how to empower the thousand as well as the "one in a thousand" with different though at times overlapping support.

When we first began this separate Fast Track Fellows Program, there was a question as to whether we would continue to invest in entrepreneurs directly through Sinapis or move to an investor match-making model to work with local investors in Nairobi. It really came down to one question: Is the primary barrier to growth for our entrepreneurs more about capability or capital?

The answer was, beyond a doubt, capability. If you asked an investor what their primary problem was, you always got the same answer: There isn't enough deal flow that is ready to receive capital now. Most of the entrepreneurs were showing up to investor meetings with inadequate financials or poorly written business plans. So, it wasn't actually that there wasn't enough investment capital available; there were too few entrepreneurs ready to receive it. So, we began to focus all of our efforts on capability, and it has paid off.

To date, without Sinapis investing anything beyond 2012, our entrepreneurs have raised about $41 million in investment capital, mostly from local sources. In fact, our impact data shows that our entrepreneurs raised over 250 percent more investment capital in the year after our program than they did in total before the program. This leads to our eighth lesson.

Lesson 8: Capability unlocks capital, but capital doesn't always unlock capability.

As Sinapis scaled, so did our alumni base. My level of interaction with our entrepreneurs is naturally quite different today than it was in the beginning. While having this number of alumni presents incredible opportunities, it also comes with challenges. Namely, how do we continue to support these businesses as they grow, while also continuing to focus on our own growth as an organization and reach more businesses?

As an example, remember the story about Buildmart? Well, after getting his factory up and running and experiencing significant trials, Daniel finally got his big break. He got a $6 million government contract to build all of the police housing units in Nairobi. His angel investors were super excited, and we gave him a three-year loan in 2012. It is now 2021, nine years later, and he is still struggling. Years of delayed payments and false promises from the government about fulfilling his contract have meant that Daniel's business has made many starts and stops over the years. So, here is the ninth lesson.

Lesson 9: It took seven days to bring down the wall of Jericho and more than seven years to support one business.

We must remember that the length of our program is not going to be long enough to support entrepreneurs through the many challenges ahead. Does that mean that our programs need to be longer than seven years? Not necessarily. But it does mean that we need to figure out how to support entrepreneurs even after they leave the nest. Sometimes this can be through our own alumni programming, and sometimes by partnering with other organizations that are already working downstream. Many hands make light work.

In late 2017, after having my second child, I transitioned from executive director to being on the board of Sinapis, and I was extremely lucky to find two amazing leaders to pass the baton to. When I transitioned, many people asked me how I wanted to see us achieve our vision of accelerating ten thousand kingdom entrepreneurs globally. My answer for that is simple.

Lesson 10: Serving a movement is better than creating an empire.

My vision for Sinapis is that we would help to catalyze a movement of faith-based accelerators that want to support kingdom entrepreneurs worldwide. There is an opportunity to join us on this adventure. After getting requests for years to license our curriculum, we designed a program just for that purpose. We began actively looking for individuals or organizations that wanted to start or grow a faith-based accelerator in their own communities to empower God-glorifying enterprises around the world. So, what are we looking for?

We are looking for those who have a heart for our mission, have the deep business skills required to effectively train entrepreneurs with the curriculum, have intimate knowledge of the region where they want to launch, have the ability to raise the funding to get the program started and to sustain it, and can commit to a longer-term presence, not just a "fly in" approach. We weren't just looking for people who solely want to copy our program just as it is. Instead, we really want fellow creators—people who will create new value, and in return share their knowledge back with us and with others.

We have been fortunate to find several partners we feel God called just for this work! We have partnered with groups in Brazil, Ghana, Egypt, Burundi, and Mongolia. We give the selected groups access to all forty modules of our curriculum, toolkits where we provide step by step guidance on how to do all parts of the program, and a community of like-minded people who want to share resources, knowledge, and pray for one another so that we can all grow faster together. My prayer is that this budding group of partners will eventually bloom into a movement of kingdom-focused entrepreneur supported organizations worldwide.

I thank God that I have been part of this journey of creating a faith-based accelerator. But everyone reading this has a role in the greater marketplace movement. Will you sit on the sideline, or will you join, using your skill and experience for the greater glory of God?

Sunshine Nut Company
"Hope Never Tasted So Good"

"I have never tasted roasted cashews this good. Where did you get these?" asked my wife, Vicki. I knew she had experienced harvesting and roasting cashews in Brazil many years ago and that she is somewhat of a cashew aficionado. So, she really wanted to know where I got them, since we were now living thousands of miles away from cashew country.

I had met Don Larson, CEO of Sunshine Nut Company earlier in the year and ordered three bags of cashews online to surprise my wife. She wanted to know the story.

Don is the first to tell you that the idea came from the Triune God who cares more than any of us about injustice, poverty, joblessness, and alienation from our creator. At the top of his career as an executive at the Hershey Company, he felt that he came face to face with God at an oceanside retreat. His response: "God, I totally surrender. I fully commit to you. Use me completely." And he meant it.

He did not realize at the time how freeing it would be to give up his affluent lifestyle, sell his expensive toys, give up the pride of knowing he controlled 10 percent of the world's cocoa market and that he had been successful in bringing innovation to Hershey. The company had even greater things in mind for Don when he turned away and asked God what was next. His Christian friends at church advised him to go to seminary. After all, he thought, isn't that what spiritual people do? But while in his second year at seminary, God told him, "No, I have other plans for you. Spiritual people listen to me and pay attention to how I made you." Like Moses in Exodus 4:2, Don felt God was asking him, "What is in your hand?"

While wondering what it all meant, Don reflected on a conversation he had while at an airport in Ghana waiting for his plane to return to the States. He was talking with some college students and when they learned he worked for Hershey, they accused him of being part of the problem of poverty. All this time, he had been proud of the amount of cocoa he was buying and thought he was part of the solution. "No!" the students claimed. "You are part of the problem because of the low price you pay the farmers." As he thought about it, he remained confused, while analyzing the laws of supply and demand, principles of fair trade, and the profit ratios expected of him on his quarterly reports.

It was then that God affirmed that in his hand was twenty-five years of experience in the food industry. God wanted to use that to build food factories in developing world nations to bring lasting economic and spiritual transformation. In 2007, Don turned down a major career move after building the largest cocoa processing factory outside of Philadelphia for a group of investors. Through prayer and solitude, he then developed the Sunshine Approach business model, focusing on transforming lives at every level of the business. Along the way, God led him to a book of sermons by D. L. Moody and a sermon on obedience that validated his surrender to God.

Not long after, Don and Terri were on their way to Mozambique with its abundance of amazing cashews to start their grand adventure. Faced with a calling he had little desire to fulfill, they chose to be obedient, sold everything they owned, and moved their family to Mozambique in 2011.

Mozambique ranks 181 out of 187 on the world's Human Development Index.[12] This reflects years of bad economic policies, extreme climate conditions, and a long civil war so that still today one-third of the population is malnourished, over half do not have access to clean water, 80 percent of the population lives on less than $2 a day, and the literacy rate is only 47 percent.

In the 1970s, the country was the number one cashew producer in the world, but no longer. Although today cashews are making a comeback, still only 25 percent are shelled in-country and farmers are being exploited. Raw cashews are shipped to countries like India and Vietnam, taking jobs away from needy Mozambicans and mitigating the quality of the product. Most analysts agree that the solution to issues of poverty in countries like Mozambique rests with investment in the lives of people, and that is exactly what the Larsons set out to do, with God's help.

It was the beginning of a partnership with God, which included years of obstacles, hardship, and concentrated times of prayer. They had to learn about exploitation, Satan's strongholds, persecution, how start-ups work, how to develop a business model and pivot— over and over! Then, in 2014, they exported their first quality cashew product to overseas markets.

Although it may seem trite to say it has all been a miracle, Don readily affirms that "it's a God thing." How else can one explain how a successful industrial engineer turned business executive could launch into the unknown in one of the poorest countries in the world? How else can one explain that someone who studied automation and robotics at Penn State University could become an advocate for putting people back to work instead of automating? How else can one explain success when Satan is so alive and well in that spiritually oppressive land? "It's a God thing."

Don and Terri are quick to remember that their own lives were transformed in ways otherwise impossible. It has been through God at work in them that they have been able to bring the kingdom of God to others through the workplace. They believe that work is the best way to demonstrate God's character and intent for his people on earth. That is what's happening at the Sunshine Nut Company, which Don insists is owned by God. "This is his company," he says. "We have not given up anything; we are living the abundant life."

Today, a factory of fifty employees is supported by one thousand workers in the shelling sector, and they purchase the freshly harvested cashews from fifty thousand small farmers. They are truly providing jobs for tens of thousands. It is a values-driven transformational company. Dignity, love, and community drives everything they do. These values are manifested in the way they run their business:

1. Buy cashews at fair prices from the local Mozambican community.

2. Roast and package in-country to assure freshness, quality, and the best tasting cashews in the world.

3. Hire impoverished adults who have been abandoned and orphaned.

4. Sell at competitive prices and eliminate the middlemen.

5. Give 90 percent of the profits back to the people (30 percent to uplift the farming communities with better education, water supply, etc.; 30 percent to care for the most vulnerable in the community; 30 percent to build new Sunshine companies in Africa).

Don often refers to the Sunshine business model. It is not only about producing the best cashews in the world. It is about transforming lives—economically, socially, and spiritually. It is about pride, dignity, character, independent choices, opportunity, and community.

It is no secret that the success of the Sunshine Nut Company is totally integrated with the Larson's faith. He is a regular speaker at development events such as the African Leadership Institute,

World Economic Forum, Aspen Institute, Grow Africa, and Oxford Business School. In 2016, Don was awarded the silver medal at the International Peace Award ceremonies in Rio de Janeiro. At that time, a top United Nations official invited Don to the UN to tell his story, particularly the part about the role of faith in bringing peace and economic prosperity. Don is quick to remind people in these contexts that it is God's company and that he is building it for his glory.

Early on in his spiritual journey, Don was influenced by the famous words of Søren Kierkegaard; "The key is to find purpose, whatever it truly is that God wills me to do; it's crucial to find a truth which is true to me, to find the idea which I am willing to live and to die for." Don and Terri found that purpose, God's will, the essence of truth, something to spend the rest of their lives doing. As we ended our conversation, Don said that in the end, he really only wants one thing: To hear the Lord say, "Well done, good and faithful servant" (Matt. 25:23). Or, as Don also says, "Hope never tasted so good."

Tim's Coffee and Bakery
"God Is the Chairman"

Sometimes I imagine what heaven will be like, particularly during lunchtime or coffee breaks. I imagine some of the amazing coffee shops and bakeries around the world where creative minds and hands have developed the best of delicacies. Their owners understand that we are co-creators with God, whether in a kitchen, business office, classroom, or anywhere that humankind is being served. The pastries that seem to be a taste of heaven are delightful to the eyes and the taste; the tropical drinks, coconut milk, coffee affogatos, and bubble tea defy one's imagination. They are, without doubt, heavenly.

Such divine creations can actually be found on the cobblestone streets of the old Medina of Fez, the ancient piazzas of Milano, in Istanbul's Galata area, in the Tay Ho district of Hanoi, in the public square of Bangkok, in the Russian Market area of Phnom Penh, the top of the world in Katmandu, old Shanghai, or hundreds more cultural and economic centers in the world. Among the best is a chain of cafés/bakeries in multiple cities in south Asia—all of which represent the quadruple bottom line of Business as Mission. They are profitable, job-creating, disciple-making, and caring of God's creation.

For two and a half decades, Tim's Coffee and Bakery, Inc. has been providing quality pastries, specialty coffee and tea, and meaningful employment in major Asian cities. The seed idea began in the home of a Western immigrant to Asia when a local friend discovered her delicious homemade bread and wanted to buy some. This kitchen became the start of a small business that allowed her to remain in the country with a livable income. Within three years, there was a staff of five operating the small bakery, which only two years later became a café with thirty employees.

As often happens with start-ups, the business was sold, and the entrepreneur moved on to other opportunities. The buyers were two couples from North America who bought the bakery with a vision for growth. One of the couples, Stan and Tan, is still the majority owner today of a chain with about four hundred employees, fourteen cafés, ten food service contracts, and four bakeries in multiple cities. Stan likes to quote Matthew 13:33 (NLT): "Jesus also used this illustration: The Kingdom of Heaven is like the yeast a woman used in making bread. Even though she put only a little yeast in three measures of flour, it permeated every part of the dough." Today, Tim's is permeating markets in Asia with bread-making yeast—but more importantly, with transformed lives, with jobs, and with the message of the gospel.

Although it's a long way from a tiny town in the Kootenay mountains of Canada to the megacities of Asia, Stan readily adapted to the challenge, realizing God had given him a passion for people and an eye for business. Bringing the two together was a recipe for the transformative power of business to change lives. Stan says it is their calling.

The number one seller at Tim's Coffee and Bakery is coconut cake—but this is not like any coconut cake you have tasted before.

Each one, like all their bakery products, is made daily with fresh ingredients and well-trained bakers. Whether you're a traveling businessperson from Europe, an Australian shoe importer, a resident expat, a multinational executive, a tourist, or a local resident, there is something for everyone from dozens of choices. How does one choose from an assortment of tropical juices, coffee freezes, chai, or English breakfast tea? Want a New York bagel, a Canadian Nanaimo bar, an almond croissant, or the bestselling Egger bagel? Yes, they really do have cheese steaks eight thousand miles from Philadelphia.

It is also a long way from a mom-and-pop home kitchen with a few employees to hundreds of employees in multiple locations. Stan didn't have time to tell me about all the challenges he had faced in building an international brand, leading multinational teams in multiple countries and languages, and developing a training program with a focus on development of employees. But he mentioned one story from the COVID-19 pandemic challenge of 2020.

While food and beverage operators around the world were experiencing disastrous consequences from the effects of the pandemic, Tim's not only survived but thrived in its wake of the pandemic. In March 2020, Stan called a meeting of the forty top managers and supervisors from facilities in each country. He declared to everyone that Tim's is God's company and that "God is the chairman." He shared that God is a God of miracles and then cited several miracles in the Bible. As they prayed in three languages, many wondered what might happen next.

In the following months, while other similar businesses experienced major losses, cutbacks, layoffs, and even liquidation, Tim's experienced success. In fact, all regions posted a positive measure of profitability, while adding nearly fifty staff members during the final months of 2020. Much of this recent success is due to the opportunity Tim's had to pivot and procure major food service contracts, many at international schools. This gave the company triple the number of students served by the food services department of Tim's. Stan is the first to give thanks for the faithfulness of God. I was reminded of Elijah's victory on Mount Carmel when the people cried, "The LORD—he is God!" (1 Kings 18:39).

Good food and drink provide evidence of Tim's pursuit of excellence. Profitability is evidence of Tim's good service and customer loyalty. But these things have a deeper purpose and "the story is told in the changed lives of people."[13]

Mari, a project manager, says, "I have learned a lot from our senior managers who care for us as people and create a family environment." Huy says, "I love being part of the Tim's team as I can improve and develop to be a better person and leader in such a positive working environment." Jason affirms that after working at Tim's, he now knows that in whatever field he enters in the future, he wants to serve and help people—something he experienced at the company.

A hot-tempered young woman on a design team received a last-chance warning letter before God got a hold of her heart. Here, in her own words, she reflects the beautiful transformation that others saw in her life through the company, which she carried forward to her children and colleagues:

> I grew up in a nonbelieving family where my mom loved to go to the temple of Buddha. I joined Tim's Coffee and Bakery almost eleven years ago and was working closely with the founders who were two of my first Christian friends. Watching the way that they worked, the families they cared for, and the love they gave to people, changed my thoughts about believers. I started to follow them to a fellowship most every weekend. I still remember, after attending for a few months, that one day everyone took Communion. Stan told me that if I feel ready and believed, that I could join with them. That moment changed my life totally. In November 2011, I told Stan and other Christian friends in the company that I believe, but I didn't get baptized at that time. In January 2018, after a long time reading, studying, joining in fellowship with others in the company, I was baptized. Thanks be to God for bringing Tim's, which changed my life, changed my personal actions, and led me to the path of knowing Jesus.

Stan says that over twenty years, many have come to faith and been baptized because of the way Tim's has embraced a holistic approach of caring for the well-being of staff and their families. Tim's ethos reminds me of the quote by Theodore Roosevelt: "Nobody cares about how much you know, until they know how much you care"—or more importantly, until they have captured in a contextualized way the second half of the Great Commandment of Jesus to "love your neighbor as yourself." At Tim's, they have developed a DNA of living and loving like Jesus.

In the context of many places in Asia, there is another component of loving your neighbor: "Religion that God our Father accepts as pure and faultless is this: to look after orphans and widows in their distress" (James 1:27). They recognize that the Lord takes special concern with those who live on the margins of society.

A primary way that Tim's leadership demonstrates the heart of Jesus Christ is by taking a special and strategic concern with the blind and deaf in their community. In their context, as is true for nearly everywhere in the world today, the blind and deaf are largely ignored, discriminated against, and have great difficulty in providing a livelihood for themselves. Tim's believes in the dignity of every person and their intrinsic God-given worth. To that end, they have undertaken to hire and train these individuals so that they may use their talents to gainfully provide for themselves. Over 20 percent of Tim's staff in one country are blind or deaf. The company is actively translating and expanding their training material into sign language and partnering with a local NGO to make additional strategic hires in this category. In another country, forty employees are disabled and work in several locations, and twenty are deaf. As of this writing, about one hundred disadvantaged people have been employed—people the competition would not even interview. Most have done well, and now have a fair chance with life.

Tim's has hired employees from the care agencies that have rescued victims of human slavery, giving them a safe work environment and a chance to learn a skill and develop real dignity. In doing so, they rely on a philosophy based on the dignity of all people: that when given a chance, anyone can rise to the occasion of healthy living. It is in contrast to the perspective of finding the best qualified people and hiring them. Instead, Tim's prepares its managers for the high and satisfying goal of helping disadvantaged people live a normal life. When Ken Wessner was the CEO of Service-Master, he said the same thing this way: "Our responsibility . . . is to stir up the gift, the abilities, of each individual so each person becomes fully developed and mature for making his or her contribution to the winning team and then goes on to being a leader on his own team."[14]

Even though the practical action steps described above are the most important in understanding a real profit-making, job-creating business, I had to ask what this looked like in written form. Stan had an easy answer, but he reminded me that the real test is the way it works in personal transformed lives. He then explained it to me.

The foundation for everything Tim's does is based on biblical principles, and there are three main ways Tim's achieves its mission:

Character. Tim's is built on biblical principles which include upholding all laws to the best of our ability (Rom. 13:1–7), making ethical and moral decisions (Deut. 25:13–15), supporting the needs of our clients (Prov. 3:27), and appropriately handling money and wealth (Prov. 28:6).

Craftsmanship. Tim's views its employees and vendors as its greatest resource and treats them accordingly by providing excellent compensation, practicing fair trade, and providing a safe and flexible working environment (Matt. 22:39). This is intended to create an environment in which each of our employees can achieve excellence in their craft, and ultimately, serve our customers well with high quality product and customer service (Exod. 31:3).

Connection. Tim's actively pursues opportunities to connect with the community in which it operates. This includes understanding the language and values of the people in our community as well as participating in donations, sponsorships, and networking (Matt. 5:16). Tim's also seeks to provide opportunities for employment to those who are disabled or disadvantaged so that they can have a sustainable means of self-sufficiency (Phil. 2:4).

I talked to Stan about how this all developed and matured to become a powerful quadruple bottom line company. Although he recalled his childhood and his faithful obedience to the tithing principle, he wisely saw that something was missing. As early as ten years old, he wanted to see something sustainable, growing, and perpetual. As he grew older, he understood more and more, and began to believe in the transformative power of business. An internship in southeast Asia in 1996 became a meaningful learning experience for him. After he permanently moved overseas, he understood that traditional mission methodologies were struggling and that God had opened the way for Tan and him to purchase a for-profit bakery, which they then called Tim's. Although they had roots in a church in Stan's homeland, there was no formal partnership with the church or with any mission organization. It was grass-roots entrepreneurship, with God as the chair.

But it didn't stop there. It never does for visionary types. Leaders like Stan tend to see where others do not. Stan, Tan, and the other leaders continue to notice the personal and social issues in the lives of their staff and the community. For them, it is all about improving lives and developing people. In that spirit, Tim's partners with sports ministries, human trafficking rescue NGOs, and community development programs, and they have helped fund initiatives focused on clean water, rural school projects, counseling, literacy, organic farming, hygiene training, and rehabilitation centers.

Tim's is also a destination for interns from abroad who become exposed to a kingdom-focused business, which changes and expands their perceptions of a missional God at work in the world. Tim's helped start a marriage ministry and so far, more than fifteen hundred people have attended one of the eighteen weekend encounters. Many marriages have radically changed, and some couples have even come to faith and become followers of Jesus.

Stan reminded me that it has not been clear sailing; there have been ups and downs with a "wide range of successes and failures."

> It can be stressful and messy. . . . We have failed when we've lost vision, felt the pressures of operating in changing markets. We have had to lay off staff, fire many others, deal with painful conflicts,

negotiate with bad landlords, suffer theft, and worry about cash flow, food troubles, and injustices.

Yet even at these low points, the Lord graciously sent people to encourage us. He provided key scriptures to speak to us in our darkest moments to urge us to keep going. The Lord remains faithful! I believe the Lord still has much more in store for us. He is the light unto our path; it is his journey, and we will walk it as best we can!

Is it worth it? Are businesspeople worship leaders? Think of the testimony of Lin, a manager at one of the Tim's stores, who started out as an intern. She said that while she was trusting in local fortune-tellers, she was also watching Christian leaders and families at Tim's and saw them doing things the right way when other businesses weren't. Because they were different, this made her want to know more about God. They took time to answer her questions, and she responded to their challenge to trust Jesus. Today, she is a faithful follower.

Hamara Feed, Zimbabwe
"The Goal Is to Feed and Disciple the Nation"

*"The goal is to disciple the nation—and
it starts right here with me!"*

—Peter Cunningham

I had waited a long time for the opportunity to travel to Africa to experience a true integration of a profitable business with disciple-making intention on that continent. And this time I could take my grandson Korbin with me.

Dave Kier is a good friend and business owner in the agricultural sector in Iowa with influence throughout the state and beyond. It was an answer to prayer when he asked me to go with him to Zimbabwe where he was making a substantial investment in a feed mill that would provide quality feed for dairy and poultry farms. He said I would experience firsthand what I wanted to see:

an integrated quadruple bottom line of Business as Mission proven over a couple of decades.

He explained how God had blessed the Cunningham family for over thirty years in some of the most difficult circumstances in Africa: the Mugabe years in Zimbabwe. Through the Cunning-hams, agricultural projects had scaled to high levels of profitability; thousands of jobs had been created, and (in close liaison with the national church) people were being discipled as followers of Jesus.

Zimbabwe is one of the poorest countries on earth—perhaps even the poorest in Africa: 72 percent live in chronic poverty and 1.5 million face starvation every day.[15] How did what was once the breadbasket of Africa deteriorate like this? Certainly, the situation is complex and the answers far from simple.

Peter Cunningham, who has spent the last thirty years in the agricultural sector in the Matabeleland region, offers his story in the context of the "eternal story of God." During his adult years, crisis after crisis in the country have caused him to value the grace of God and the bigger picture of what God is doing.

Since its independence in 1980 from Britain, it would be easy to look at Zimbabwe through the lens of a crisis of "economic con-traction" and increased poverty, unemployment, and corruption. Peter, however, prefers to focus on opportunity: 63 percent of the population is under the age of twenty-four, and there is arable land available for cultivation—if the obstacles could be overcome.

Successful businesspeople solve problems, and those who call themselves Christians do it in the name of Jesus and for his glory. Asking "What would Jesus Do?"[16] in the twenty-first century, they find ways to help with education, job creation, and an increased standard of living in parts of the world today that are struggling. That is certainly how the Cunningham family sees it, and God is blessing Hamara and its subsidiaries despite the fastest shrinking economy in the world, hyper-inflation, government corruption, and years of drought. They know that God is in this operation.

The first clue is that these companies have learned how to integrate profitable business, job creation, and disciple-making, with all the credit going to God. Second, they base their business decisions on the food needs of the people instead of high-revenue export crops. Third, they have a measured focus on creating jobs to increase the income of poor families.

One might say it all started when Peter's parents, David and Janet, arrived as missionaries from Scotland as members of the Scripture Union. When Peter was eight years old, his parents noticed his interest in farming, so his birthday present that year was fifty baby chicks. This was the beginning of a career in agriculture. By the time he was thirteen, he was producing three thousand chickens a week, and ten thousand per week by the time he was seventeen.

Ostrich Farming and Miracles

After a university education in Scotland, Peter returned to a decade of turmoil: the 1990s in Zimbabwe. President Robert Mugabe solidified his one-party state with the beginning of forced land distribution, which meant taking land from the white farmers. During this decade, Zimbabwe experienced high levels of HIV infection (25 percent of the population), widespread drought, 40 percent devaluation in the Zimbabwean dollar, and general violence and political upheaval. It was hardly a time for a young, energetic agriculturalist to start his career in the country of his birth—unless, of course, God was with him in this.

The ostrich is the world's largest bird, and ostrich farming is a gigantic industry in neighboring South Africa. There seemed no reason not to pursue it in Zimbabwe, especially in the southwest. The potential of ostrich meat, eggs, and leather captured young Peter's mind. In partnership with the National Parks Service, he started collecting eggs from the wild. It wasn't long until he was the biggest ostrich farmer in Zimbabwe, raising thousands of ostriches, and operating an abattoir and a tannery in Bulawayo.

To this day, he continually reminds neighbors, visitors, government officials, and colleagues that there is a greater purpose for him—and them—in life than just profits: that is, one that brings honor to God more than anything. He has never forgotten the miracles along the way.

When he was in his early twenties, he prepared to sell his ostriches and those of fellow farmers to a buyer in China. He made a
contract with a cargo plane he brought to Bulawayo from Amsterdam, but as the plane arrived the obstacles started to mount. The
Chinese government refused to grant air space to the jumbo jet,
and the weather was too hot to take off with a fully loaded airplane,
so the birds were unloaded. In hopes of finding a cool time early in
the morning, he loaded the birds again and then unloaded them
again off and on for two days, but he still didn't receive the permission he needed. During that time, he was afraid he was going to
lose it all. Bankruptcy loomed, as well as the loss of his honor and
trustworthiness with the other ostrich farmers.

After two days, the pilot informed Peter that he needed to return to Amsterdam for another job, and they prepared to unload the
birds for the last time, back into the trucks. He had been there all
night, waiting for permission and the weather to cool. At dawn, his
mother arrived with some breakfast for him. He was one discour-
aged ostrich farmer. He would never be able to repay the farmers
or the contracted plane. The pilot still had no permission to fly, and
the weather was approaching the 25 degrees Celsius, the threshold
temperature allowed for take-off. He unloaded the birds . . . again.

God, however, was watching, and his mother was listening to
him. When she felt the Lord tell her "Go ask the pilot what was
needed right then," she did just that. "In twenty minutes," he said,
"I need to close the doors. The temperature is too hot, and I still
have no permission." She then headed to the tarmac in front of
this gigantic cargo plane, got down on her knees, and raised both
arms in prayer to God in heaven. After this, she headed back to
the cargo building.

Five minutes later, a rare cold wind blew across the city, a bank
of dark clouds hovered, and the temperature dropped to 15 degrees
Celsius in fifteen minutes. When this happened, Mrs. Cunningham
rushed out of the building and up the stairs to the cockpit, and said,
"Mr. Pilot, here is the telex from China." A shocked pilot ordered
the birds back on board and took off within the hour. Peter never
forgot that it is God who supervises the affairs of man, the winds,

and the clouds. And although he had been embarrassed that Mum had intruded, he was certainly grateful to her for this critical turn in events.

That was a turning point for Peter. The profits from the sale of the birds in China provided him with money for the first time in his life. More importantly, it was one lesson among many that challenged Peter to study the Scriptures and honor all that God says about money, profit, motives.

Some months after the miracle on the tarmac, he was reading the passage in Matthew 6:24 where Jesus says, "No one can serve two masters. For you will hate one and love the other; you will be devoted to one and despise the other. You cannot serve both God and money." That bothered him because he did not despise money. He loved God, but he also loved business and knew that God had wired him for it. At the age of twenty-seven, he grappled with God and came out of it determined that money would not control him. Everything he did would be in response to God's vision of a bigger picture than Peter's prosperity: that of a prosperous Africa and a partnership with God in what God wanted to do on the continent.

God showed him that the only way to be free of the love of money was to live for a larger reason—to be part of God's eternal story. He saw that this world is just a passing whisper in time, and that our security and life come from the presence of Jesus with us, not from the illusion of control that money gives. The God of the miracles of the Bible is the same God of miracles today. Peter then committed himself to lay up treasures in heaven (Matt. 6:20).

Although the ostrich industry has since collapsed in Zimbabwe, Peter still keeps a few pedigree birds for breeding purposes, anticipating that at some point the industry will rise again. In the meantime, he returned his attention to poultry and discovered a new vision from God—and the miracles continued.

While Zimbabwe continued to expropriate land from thousands of white farmers, God spared him from losing his land. When officials demanded that he leave his Maleme farm—which included his parents' camp, his agricultural college, and massive tracts of farmland—employees and neighbors rose up in his defense. Even a vice president of the country stood up for him when he realized how much Cunningham assisted villagers with various projects by teaching them chicken production and modern farming methods. He was helping more than eight hundred families and donating chicks to communities around the country in order to economically empower small farmers.

Another miracle was the building of a water dam, which spared them from the drought in those years. Then in 2004, he was abducted by a warring faction and held at AK47 gunpoint. "It is not my fault that I am white," he explained as they prepared to kill him. When he explained the time and place that he was born, it turned out that the man with the gun happened to be born in that same ward at the same time. He changed from animosity to agreeing that neither of them had any control over what color they were born. Peter prayed and asked God for another miracle. Then, without any humanly understood reason, they let him go.

A Diversified Agribusiness: Hamara Feed and Food

Not much has changed in what some call the "failed state" of Zimbabwe. There is still corruption, bad fiscal policies, natural disasters, and massive poverty. But what has changed is that God is honoring the obedience of one man and his family to put God first in the spirit of Matthew 6:20–24. There is light in a dark place with hope for a brighter future.

The vision given by God to Peter Cunningham was to unlock the productive engine of Zimbabwe with a focus on small-scale farmers who would first feed themselves and then export produce to other areas of Africa. The genius of the vision is that it is a partnership between business, church, community, and government. The leaders of the Turning Matabeleland Green (TMG) movement are none other than Peter and Diane Cunningham (and his conglomerate of businesses) and Bishop Patson Netha (representing various churches in Southeast Zimbabwe-Matabeleland). Formed in 2013, TMG seeks to develop a network of competent farmer partners to meet the country's growing food and export needs.

What does a landmark successful agribusiness look like in a country like Zimbabwe? To date, over thirteen thousand small-scale farmers have been trained under its programs. What started with fifty chicks in the care of an eight-year-old schoolboy has become one of the biggest chicken distributors in Zimbabwe, with fourteen franchise sites across the nation. Hamara Chicks is a division under Sondelani Ranching, a diversified farming and agribusiness concern, which focuses on broiler and layer day-old chick production as well as a producing point of lay birds. Around 160,000 chicks a week are produced for both layer and broiler birds. The HiGrow outlet in Bulawayo alone supplies more than ten thousand farmers a month with chicken stock.

Since chickens need quality feed, Hamara Feed produces four hundred tons a week and is a leading producer of feed for birds and livestock in Zimbabwe. Gigantic trucks pull out from the mills and distribute to more than five thousand customers weekly. But how does all this begin with the small farmer and then scale to the size it is today? How does a poor small farmer get started?

Peter says it this way: A poor family can start with thirty egg-laying hens, which provide about twenty-two eggs a day. The family can keep five and sell seventeen. As simple as that seems, it is a great leap forward in family income. Things can only grow from there.

This is not old-time subsistence farming, but a modern, efficient, and technically well-managed network, organized around hubs for training in the latest techniques, supply-chain management, processing, and sales. It is an input-driven and a market-pulled vertically integrated chain that includes training centers around the country, Ebenezer Agricultural College, and a model farmer incentive program with commercial centers. All of this brings economies of scale and increased business profitability with the Hamara chain of retail outlets, where out-grower famers can sell their product.

In 2018, the Sondelani Ranching division built a $2 million state-of-the-art tomato processing plant that can process 150 tons of tomatoes a day as it produces tomato paste for export. The soil and climate are ideal for crops such as tomatoes, squash, maize, and potatoes.

All of this—and much more—is possible with clear guidelines based on biblical principles, church mentorship, political liaison with regional chiefs, agricultural expertise, college apprentices, technical road maps, vision days, TMG training, and a plan to scale. The farmer support includes well-developed financial models, business contracts, a stewardship bank, TMG training, pastoral support, and a buy-back store.

Peter and Pastor Patson like to use the image of an eagle, which requires two wings to fly. One wing is the spiritual-religious wing, and the other is the practical wing. Both are necessary and tied together in one entity—spiritual disciple-making and job and food creation. One without the other is a one-winged eagle, explained Patson. That spells disaster.

Ebenezer Agricultural Training Centre and Other Educational Visions

I wanted to see Ebenezer Agricultural Training Centre first-hand with its more than one hundred students who study in the morning and work in the fields in the afternoon.

We asked Anthony, an agricultural student, what was happening at the college and why he was there. Without hesitation, Anthony said, "I have always wanted to be a small-scale farmer and to know God and have a greater relationship with him." He went on to describe the "life" he felt the moment he stepped on the grounds of the center. "Ebenezer has changed me," he said. "And now I want to pass it on to others."

Ebenezer started in 2007 as the vision of Peter's sister, Renee Cunningham. Since then, the two-year program, along with its outlying shorter courses, has graduated hundreds of students. On a yearly basis, they are now responsible for 10 percent of the agricultural graduates in the entire country. With two-thirds of the nation's population under twenty-four, it makes sense to focus on this age group. They come interested in "cropping"—planting food crops, poultry (layers, hatcheries, and broilers), or dairy. Each day, trucks carry thousands of eggs and tons of milk to town. In a recent month, they reported harvesting 6,452 watermelons, 72 tons of butternut squash, and 88 tons of tomatoes—not bad for the work of students who are learning the trade.

Each morning begins with devotions. Sometimes the students meet together in the simple thatched pavilions, and sometimes on their simple frame beds in the dorm. One day, we walked in on 120 students listening to some teachers, and soon they were dancing and singing praises to God. Family nights add to the fellowship and focus on the greater good and glory of God. This is truly work as worship.

But Ebenezer is not just an agricultural microcosm. Renee, who is the center's coordinator, dreams of revolution in Africa—not just in Zimbabwe. It starts with God and education. With 1.2 million Zimbabwean children and 300 million in all Africa not attending school, she dreams big. The answer is e-learning. Without rural electrification, money, or much of anything, how is this possible?

"The solution," she asserts, "is a mini-computer and trained facilitators." Her dream is to set up Africa's first learning platform providing a free and accessible education. Nelson Mandela stated that the biggest weapon for changing a nation is education. And as Renee suggests, a Christian education is an even bigger weapon. Although there is much to be done to realize this vision, the Hamara agricultural juggernaut will surely prevail with God's help.

Renee took us to Hope Primary School in Bulawayo where we met Nkosi, who arrived early for class that day. Martha, the headmistress, welcomed him and I asked her to tell me his story. She said that he was the eldest of three children and that when the third was born, his mother died, followed shortly by his father.

Sixth-grader Lucy then wandered by. She loves school and is always early. It is a safe place for her, far removed from her abusive uncle. Orphans, Nkosi and his siblings were poor and without hope. Likewise, Lucy saw no hope for herself for justice or a normal childhood. But hope is what they found in this school.

Martha and Ezra, who both work with Peter, wanted to provide quality education to the local children who didn't have access to attend school. They hired good teachers and opened the Hope

Primary School in an old church building, and they expanded with
secondary grades, athletic facilities, and quality education. Not
only is there renewed hope for an education, but there is hope also
in Christ, as teachers focus on what it means to be a disciple of
Jesus. Since then, they have also taken over Nduna, which was a
government school without the resources to continue. After they
took it over, this school had the best improved grades in the district.

That is what kingdom businesses like Hamara can do. They
are disciple-making, kingdom-focused, job-creating, and servant-
minded. They think differently about how business, the church, government, and the community can work together for the greater good.
They can change a country like Zimbabwe for the glory of God.

In one week, I had an answer to my question. "Where is it
possible to observe tangible evidence of a profitable business integrated with lifting people out of poverty in the name of Jesus so that
his church grows?" I saw it in the context of a humble, God-fearing
family who were "living by grace in relationship with God." They
count it a privilege to serve Africa.

Onward to Zambia

Visionary, entrepreneurial, obedient, God-fearing people like
the Cunningham family continually ask God what's next. For them
it's Zambia, formerly Northern Rhodesia. Though not as destitute
as Zimbabwe, it too is filled with challenges. The Cunninghams'
goal in Zimbabwe repeats itself in their "Zambia Heartlands Initiative," an initiative to unlock Zambia's productive potential to
reduce poverty and actualize its vision of becoming a prosperous
middle-income nation by 2030.

I felt waves of excitement as I stood in a room with more than
a hundred leaders: a vice president in the Zambian president's cabinet, the chair of the House of Chiefs, the senior chief, the queen of
the local House of Chiefs, pastors from all over the country, business leaders like Peter Cunningham, and investors from the United
States. It was the kick-off meeting in Livingstone, named for the
famous missionary to Africa.

Zambia is the only country in the world with a constitution and a national anthem that are both profoundly Christian. Although their protocols are reflective of their historic culture, their prayers and vision are Christian in nature. But there is much work to be done for the citizens to "act Christianly." For evangelical leaders, this was an opportunity to bless the nation in the spirit of Genesis 12:2 (NLT): "I will make you into a great nation. I will bless you and make you famous, and you will be a blessing to others." Tears welled up as we sang the national anthem and reflected on the integration taking place that addressed poverty, created jobs and opportunities, and made true disciples of Jesus—all in one place! The chorus goes like this:

> Praise be to God,
> Praise be, praise be, praise be.
> Bless our great nation,
> Zambia, Zambia, Zambia.
> Free men we stand
> Under the flag of our land
> Zambia, praise to thee!
> All one, strong and free.

In Peter's speech that day, he referred to Isaiah 61 as he demonstrated how marketplace agricultural initiatives, the church, and following Jesus are inseparable. Again, I was delighted to see that integration really does work.

The Cunningham family and foreign investment groups had already begun to work in Zambia. They had already purchased an eight-thousand-acre farm, Sonrise Farm. Bio-compliant facilities were full of thousands of chickens, and six hundred employees were at work daily. Cattle were being milked and a multi-million-dollar feed mill was under construction. The philosophical, economic, and spiritual basis was the same as in Zimbabwe: address food shortage, reduce poverty through job creation, encourage the churches, and make disciples of Jesus in an integrated holistic approach. This initiative recognizes a change in the mindset of every institution in the country. Economists call it sustainable development. Christians call it fulfilling the commands of Jesus.

None of this, however, is without its challenges: 41 percent of the country is extremely poor, only 15 percent of arable land is under cultivation, there are 73 tribal groups and seven major languages, and two-thirds of the population is under twenty-four. But none of this intimidates the participants in the initiative and certainly not Peter Cunningham, who sees nothing but opportunity and the God of cattle on a thousand hills.

The opportunity is for true followers of Jesus to bring an integrated regeneration of the whole person, be a blessing to their world, and create wealth in God's name. They truly see an opportunity to raise up and mentor the next generation to put Jesus first and make disciples who will be "salt and light" in the world (Matt. 5:13ff.; Gen. 2:15–16). The initiative document concludes it all with the phrase, "A New Dawn in Zambia." As Peter Cunningham reminds us:

> All of this is founded on the cornerstone, Jesus himself, the sure foundation. It is by grace we are saved, by grace that he offers us the privilege of walking with him, and he uses us as a small part in his eternal story and the big picture.

Missional Professionals in International Small- to Medium-Scale Business Start-Ups

*There are no secrets to success. It is the result of
preparation, hard work, and learning from failures.*

—Colin Powell

Capital Roasting Company
Teaching English and Living the Faith through Coffee

"How about a cup of coffee?" is a question I have posed in almost every country I have visited. In Brazil, I asked for a *cafezinho*; in Spanish America, *café*; in Italy, *caffe*; *kuba* in Ukraine; *Koffee* in Germany; *Kape* in the Philippines; *kahawa* in Swahili speaking countries; *kopi* in Indonesia; but in most places its spelling won't work on my English keyboard. The point is that coffee is pretty much universal.

Some years ago, I found coffee in a tea-loving country in Central Asia, which I'll call "Tealand." Ten years earlier, they would have looked at me, wondering from which planet I had just arrived. But thankfully, they knew exactly where to take me: the Capital Roasting Company (CRC).

Tea is a wonderful drink with a complex history of more than two thousand years dating back to China. But it is not coffee. The most common legend describing the origin of coffee can be traced to ancient forests on the Ethiopian plateau. There a goat herder named Kaldi discovered the potential of the beans when he noticed his goats eating the berries from a certain tree. His goats became so energetic that they did not want to sleep at night. Apparently, Kaldi reported what he noticed to the abbot of a local monastery, who made a drink that kept him alert during his long hours of evening prayer. Of course, he shared it with his fellow clerics, and word of it continued to move east toward the Arabian Peninsula where it was cultivated. By the sixteenth century, it began to be exported abroad and eventually to the rest of the world.[1]

Coffee made its way to Europe, where Pope Clement VIII finally gave his approval, and it no longer was considered the "invention of Satan." By the mid-seventeenth century, there were three hundred coffee houses in London. Apparently, tea still dominated the American Colonies until the Boston Tea Party, after which Thomas Jefferson called coffee the "favorite drink of the civilized world." Who wouldn't want to switch to coffee?

After the collapse of the Soviet Empire in 1991, residents of the new Central Asia republics developed an intense interest in the rest of the world, and this included Tealand. As with some of the earlier colonial powers of the West, Russia didn't leave Tealand in the best of shape. When I arrived for my visit, I discovered how much the citizens wanted to be like the Western world. Some of the young people even wanted to leave their country to migrate to the West. The drive to build a modern Tealand and be relevant in the world meant forgoing some of their traditions, including women no longer wearing head coverings. The intense interest in the West included viewing newly broadcast television programs from the US and Western Europe, learning the English language and foreign social customs.

The Capital Roasting Company began as the vision of a small group who arrived in Tealand in 2008. As the start-up team began to learn the language and make friends, they saw an opportunity in this milieu of social change. CRC began to build their business model around the current needs.

A business idea always starts with the need or problem of the customer; some call it their pain point. A business model sets about providing a solution to the problem with a value proposition in such a way that the need is met. In typical capitalistic fashion, the entrepreneur earns a living, creates jobs, and satisfies customers.

And so it was that the owners of CRC developed a business model around the demand for coffee since it represented the West and a requisite to building a modern Tealand. Once they decided that coffee shops would be the catalyst for their business, they began with focus groups and lots of market research on everything from the sources of the best green coffee beans to what would be the best coffee tastes to intrigue the citizens of Tealand's capital.

Emily was the obvious team member to lead the product development market research. She had recently graduated with a degree in international business and had funded her way through college working at Starbucks for four years. Although the lean start-up model canvas had not been invented yet, she and her colleagues intuitively knew to ask relevant questions and pursue necessary answers, gradually determining their customer base, the primary problem to be solved along with potential solutions, a well-articulated value proposition, needed resources, and key metrics of success.

Starbucks had prepared her well. As the largest coffee company in the world with over thirty-thousand locations in seventy-six countries, Starbucks personnel have become experts in coffee, from the planting of the trees to the brewing in the retail store.[2] Emily took advantage of all of it and learned about the types of coffees grown in specific soils and at specified elevations. She understood how the cherries were harvested, she was familiar with the various methods of drying and processing, and she knew how to read grading reports. She was well prepared to lead the research necessary to buy green coffee and import it to Tealand; and once the beans were on site, she knew what machines were needed to roast and grind them. Then she set to work in finding answers to new questions.

It was not an easy task to test, pivot, test, and then start over again—everything from importing the machines to discovering the best international coffee source to experimentation with sugar coffees at the counter. Buyers were international visitors and multinational businesspeople, and they were also permanent locals with long-term buy-in interest in the success of CRC.

Emily was part of a larger team, all committed to the central values of blessing the community, making disciples of Jesus, creating jobs, and building a profitable business. The team began to meet to pray, plan, and proceed with action. In the simplest of terms, they agreed that the customer really needed three things to reach their modernization dreams, whether they stayed in Tealand or emigrated:

1. They would need to learn English, to use at home or abroad.

2. They would need to enjoy coffee, especially if moving to Western Europe or North America.

3. They would be greatly benefited if they understood the Judeo-Christian history, Protestant work ethic, and the principles of Jesus.

They knew they could help them with all of those.

Besides Emily, the team included members who were hardworking and business-minded, with a good understanding of Western economic and philosophical history, and committed disciples of Jesus.

I arrived at the CRC that day with low expectations of the place and their coffee. What I experienced was the total opposite. This place was the first of two stores, not unlike Starbucks in the US, Tim Hortons in Canada, McCafé in Frankfurt, Sofa Café in Rio de Janeiro, or a cup of Illys at Milano Roastery. CRC was meticulously clean, with multiple drink offerings, attractive artwork, efficient baristas, and relevant international food. It was an amazing experience.

The owners of CRC had captured three things: (1) They had made coffee an attractive, tasty, and fun experience; (2) they had rooms in the back where English classes were taught, as well as classes on economics, Western history, and religion; and (3) they had captured the Starbucks "experience" model and developed a place to live out Christian values and stimulate a conversation about Jesus.

I wanted to know more. How did they get to the point of having twenty-two employees in two stores? How were they making an impact in the community? How had they become profitable? How come several had become followers of Jesus and were now studying the Bible?

The answers to such questions deserve much more than a few paragraphs in a book on intercultural disruptive innovation, because they involve the expected twists and turns, ups and downs of a typical start-up. But it was clear to me that it had much to do with a clear purpose: to meet needs and bless people, to bring the truth of the gospel, to create jobs, to love people and develop them to their full potential.

They began with a clear definition of a specific business with the expertise and competency to bring it to reality. In this case, they knew coffee and could deliver it. They also knew human nature, the needs of people, and how to disciple others. They were committed to the hard work needed to learn the national language, serve customers, and pray through the tough times with resilience and long-term commitment.

They sought out mentors so they could be successful and then mentor others. They sought funding sources and communicated with them regularly with transparency and truth. The result was success: the quadruple bottom line of profitability, job creation, discipled followers, and stewardship of creation.

Today, there is a strong gospel presence connected to CRC that continues serving the community, teaching, and mentoring, and making a difference in a country that in many ways still faces the challenges of modernization. Tealand still faces ongoing corruption, discrimination, political tensions with a neighboring country, and endemic poverty, but many of their goals have been realized. CRC is profitable, independent, and a spiritual lighthouse in the capital city. Best of all, many individual lives have been changed;

some have moved on, and others who have stayed are now serving their generation.[3]

Dignity Coconuts in the Philippines
Changing Lives and Breaking the Cycle of Poverty

Every person has innate dignity. For too many, however, the cycles of poverty, war, and slavery have buried that dignity. And there are those who claim power over them, stripping away their God-given dignity. When a person believes the lie that they are powerless and insignificant, then the cycles of poverty, war, and slavery continue.

About 1.5 billion people in the world live in extreme poverty. Food, health, housing, education, and safety cannot be purchased on an income of $1.25 a day. This kind of poverty denies them the freedom of choice, and it results in desperate decisions and patterns of debt.

But a few people in the Philippines had a dream and a determination to break the chain. They asked how they could bring self-respect so that people would feel capable and worthy. How could they break the cycle and allow freedom to those suffering in slavery and poverty?

The answer was employment in a local business called Dignity, founded by Stephen Freed. They decided to tap into business as a vehicle for change—a business that would transform the future for the underprivileged. In 2012, they started with the poorest of the poor in rural Philippines, praying about what kind of business they could start that would be the engine for change. They asked questions among the locals and discovered a great asset— coconuts! Using simple coconuts with the many health benefits, they were able to transform communities. "Dignity Coconuts" was born.

This kind of transformation may be seen from many different angles. First, the group chose a location based on the needs of the community, which was rural with difficult access. The drinking water is unclean, and the unemployment rate is high. But these negative factors describe why they are there. They are bringing education, clean water, jobs, and most importantly, hope.

Community Transformation

It starts with a belief in the dignity and potential of every human being, regardless of circumstances. Since people are the reason for creating sustainable profits, the owners structured their plan to make it reproducible, not just with coconuts but also based on local values and resources.[4]

Transforming a community means *giving minimum handouts.* There certainly are times and places for handouts, but they can take away something from a person as they give something else. A handout provides temporary relief, but there often is a bigger problem looming. A handout can create unhealthy dependency. A handout can take away a person's dignity. Giving someone a job says, "You are worth the time and effort to train and empower. You are capable. You can provide for your loved ones. You matter." Handouts do not accomplish any of this, and they do not bring hope for the future.

This business *employs locals*—one hundred and twenty of them. Each employee represents a family. Plus, they source coconuts from one hundred and fifty farmers at each plant, thus affecting the lives of over two thousand people locally. In communities with high unemployment rates, this can transform everything. Dignity Coconuts is now the largest employer in the entire region.

Dignity Coconuts places *people over profits.* People can produce the best products on the market using the best methods possible. Through training, the business has become a catalyst to improve issues like unemployment rates, cycles of sickness, personal finances, education, environment, business development, leadership, and water sanitation. Training and teaching are the very things that restore the dignity in each person that is so desperately desired. Stephen Freed tells it this way:

The journey is long and hard when signing up to be a part of the first wave of a movement or new idea. You cannot do it without good people whom you trust immensely. For us, that means our key staff in the Philippines are our greatest assets. Similarly, we cannot overemphasize how crucial it has been for us that the early investors, leadership in the USA, and leadership in the Philippines have like minds and hearts.

At Dignity, they believe transformation starts with questions, not answers. There is no "one size fits all," because each community is unique. There are rarely simple answers to solve the issues of poverty, so they look to the leaders within each community to partner with them as they survey needs, develop goals, and work side-by-side to bring lasting transformation.

They use a *holistic approach*. They work toward the quadruple bottom line, and they measure success based on physical, economic, social, and faith goals established by the community.

Dignity Coconuts is a *creation care community*. Thanks to engineers and scientists, they have found ways to use 100 percent of the coconut toward achieving zero waste! They are working toward turning what is normally waste into products like eco-blankets that prevent soil erosion and renewable plastic-like material that reduces plastic in everyday products.

A Raw and Organic Product

Dignity Coconuts produces a top-quality virgin coconut oil. Within hours of opening sixteen thousand coconuts a day, the oil is packaged into jars using a unique method of production that keeps the oil cool and retains every bit of healthy goodness. Their virgin coconut oil is centrifuge extracted without heat and without refining. They use g-force to gently separate the oil, leaving the end product with the most pure and delicious virgin coconut oil a jar can hold.

Their processing plants are located in a pristine, remote area where the coconuts have always been free of pesticides and other harmful chemicals. Farmers are trained and certified in organic farming methods, which helps them farm better and smarter. The product is exported through the city of Manila to the US in solid form in jars weighing about a pound each. In the US, about fourteen hundred grocery stores carry the coconut oil, and there are marketing efforts to sell in more stores in the future.

What Do Dignity Coconut's People Say?

When I first started talking with Tim Lash, lead engineer and manager at Dignity Coconuts, I wanted to know why he chose to work for Dignity while living in the United States. I soon discovered an interesting story!

Tim graduated from Baylor University as a mechanical engineer and was mentored by engineering professor Walter Bradley, a pioneer in Sustainable and Appropriate Technology who gained some prestige for his scientific research on the utilization of underused resources to reduce world poverty. Part of that research included the use of coconut husks as a replacement for synthetic fibers. The influence of Dr. Bradley, who also is renowned for his research on the mysteries of life's origin (intelligent design), underscores the importance of mentoring in the lives of young people.[5] Tim credits him with influencing him toward many of his interests, which include business, engineering, development, and missions. When he graduated, Tim wondered where all of this could come together for him.

Two months later, Tim was hired by Dignity Coconuts, where he has primarily served in the role of lead engineer. This has meant everything from engineering new water lines from the mountains to the centrifuges needed to separate the oil from the coconut milk, which took two years to discover. He has had the opportunity to take a project from conception to completion, as well as drive an existing project toward improvement. He is also the liaison between the plants in the Philippine countryside, the offices in Manila, and US marketing operations.

There have been plenty of challenges along the way, such as frequent typhoons, lack of water accessibility, poor internet connections, lack of skilled labor, distance from specialized maintenance
help, and spiritual oppression. But there have been advantages and
joys as well. The locals are loyal and faithful, the company has favor
with the government, and there is no major organized religious
oppression. All of this brought me to the key question: What is the
relationship between faith and work, between the spiritual and the
business?

Dignity Coconuts believes that helping someone have peace
with God is part of community development, environmental stewardship, and profit sharing. When dealing with tough issues like addiction, slavery, abuse of women, and desecration of our earth, God
is at work in breaking these cycles. President Erik Olson comments,

> Unfortunately, religion has often been used to hurt people, causing
> many to keep religion and spirituality out of the workplace and any
> other environment where there could be casualties. We do not force
> religion on anyone; nevertheless, we have seen the power of God
> transform lives, break addictions and heal marriages.[6]

Shirley's story helps to demonstrate the answer to such questions of integration. Her family was struggling to survive.[7] Her
husband, Ramir, took whatever small jobs he could get to help the
family; but without land, his only options were to work on a rice
farm or a fishing boat, where he received a small share of rice or
fish. The pay was irregular and unsustainable, so he made the tough
choice to look for work in Manila and send money back to Shirley and their three young kids. In exchange for this sacrifice, they
received $33.50 per week. Since she wanted more for her children
than an absent father or just the rice with vegetables she was providing, Shirley applied to work at Dignity. She was skeptical, because she had never worked with a team and doubted her abilities.

When Dignity hired her, it changed her life and her family's.
Shirley was able to make a consistent income with a salary from
Dignity. Within the first week, she was able to increase her payment

to the school from $0.04 to $0.11 so that her kids could have bread and fruit juice at school. They now have school supplies and can pay their school fees on time. They are able to buy meat or fish to add to their family's diet of rice and vegetables. And within the first week, they had electricity connected to their house, allowing the kids to do their homework at night.

Shirley's employment at Dignity has given her hope. Before working for them, she says she had lost her hope to ever prosper. She now sees a brighter future and the potential to realize her dreams. She believes in herself and her abilities. She loves working as a part of a team. And she is also a better parent. Instead of scolding her kids for asking for a toy or food, she can confidently and lovingly say yes more often. Ramir was able to come home from Manila so that they could raise their family together. Shirley's faith has been strengthened. During daily prayers before work, she is thankful to God for his provision. She works with gratitude for what God has given to her family through Dignity.

She now has hope because she saw God and faith integrated with all of life, including the workplace. She is empowered. Her kids are being educated. They are being raised by two parents. Their diet is healthier. Their future is brighter. Their lives are better; and most of all, she is following Jesus.

Jonathan is another example of someone changed by the power of God. He is a security guard at the Dignity plant, and he also farms rice to supplement his income—though that income fed his gambling addiction. His wife almost gave up on their marriage. Then in 2012, Jonathan met Jun, Dignity's community development leader, who spent extended time with Jonathan and his wife, Jenelyn. Since that time, their lives have changed. First of all, Jonathan stopped gambling. He used to be involved in political bribes and kickbacks, and he lived without hope of paying off his many debts. But not anymore. Jonathan and his family now have hope for their future and their future generations. His marriage is getting stronger, and his wife and sister-in-law are teaching children in the area.

Jesus changes people like Jonathan and transforms whole families like his, and it continues on into the community.

Tim travels periodically to the Philippines to keep in touch with the projects and see the results of a company committed to integrating faith into the workplace. He regularly sees the economic impact, like in Arnold, who was empowered to start his own micro-business. God used him to share a Bible verse and help another employee come back to Christ. Dexter, who recently joined the engineering team, is another employee seeking truth.

Tim is glad he has continued with Dignity for more than five years because he can see the big picture of God at work changing lives, breaking the cycle of poverty, and transforming an entire community—all because of a commitment to an integrated life of faith on the job and everywhere.

Teaching English in Thailand
"We Are Building a Cumulative Case for Jesus"

Thanks to my colleague Sharon, who told me that I had to talk to Grant Wooten because he had an amazing story, I was able to meet him via video conferencing.

He lives in central Thailand, where he teaches in government schools. He came prepared with his story segmented into his early years, college, marriage, teaching history in Thailand, and his dream for software development for the glory of God. Who wouldn't want to listen? I always love it when someone starts his story by crediting mentors who provided solid counsel and paved the way for his career. For Grant, one of those mentors was Dwight Martin, who was born to missionary parents in Thailand sixty years ago.[8] After eighteen years in Thailand, Dwight headed to college in the States and a thirty-year career in the tech industry, which included founding his own software company and earning an MBA in technology. Ten years ago, Dwight returned to Thailand to serve the church with his technical skills.

Dwight has seen all sides of missionary activity, and it bothered him to see traditional missionaries having minimal impact, especially those who stayed for such short periods of time. He knew a new model was necessary, one that focused on native Thai leaders being motivated by their faith and supported by technology. "We need to think about missions differently. The old method of sending American missionaries to foreign countries is expensive and not efficient. It's not working."[9] Dwight maintains that by focusing on indigenous leaders, the cost goes down and the effectiveness goes up.

During his early years, Grant was a directionless teen, and a poor student who played video games for twelve hours a day. His dad was a marine officer and had only one solution for young Grant to find that direction: the military. This scared Grant to death and at the end of the eleventh grade, he randomly searched for colleges on the internet. The first one to catch his attention was Bethany College in Minneapolis. Grant has only one explanation for why he attended there, since he had never heard of Bethany, knew nothing of Minneapolis, and had no idea of what to study. It was the Spirit of God.

But how could he go to college with straight Ds and Fs? He was a guy with above-average intelligence, however, so he dove into AP classes during his final year of high school. With a lot of hard work and the grace of God, he was accepted to Bethany. The year was 2010 and he was eighteen years old.

During his first month in Minneapolis, he met Michelle, and God spoke to him, saying, "This is to be your wife." This was another miracle that gave him even more direction and purpose. They began to pray for the unreached of the world, and God pointed them toward Southeast Asia. In 2012, they left for an internship in Thailand.

Grant is not only intensely in tune with the Spirit of God, but he is a common-sense guy. He wanted to go where the need was the greatest, and he wanted to do something productive in the eyes of the local people so they would welcome him. This is where Dwight Martin came in with the challenge of teaching English in government schools. Dwight was part of the internship program and taught lessons on Thai language and culture. Grant dove into the study and began to excel.

Both Grant and Michelle returned to college, graduated with degrees in Teaching English to Speakers of Foreign Languages (TEFL), and passed the exams for a credential. They were married and back in Thailand by December 2014, with diplomas and job invitations in hand. They were both twenty-two years old.

Dwight knew people all over the country, spoke the language like a native, and had ideas for a place for Grant and Michelle to work. Where else but the most Buddhist cultural center in the country? As the first capital of Siam, the Sukhothai Kingdom (1238–1438) was the cradle of Thai civilization, the birthplace of Thai art, architecture, and language. *Sukhothai* means "the dawn of happiness." School children are taught that they are the guardians of Buddhism. The area is seventy years behind the rest of Thailand in openness to outside ideas, and there is plenty of resistance to other religions, particularly to Jesus-followers. There were no other expatriates for more than sixty miles. It was a great place to start for a couple that loves challenges and is committed to the call of God.

From the start, their model was that their identity would be as professional English teachers with the goal of being the best language teachers they could be, even exceeding the professional requirements. In addition, they set personal standards for their character, meaning the highest code of conduct, morality, integrity, respect for authority, love for the people, and a commitment to being law-abiding residents. They would integrate relevant values into the curriculum, and they would never use the classroom as a platform for proselytism or base the lessons on Bible stories. When asked (and when appropriate), they would take the opportunity to respond to questions and share their faith.

Grant and Michelle took their cues from the spirit of Abraham in a story from Genesis 12. Abraham, who had considerable wealth, was asked by God to go to a new, faraway land with God's promise to bless him. But that was not the end of the story. God said, "You will be a blessing." That was a key follow up phrase for the Wootens as they set out to build into their model the idea of being a blessing—not only in the classroom but also in the community, to local authorities, and to everyone they encountered.

They discovered that in a country with a strong commitment to Buddhism, there is great respect for "people of faith," in contrast to other expatriate teachers they had known who may have been atheists or without a respectable moral code. But that just meant they were respected, welcomed in the community, and accepted as teachers in the schools. What about their desire to share Jesus?

The road was not easy. For more than three years, they were the only foreigners in the whole area. They wondered why more Christian English speakers did not respond to the challenge to take their profession and create value for a community in Thailand. They saw what they were doing as a divine calling, and they saw teaching English as ministry. Teaching English, especially in the context of Sukhothai, was not easy. But they were determined to become proficient in the Thai language and to cope appropriately with a corrupt administration, a hot and humid climate, and an ambivalence to their Christian faith.

Finally, things started to change. Grant had observed that the government schools celebrated Christmas as a respect to Western tradition, yet the Thai people only knew about Santa, elves, reindeer, and colored lights. One day, Grant reminded them that he knew something about Christmas, which landed him the job of writing the Christmas play in the Thai language that year. Of course, they saw the Christmas story as historical and ethical; but more importantly, two thousand students and more than a hundred teachers heard the gospel, most for the first time. The play was repeated the next year and has now spread to other schools.

Almost every day, someone asks Grant, "Why are you here?" They want to know why he came to Sukhothai, of all places. His standard answer is that Jesus wants him here. This initiates more questions about their lives, about America, about family, about their faith. He affirms, "I now have more opportunity to share my faith than any missionary." He has established credibility. They are valued in the community and have accomplished the goals they set in the beginning: to be excellent teachers, to have high standards, with an opportunity to live out their values. Think about it: every day, two thousand people gather for school from various socioeconomic Buddhist backgrounds. In town, there are more than thirty thousand people, and everyone knows him. They all talk about how Christians are different and ask why. In Grant's words, "We are building a cumulative case for Jesus."

This paid off in an interesting way when the leader of a local community group called Grant and asked him to come and tell them about Jesus. This leader said that he already had been introduced to Jesus through a vision but needed to know more. He called Grant because a student from his English class said he might have answers. As a result, ten members of the group decided to follow Jesus. Since then, hardly a day goes by when someone doesn't ask for more knowledge about Jesus. Grant and Michelle believe this is just the beginning, and they are so grateful they didn't give up after only a few years like so many others. Through his experiences, he sees a pattern:

- The seeds of faith are planted via a life well lived as a witness.

- People begin to ask questions.

- The seed is watered with a life testimony, example, and love.

- The Spirit of God guides them to a "tipping point" and they open the door.

- A new life is born as the Spirit answers with his presence.

During another video conference that day, Grant told me about his struggles to launch a start-up related to educational technology. It all started in his third year in Thailand when the school administration announced that they were no longer purchasing curricular materials for six grade levels. This meant that Grant and Michelle were on their own. His graduate school professor in the States advised him to "run," but Grant and Michelle face challenges head on. For a full year, they created the program on a day-to-day basis, keeping themselves only a few days ahead of the students. In Grant's words, "They built it as they flew the plane." He discovered that much of what he found on the internet wasn't helpful and needed to be individualized to the unique group of students, the teaching context, and each teacher.

They made it through 2018, but this experience launched Grant and another teacher into a start-up business building a database. Using the latest technology, they built a database that accounted for individual ages, culture, energy, proficiency, range of ability, and content. At the time of this writing, the project is still in process, but it may be what Grant calls a "game changer." It has gained attention with database specialists, educators, professors, and technology experts in the States who are intrigued with this effort to wean teachers from their dependence on textbooks and standardized curriculum. "We incorporate student retention data and correlate it with teaching content to create a student module," he explained. It is called a "Learning Optimization Product." It is a lean high-tech start-up, with a viable product design. Although there is a long road ahead, it is promising.

This couple never stops. And I can't help but admire and appreciate the way they have integrated their faith with their profession, hung in there during difficult times, and built on the small wins they achieved in a foreign country. Grant and Michelle are wonderful examples of the work missional professionals can do around the world.

Information Technology Jobs
A Software Company with a Mission

As I listened to Mike tell the story of Information Technology Jobs (ITJ), I thought how amazing it was that these guys built into the company from the start what many Fortune 500 companies were just now beginning to adjust to. True, some, like the ServiceMaster Company, believed for decades that the development of employees is key and that their empowerment and sense of purpose comes first. Contrary to the famous statement of Nobel Prize-winner Milton Friedman in 1970 that the sole purpose of business is profit, businesses today are taking into consideration their social responsibility, the environment, and employee development. Christian businessman Don Flow states, "We have to have a profit . . . but profit is not the goal. I don't know a healthy person who gets up on the morning and looks in the mirror and says, "I live for my blood." But I don't know a person alive who doesn't have blood. Blood is like profit—necessary to live, but not the reason for living."[10] ITJ models a priority on their employees—on their dignity, their growth, and their empowerment. Their whole lives are important.

Mike and Jason were studying the local language of the people when they took a vision trip to a small city in South Asia in 1996 with the purpose of analyzing the needs of the city. They found that the greatest need was for jobs for the growing population of young people. A local focus on technical education had resulted in the community's interest in developing computer skills, but there wasn't a single software company anywhere locally to offer employment. Mike and Jason agreed that such a company would be a great way to bless the community by creating jobs so people could stay in town and provide for their families, while at the same time pointing them in the direction of spiritual hope.

And so, Information Technology Jobs (ITJ) was born in the "sticks" of South Asia. The two families acted on their impossible dream to provide a low-cost solution for businesses in the West (mostly in the United States but with some in Europe, the Middle East, and the Pacific region), using locals they trained and mentored on how to serve clients' needs with appropriate software. The past seventeen years have proven their commitment to provide excellent solutions to the satisfaction of their clients. Mike and Jason see it as being good stewards for God.

ITJ's main business is creating custom software, with a specialization in building web applications and mobile apps. Due to their economies of scale with about 150 employees, they have established excellent capacity, competence, cost-effectiveness, intercultural communication, and consulting expertise. In 2012, ITJ decided to open a second location, which gave them more access to people who had limited opportunity to hear the gospel.

This second location also opened a new pool of local talent from which to draw.

One of the biggest challenges in operating a software company is in retaining talent. Small software companies are often only training grounds for larger IT companies that recruit from the smaller ones. This cycle leaves the smaller businesses continuously struggling. By God's grace, ITJ has several factors that help it thrive, one of which is a deep focus on building a company culture that fosters a vibrant personal family atmosphere. One former employee stated that she likes ITJ because when she walks into the office, she senses that God is there. ITJ intentionally nurtures a company culture where employees have the freedom to express themselves openly and honestly. Employees look forward to development days, seminars, and outings that further promote the spirit of unity. Most importantly, the team values are modeled by leadership at all levels.

Because their faith is important to co-owners Jason and Mike and integrating it into every aspect of their lives had become central to their strategy, they developed a plan to fit the context of the local culture. Their goal was to bless the local community by offering young people a job and the training required to be successful. They then point them to Jesus as they build relationships through conversations about their family and life issues. In Mike's words, "When one key employee was going through a difficult time emotionally, we had the opportunity to share about healing and peace that could only come through Jesus Christ."

Living in the community has also created many opportunities to share the good news with company families and with their neighbors. Host country nationals always value foreigners when they learn their language and culture. Such integration, however, is not without its challenges related to the culture—on the job and in the community.

Mike mentions, "For instance, the locals tend not to say no directly. Hence, when they say yes, it may not necessarily mean yes." Western staff or clients may have difficulty discerning whether yes actually means yes. Having Western team members working onsite has enabled not only cross-cultural training for the locals so they can serve a Western client more excellently, but it also provides opportunity to model servant leadership, which is one of the core values of the company.

Cultural differences also affect the design and development process. While the actual software coding transcends cultures more easily, the design side—which includes user experience, colors, layout, look and appeal, graphics, etc.—depends on individual style. Asians and Westerners typically have different preferences.

ITJ must be proactive in addressing cultural differences like this. To bridge such cultural gaps, it helps to have Western staff living onsite to help train local staff to see projects from a foreign perspective. Interns from abroad who are gifted in web development, design, marketing, human resources, or business management are sought to demonstrate the Western client style and thus advance the skills of local staff who are already strong in math, science, and coding.

Company values include Jesus' commandments to love God and love others. It is a key value for leadership to be able to express their faith in Christ while at work.

Building a company as robust as ITJ is not without its challenges. Since its inception in 2003, there have been low points, such as 2014 when cash flow reached a critically low level. Competition is especially stiff with other small- to medium-sized companies located in Eastern Europe and South Asia. In fact, a dozen other new software development companies are now located near ITJ in their two cities, but they work hard to maintain a competitive advantage with differentiation in the areas of cultural uniqueness, historical core competence, and cross-industry understanding.

Another significant challenge is that the perceived value of outsourcing for US companies is decreasing while costs in South Asia are increasing. It is taking more time to find suitable clients and to define and work out suitable projects for them. Furthermore, the information technology world is constantly and rapidly changing, and it takes increasingly more time to stay ahead of the changes.

Developing a consistent sales pipeline, as well as hiring and training a sales team, has been a challenge. The sales cycle takes more time and sourcing new clients has become more crucial. When it takes several months to close projects, more sales representatives are needed and cash flow is affected. At this writing, there are five sales representatives working throughout the eastern United States, and the goal is to see more strategic and sustainable initiatives in the US.

The Jesus-followers who work for ITJ strive to simply live out their faith transparently in order to promote authentic conversations. Although the majority of the employees do not follow Christ, they are hospitable and interested in spiritual conversations. Jesus, however, is often considered to be a Western God and irrelevant in this part of the world. Their views, including the concept of sin, are very different; therefore, a savior is often dismissed as unnecessary for salvation. Because of these and other differences, there is considerable pressure from family and society if a person rejects their traditional faith and turns to follow Jesus.

As I listened to Mike, I sensed a robust understanding of what it means to follow Jesus in the modality of *missio Dei*. It is not about the making of converts or about planting a church (although that is the natural outcome of sharing the gospel); it is about the opportunity and freedom they have as business owners to integrate faith with business. As they pursue that end, they are sowers of the values and the good news of the gospel of Jesus. For example, during the recent Easter seasons, many of the staff met together on company time to pursue the question, "Why is Good Friday good?" Imagine over forty employees assembled for a time of interaction, fellowship, and learning. They were divided into teams and watched animated videos demonstrating the biblical narrative leading up to the meaning of the Easter event. They watched these videos in separate rooms, and each team was responsible for learning the message of their video and then presenting it to the entire group. They spent time practicing the telling of the story to one another, and when they were ready to make a presentation, they told their story in front of their peers, complete with factual detail and the inherent meaning. Everyone in each team shared with the larger group, and everyone listened to one another's stories. After a coffee break, one believer shared the meaning of the atonement while another shared her testimony. It was amazingly relational, relevant, natural, and interactive.

The company schedules these types of events throughout the year. They are all relational-driven topics like marriage, leadership, personal development, new technology, and similar relevant topics, all based on biblical values with Christ at the center. Such opportunities are totally natural, legal, and appropriate—something unknown in most countries in the West. It is one way of bringing the Christian worldview into the context of the workplace.

Another example of integration emerges from within the HR domain. Every manager has experienced letting a worker go, but how does that manager release a person in a culturally relevant and biblical manner? How is it done right? While all businesses need to release employees who are no longer a good fit, in Asia there is the added complexity of doing it within a shame culture.

Shame-honor cultures, such as those in most of Asia, are based on the need for the appearance of honor. Unlike guilt cultures that have a baseline of absolute standards that when violated produce guilt, shame cultures use external sanctions as the enforcer of good behavior. Appearances are what count, and the idea of being dismissed from a job brings shame—something worse than violating any criteria based on a code. Don Flow, who is well acquainted with this type of culture, says:

> In a guilt culture you know you are good or bad by what your conscience feels. In a shame culture you know you are good or bad by what your community says about you, by whether it honors or excludes you. In a guilt culture people sometimes feel they do bad things; in a shame culture social exclusion makes people feel they *are* bad.[11]

In the case of one employee's dismissal, Jason and Mike took him out for coffee, listened to him, reminded him that it was not the end of the world for him, shared how Christ could help him through this, and assured him they would support him through the transition. Although he still needed to move on, management assisted in a cordial, respectful way, and they prayed with him. This was an example of living out their faith in a godly, encouraging, and respectful way.

Mike shared another example, this time from a disciplinary case. A midlevel manager named George had used his leadership position inappropriately. But top management saw this as an opportunity to help him learn how to change if he was willing to do so. Company owners knew they needed to remain consistent in following company guidelines, but George agreed to be on probation for three months while they worked with him and taught him how to lead appropriately. In the process, he learned the difference between penance and repentance, and he agreed that he wanted to learn. All middle management (none of whom are Jesus-followers) worked together in the learning process; and at the end of three months, George was a changed man and clearly understood the gospel. All of this was possible because ITJ leadership had created a culture of living out faith in every aspect of the business with a focus on the worker and God's redemptive grace.

Mike was quick to recognize that he too makes mistakes, and as he and Jason humbly ask forgiveness from employees, it is an amazing learning experience for all. The proof that the employees are "getting it" is that they are starting to put into daily practice principles found in the Scriptures. "Discipleship happens prior to coming to faith," Mike affirms as an encouragement to all of Jesus-followers no matter where they serve in the world.

As with all such companies both in North America and in the developing world, it is a struggle to maintain professional business goals with missional faith goals. It can get complicated when sales take a dip, making layoffs a necessity. But ITJ maintains to this day that people are as important as profit, and their company exists to employ people, serve them, and provide resources so they can adequately provide for their families and contribute positively to their community. Maintaining the balance between profitability, job creation, people care, and living and sharing biblical values and truths has not been easy, but the owners credit the grace of God and his provision for these past seventeen years of growth and fulfillment.

Continuing *Missio Dei* after "Retiring"
Dave Kier's Other Life

Then I heard the voice of the Lord, saying, "Whom shall I send, and who will go for Us?" Then I said, "Here am I. Send me!"

—Isaiah 6:8 (NASB)

Although my primary purpose in writing this book and citing these stories is to challenge younger generations to follow in the footsteps of those who have used their profession for the glory of God, I feel it is also appropriate to include the story of a retirement-aged business owner who is using his talents to strengthen the economic and spiritual condition of people in the developing world. Such is the case of Dave Kier (cited earlier in chapter 4).

The story of this kingdom-minded business guy in the Iowa feed industry didn't stop when he sold his business. He calls this his "other life," which actually began when he was busy building his animal feed business. His ministry had always been in the US, and he had never heard of places like Tajikistan and Kyrgyzstan when he agreed to take a trip with other businesspeople. It was there in central Asia that he learned the connection between chickens, eggs, feed, education, and training—and sharing his life in Christ.

Some years after selling his business, a friend introduced him to a business in Africa, one that needed his skills in the feed industry. By then, he realized that the good life was found in serving and giving. Off he went to Zimbabwe in southern Africa to meet Peter, Diane, and Renee Cunningham, whose story is told in chapter 7.

As we saw in the Cunningham story, Peter believed that we must meet the needs of the entire person, because someone who is concerned how they'll get their next meal isn't going to be very receptive to listening to the good news of Jesus. This made sense to Dave; and from that time forward, he invested time and talent in the Cunningham expansion into neighboring Zambia. Dave and his son were asked to lead the commercial aspect in Zambia where a feed mill, abattoir, and soy-processing plant were being built.

These days, Dave makes frequent trips to Zambia to keep up with the projects that integrate value-creating economic development with personal discipleship and church growth. Dave challenges everyone he sees to use their skills, talents, and professions in ways that can change the world. Although he was at first skeptical about Peter's goal to reach all of sub-Saharan Africa for Christ, he's now happy to be part of it.

Nguvu Dairy
A Trauma-Informed Workplace in Uganda

Abducted by the Lord's Resistance Army (LRA), Gloria was forced to be a child soldier in northern Uganda. Although girls sometimes carried rifles on the front lines, they usually did the cooking for the boys involved in guerilla warfare and served the sexual wishes of the commanders. After eight years, she managed to escape the LRA and walked back home. Life, however, continued to be hard. No one trusted her, not even her sisters. They thought she was a killer and to be avoided at all costs. She couldn't find work and barely survived on the few things she could grow on a tiny subsistence plot of land. But then her life changed:

> The moment I stepped inside the gates of Nguvu Dairy I felt a sense of peace. James was so kind and friendly, and he taught all of us victims how to make yogurt. He was patient and encouraging. Nguvu Dairy has changed my life. I have a job and can rent a little house in town and afford school fees for my son.

Gloria is a survivor of human trafficking. The International Labor Organization estimates that there are 40.3 million people affected by human trafficking globally. According to an official definition, there are three groups of human trafficking victims: (1) Children under the age of eighteen induced into commercial sex; (2) adults (age eighteen or over) induced into commercial sex through force, fraud, or coercion; and (3) children and adults induced to perform labor or services through force, fraud, or coercion.[12]

Gloria is in the third category. At a young age she was en-slaved, brain-washed, exploited—without hope. By God's grace, she was one of the few who successfully escaped and returned to her home area in northern Uganda, though as a highly traumatized young woman.

The troubled history of northern Uganda is complex and dates back to British colonial rule (1894–1962). The LRA rose up dur-ing the independence of 1962 as a resistance group among ethnic entities in the north and was led by superstitious cult-like person-alities, the most well-known being Joseph Kony. During a twenty-year campaign of terror across Uganda and nearby states, the LRA forced tens of thousands of children to fight, perform menial tasks, and commit atrocities.

The children endured harsh training and were told that it was necessary to make them into fighters. The LRA forced them to commit terrible crimes, including beating to death other children or even adult fighters. Afterwards, they would tell the children that because of what they did, they could never return home again and that their families and communities would shun or even hurt them. On top of the ritualized violence, kidnapped girls were forced to marry LRA commanders, subjected to sexual violence, and forced to bear their children.

Though now a shadow of its former self in Uganda, the LRA still has several hundred children fighting in its ranks. Northern and eastern Uganda still suffer from the devastating consequences of Joseph Kony's reign of terror. The International Criminal Court (ICC) has charged him with the enslavement of twenty-four thou-sand children and ten thousand murders. During those years, pov-erty increased in those regions of Uganda from 68 percent to 84 percent.[13] While the LRA has little direct impact today in Uganda, it still violently demonstrates its power in the Central African Republic, South Sudan, and the Democratic Republic of the Congo.

In 2017, the advocacy group Child Soldiers International estimated that more than one hundred thousand children were forced to become soldiers in state and non-state military organizations in at least eighteen armed conflicts worldwide. The UN further reported that a majority of these children were actually under the age of fifteen and that 40 percent of them were girls. This is a global problem that is only getting worse.

The roots of Nguvu Dairy's story lie in the efforts of several organizations to rescue and provide recovery to these survivors of enslavement. Though the work of the rescue organizations was highly valuable, something was missing. Successful US entrepreneur James Dirksen of The Market Project asked the question, "What happens to survivors when they finish the program at the care organizations?" While researching the operations of NGOs and rescue agencies, he discovered that all activity was in the "program" category of rescue, health care, and counseling, and that 95 percent of this was funded by foreign donors, which seemed to be unsustainable.

Being a seasoned entrepreneur and business owner, James conducted a market analysis of the Gulu district in northern Uganda and engaged in entrepreneurial thinking. This work was done as part of The Market Project, which starts real businesses that take the next critical step to bring healing to survivors and provide full-time employment. Although he and his colleagues realized the NGOs and Care Organizations had a critical role in bringing health, spiritual care, and counseling, they saw the need and potential to build a profitable job-creating, disciple-making, sustainable business. And so Nguvu Dairy was born.

James realized that while microbusinesses have their place, he understood that only a small percentage of traumatized people can take out a loan, start a microbusiness, and support their family; and he knew that a company needs at least a hundred employees to have any economic or social impact in a community.

James also believed that he didn't know much about trauma and its effect on human potential. It's one thing to be a seasoned business start-up guy with several tech businesses that he's grown and then sold. It's quite another to try to start a business in a rural city in northern Uganda with a population of traumatized survivors. How could he embrace a community of survivors while preserving the dignity of each person and provide the hope of healing with a belief in a God who loved them?

He turned to his colleagues at The Market Project, who had published detailed research in "Trauma-Informed Approach: Understanding Trauma and Its Implications," which is possibly one of the best programs for preparing the workplace for hiring victimized employees. Their foundational principle states:

> We believe that healing and recovery from trauma and exploitation is possible for each man and woman, regardless of current vulnerability. TMP aims to instill hope by providing opportunities to work in a safe environment and to be involved at all levels of the business. We focus on an individual's strengths and resilience, and we encourage them to articulate future goals.[14]

This approach clearly explains the importance of becoming informed about trauma and committed to business. All the while, they acknowledge the importance of safety, trustworthiness, transparency, peer support, and empowerment, as well as cultural, historical, and gender issues.

The Market Project partners with Care Organizations to source employees for Nguvu Dairy. Willow International is one example, with a program called "Aftercare" described below:

> The aftercare process for survivors is complex and unique for each individual. Program duration varies depending on the severity of the beneficiary's victimization and the stability/safety of their family. Survivors work directly with a case manager who provides them with an individualized care plan that addresses the following areas of intervention:
>
> - *Safety*: Family reconciliation and home visits

- *Health:* Medical care, access to HIV treatment and support

- *Education & Economic Development:* Vocational and formal education scholarships and access to business skills training, tutoring, literacy programs

- *Psychosocial:* Counseling and therapeutic interventions, social connectivity opportunities, support groups, mentorship, yoga, art therapy, play therapy

- *Social & Spiritual:* Spiritual care and mentorship, access to church and social activities including choir and youth group

Willow is committed to programs that are survivor-led and informed. Survivor voices are essential to the programming, monitoring and evaluation, and the overall vision of the organization. Our mission in the aftercare program is to empower each survivor with the tools they need to heal from trauma, reconcile with family, resettle independently or with relatives, and live a healthy life free from re-victimization.[15]

The Market Project provides a twelve-week training program that equips self-identified survivors and others to understand their trauma and begin to process their experiences in a way that safely leads them to heal their wounded hearts, grieve their losses, and build trust in their relationships at home and at work. Regular employee surveys help Nguvu's managers understand where further training is needed.

Nguvu Dairy is the first business started by The Market Project in Gulu, a city in the heart of the former LRA territory in northern Uganda. "Nguvu" means "strength" in Swahili—exactly what the dairy's healthy yogurt products promote! The yogurt comes in lemon, vanilla, and strawberry flavors and is sold at the lowest possible price, in order to be accessible to all. The yogurt is produced from milk sourced from cows on twenty dairy farms. Distribution is coordinated in nine sales centers. A team of salespeople in purple shirts hit the streets of Gulu on custom bicycles with coolers attached on the back, peddling the tasty treats along the way.

Nguvu employs over two hundred resilient, industrious men and women of northern Uganda. More than 65 percent of the employees have endured multiple severe traumas, but management walks alongside them as they heal, grow, regain their dignity, and support their families. The company is unique in that it delivers the yogurt to the doorstep of the customers in the villages, allowing employees to engage with and build up the community through quality, nutritious options previously out of reach of customers.

The Market Project's Nguvu Dairy continues the care and training started by the Care Organizations and ensures that women and men are further equipped with transferable job skills, robust training, and mentoring that encourages stability and integration into community. Trafficking survivors—whether child soldiers, forced brides, or those freed from trafficking for sex—bear heavy shame and are often shunned by family and friends. These jobs enable each wage-earner to care for an average of seven family members. They now earn enough to pay rent, receive medical care, feed their families, and even pay the school fees for their children. Work brings self-respect and gradually erases stigma.

As a trauma-informed workplace, Nguvu Dairy cares just as much about making disciples as they care about making profit. They hire trained pastors to work at each distribution center. These pastors then lead Bible studies, provide counseling to the employees, pray with them, and encourage them. Each pastor also starts a church near the distribution center. To this date, nine churches have been started.

The Market Project does the hard work of market research and product development on the front end, with bridges built to Care Organizations, a focus on building medium-sized companies, rigorous research, respect for the environment and culture, business planning, raising capital, and employee development. A document titled "How the Market Project Creates its Businesses" is a model for any start-up in most any industry and environment.[16]

Winifred is one who owes her life to the Willow team and a business like Nguvu. "I did not know that the world still has good people," she said when meeting the Willow family after returning from her slavery in Saudi Arabia. She was in severe pain from the abuse she endured at the hands of her perpetrators, and she was at risk of losing her uterus from extensive trauma. But Winifred's physical ailments were only part of her struggle upon arriving at Willow. She was emotionally unstable, bitter, and short-tempered. She would isolate herself from others and refuse to take her medication because she had no hope of ever living a healthy life again. She wanted to harm herself. She wanted to end the pain for good.

Through frequent one-on-one counseling sessions and group therapy with compassionate case managers, Winifred began to connect with other survivors and started to share her story with increasing comfort. She began to see the good in others. She focused on changing her actions and working to help however she could around the home each day. Through these small acts, she began to discover who she was in this new life. She embraced her strengths and accepted her weaknesses.

Winifred is now physically, emotionally, and socially stable. While her journey has been painful, Winifred composed a song (excerpt below) thanking God for her life and the happiness she has found with Willow International's support.

> I thought that when someone is born, that is how she will live until she dies. That is how I felt when I had a lot of pain, challenges. . . . As I was wondering where God who changes all situations was and at that last minute He came and changed my life. He has done so many wonderful things, most of His wonders have brought tears of joy yet I used to be filled with bitterness and anger.
>
> When I remember the love God showed me, it makes me cry tears of joy. He has done so many mighty things my dear, so many wonders. He has made me glad, and I strongly realized that it is God. When mummy died, He brought my life back again. . . . Ah, God is truly my friend. He deserves all the glory, and praise, there is nothing that can be compared to His love just like how He promised that He will bring back all that I lost.

Stephen, another survivor who now works at Nguvu Dairy, tells his story:

I went through many bad things. I was abducted by the LRA and stayed in the bush for many years and did many bad things when I was still in the bush. My father was killed by the LRA and my mother who was left also died when I was still in the bush. But after the Nguvu trauma healing program lesson [on grief] was taught, I have found there is a problem that I used to keep thinking of my late father. Today I am happy because now I know how to handle the idea [of what I went] through. I can now share my problems with friends . . . even now I can share with my wife. I have a good understanding with my fellow workers. It is Nguvu which has brought good change into my life.

The stories of Gloria, Stephen, and Winifred are typical of most Nguvu employees. Theirs is the story of pain and suffering. But theirs is also the story of someone who cared, a story of rescue and restoration, a story of productive work and healing—and a story of beginning to follow Jesus as his disciple.

Outland Denim
The Power of Obedience

The Royal Australian Air Force Bombardier Challenger 604 jet touched gently down in the Outback town of Dubbo, Australia, to a cheering crowd of fifteen thousand anxiously awaiting the arrival of the duke and duchess of Sussex. It was October 18, 2018, and the first full day of the royal tour of Prince Harry and Meghan in the South Pacific. The activities in Australia included Aboriginal dances, a barbecue lunch, a boomerang lesson for Harry, baking banana bread for Meghan, and lots of hugs for excited students. Their visit even brought joy to farmers suffering from the two-year drought that had afflicted so many in the region.

I first observed a royal tour in Canada when I was seven and Princess Elizabeth, the duchess of Edinburgh, toured Vancouver in 1951. Teary-eyed, my mother enjoyed every minute of her brief view of the motorcade as the future queen drove by. Then, as with contemporary visits, every aspect of the royal's appearance was scrutinized. On that October day nearly seventy years later in the Australian Outback, everyone noticed the black stove-pipe jeans the duchess was wearing, and it wasn't long until the story hit the media. By wearing these particular jeans, Meghan was making a statement in support of those fighting human slavery and trafficking. Her jeans were manufactured by Outland Denim, a company owned by a kingdom-minded Australian couple with a factory located in Cambodia.

Human trafficking is a lucrative multi-national 150 billion-dollar per year illegal industry of exploitation and enslavement; and two-thirds of that total comes from sexual slavery. It is estimated that up to 40 million people are trapped in this modern slavery and most are children and women—a crisis of epic proportions. It is something that people should and can do something about; it certainly is something Christians must do something about.

In 2017, I accepted the challenge of joining the Freedom Business Alliance as an advisory board member. As with anyone facing a new challenge like this, I realized I had much to learn. After reading many articles and books, listening intently to speakers at conferences, encouraging people working with victims, and praying that God would help restore this vulnerable population, I boarded a plane to Cambodia with my wife, Vicki and, our teenage grandchildren, Korbin, Hayden, and Sadie. We were traveling to Phnom Penh where our daughter Trudy served as the HR director for World Vision. We had plans to visit seven freedom businesses in the country, one of which was Outland Denim.

There we learned about the three phases used to help bring change to the lives of those who have been victimized: (1) rescue, (2) restore, and (3) reintegrate. Most of the activity we found seemed to concentrate on the first two phases of rescuing victims and working to restore them, which left the third stage short-handed. What happens when those becoming restored with a desire for a better life are ready to reintegrate into society? Do they have the appropriate skills, a trade, or options for remunerative employment? These were the questions that drove the owners and corporate officers of Outland Denim, James and Erica Bartle, to do something.

Managers Caleb and Katie did a great job showing us around the factory on March 23, 2018. We heard brief stories of the passion of the staff to make a difference in the lives of the employees, elements of their business model, ethical practices, and the environmentally savvy supply chain they used. We observed as approximately fifty women learned the production process, from pulling the Turkish denim from the rolls, which they verified had been ethically sourced, to the finished product with the seamstresses' stories written on the pocket linings. We saw them hold the pair of jeans they had produced, and we could clearly see that their sense of dignity had been restored as they were reintegrated back into society.

History of Outland Denim

As a journalist, Erica Bartle has over twenty years of experience in the communications sector, and her passion for justice evolved from her decision as an adult to follow Jesus. When she was in her mid-twenties, she first encountered victims of the sex industry while on a Contiki tour with her friends, and she realized that there was more to life than her planned career as a glamour girl and beauty editor of a popular teen girls' magazine in Sydney.

James, a one-time career motocross racer, was riding one day at a music festival when he came upon an anti-trafficking group. While in prayer during the festival, he was overcome by a vision of women in need in Asia. The impact never left him. Then, after their marriage, Erica and James watched the highly disturbing film *Taken*, which further exposed them to the nightmare reality of human trafficking.

While Erica continued to grow in her understanding of exploited women and girls, James decided to travel to Southeast Asia. There, he observed the devastation that traffickers bring to young girls.[17] James learned that once a woman is rescued from sex-trafficking and then supported through recovery and restoration, it is vital for her to find a sustainable career path in order to reintegrate into society. It was from here that the foundations of Outland Denim were laid as an avenue for training, employment, and career progression for these vulnerable women.

When I asked James about motivation, he said that it came down to being obedient to God and his calling: meeting the real needs of people, while also respecting the environment. The Outland Denim team spent over six years developing a business model before they took it to market, all the while being guided by a desire to help people permanently out of poverty.

James told me, "We were not about generating sales so we could have impact; but we strove to concentrate on impact as a driver of sales. At one music festival in Australia, we sold $28,000 worth of a test model of jeans because people saw we were producing jeans the right way, not by using cheap slave labour." He wanted to get away from an exploitation mindset and when he saw that the church was failing in this area, he determined that business must lead the way: "Honest and authentic industry can model genuine care as part of the solution—not part of the problem."

With the corporate office in Australia, they set up production in Cambodia. James says,

> We first welcomed a small group of five aspiring seamstresses who had been recommended to us by a non-government organization (NGO) with frontline operations in Cambodia. These women needed work in a safe space owing to their experiences of exploitation.

> So, with these small, humble beginnings began the steep learning curve that is picking up a highly specialized craft from scratch, from experiments in pattern making, sourcing raw materials and stone washing in a cement mixer, to setting up a manufacturing process that began with pedal press sewing machines and hot-coal irons in remote Cambodian villages. They called it the "Denim Project" and began to train vulnerable women, giving them jobs in a stable and safe environment while creating the brand's premium denim.

> Beyond Outland's commitment to preventing vulnerable women from falling back into poverty—and a broader mission to set a high standard for the treatment of young female workers in the garment manufacturing industry—there is also the brand's dedication to sourcing ethical and environmentally sound raw materials from organic cotton to recycled packaging.[18]

James recalls that his closest friends advised against a business start-up in a country like Cambodia. "There are simply too many risks," they counseled him. But he readily admits even today that "it would be scary if we didn't know that God's got this and that he has called us to do it. . . . There have been so many miraculous confirmations from God along the way." Erica emphasizes their commitment to "creating sustainable career paths," producing a useful product and paying a living wage while minimizing the negative impact on the environment. "The jeans are made in an entirely ethical way," she says, "by a community of young women who have wonderful working conditions. Why shouldn't they go to work in a beautiful space where they feel a sense of family and community, which reflects our Christian values?"

As James reflected on the obstacles along the way, he mused about the difficulty in developing proof-of-concept and issues of cash flow. His church helped in the beginning with capital and encouragement, but until they started to scale, it was a struggle to get wide support. After starting as a nonprofit, they set up a for-profit business alongside it, realizing the importance of economic sustainability for true success.

He reminded me of the initial motivation that kept him going during the hard times: being obedient to the Great Commandment to love God and to love others. Using biblical examples of characters who made an impact, he said that "they all had to go through it. . . . It would be wrong to avoid the challenges one faces in a business. . . . It is all about obedience and perseverance in the call of God." Reflecting on miraculous moments, such as receiving the right advice or cash just in time, he says that staying on the path of obedience helped them even when it was hard going.

Outland Denim Today

After that royal visit in October 2018, there was an immediate 3,000 percent increase in web traffic, and sales grew by 640 percent in the week following the duchess's first appearance in the jeans. In Australia and the US, the Harriet style she wore sold out in twenty-four hours and went on backorder twice. In a 2019 *Town & Country* article, Roxanne Adamivatt writes:

> The denim maker has since been able to hire forty-six new seam-stresses in Cambodia, raising their total number of employees to around one hundred and twenty. Employment for these women is completely life-changing in the sense that it acts as a protective mechanism against the very things that led to their exploitation in the first place. Poverty and the stigma and shame within specific cultural settings that so many exploitation victims suffer from af-fects every aspect of their lives, from educational attainment to employment.[19]

Since Outland Denim fit the Business as Mission mandate of the quadruple bottom line, I was on the lookout for all four ele-ments of it during my visit that day—and it was clearly obvious.

As a private company interested in profit (the first p), Outland Denim has invested significant capital into growing their opera-tions. They recently initiated an equity crowd-funding campaign, partially because they want others to participate in serving the poor in an honorable and tangible way. Says James,

> As a profit-for-purpose company, we are ensuring the economic sustainability of our operations by making a profit to reinvest into Outland. This money can then increase the social or environmental sustainability as it can be used to hire more seamstresses or invest in more environmentally sound materials.

Outland Denim also focuses on people (the second p). They do this by including a spiritual disciple-making component and a social job creating element. The business creates jobs—now more than one hundred—giving dignity through training and encourag-ing demonstrable skills in the workplace. For some business own-ers, they have the satisfaction of knowing they have helped provide for the survival of families, opening doors for them to thrive. But for Outland Denim, "sustainability" is achieved only by treating people and the planet right.

This is a social enterprise, which is sometimes defined as a business committed to a sense of responsibility and an attitude of sensitivity toward injustice and societal problems in the world. In their book *Social Entrepreneurship*, David Bernstein and Susan Davis say that "social entrepreneurship is the process by which citizens build or transform institutions to advance solutions to social problems, such as poverty, illness, illiteracy, environmental destruction, human rights abuses and corruption, in order to make life better for many."[20] Success has a metric beyond the essential profit motive and includes a strategy for solving social problems and creating value that brings a direct positive return to society. The Outland Denim website succinctly states this:

> Here at Outland, we are contributing to social sustainability primarily through working with rescued victims of human trafficking and sexual exploitation. By providing these women with permanent, secure and fair paying jobs, we give these women a chance to increase their quality of life. This is achieved through paying a living wage, which increases the physical and mental wellbeing of the workers and their families. As a result, these women can afford to place their children in school, meaning their sons and daughters are at a lower risk of being sold into slavery in order to provide the family with money. Through achieving an education, these children are more likely to attain a high paying, more secure job which will give them a higher income and quality of life. This in turn will reduce the risk of them ever needing to sell their own children, and thus eventually the cycle of poverty and exploitation will be stopped. Many of these women lose the respect of themselves and their families and communities after enduring exploitation. We help these women regain the respect they deserve by providing them with a meaningful and well-paid job which gives them a sense of purpose and pride by enabling them to provide for their families while learning a transferable skill set.[21]

For the Bartles, the people component includes ethics and Christian values lived out in the workplace. Here, employees see what love means and how it relates to faith. For example, in our visit we saw how the workers prayed before starting the day, an activity that reminds them about who God is, their love for God, and their dependence on him, along with lessons they learn about justice and faith. Someone once said, "Live your business life in such a way as to provoke the question [of faith]," which of course is predicated in 1 Peter 3:15: "Always be prepared to give an answer to everyone who asks you to give the reason for the hope that you have. But do this with gentleness and respect."

Also important to Outland Denim is the third *p*: the planet. Accountability for an ethically sourced supply chain is unique in today's world of environmental exploitation. When we visited, an employee had just returned from Turkey where he had confirmed that the denim was produced in ways that protect God's creation and reduce environmental impact as stated on the company website:

> Through selective sourcing of materials and suppliers, we are aiming to reduce the potentially harmful environmental impacts of our operations. Sourcing organic cotton, natural indigo dyes and vegetable tannins, and utilizing recycled and sustainable materials, are all aiding in reducing our environmental impact in regards to water and air pollution, raw material use, environmental toxicity and ecosystem and biodiversity health.[22]

Outland Denim is not an assembly line factory or a sweat shop. By design, it benefits employees in daily operations and over the long haul.

> Unlike conventional production facilities, our staff are trained in twenty skills across the cutting, finishing, and stitching departments. Our method of recording each staff member's progress involves scoring on a 0–5 scale, with a five indicating that the individual has achieved expertise in that skill. By December 2018, 69.5 percent of our new employees were undergoing training in more than one area of production, with 70.8 percent of new employees already progressing above a level 2 in at least one area of their training areas.[23]

It was clear that lives were being changed socially, economically, and spiritually. James told me about one woman who benefited from her training in the job and then she helped another vulnerable woman begin her own microbusiness as a tailor. Regarding the duchess's promotion of their jeans, the company website states:

> Behind the scenes, we have been given the opportunity to tell our story to thousands of people at conferences around the world, to launch Outland Denim to the market, to be recognized by industry bodies, and to reach new customers in some of the world's best-known department stores. The "Markle Effect" is real, but the reality is that it takes hard work from hundreds of people to create a brand good enough for royalty, and this includes the women sitting at their sewing machines crafting your beautiful jeans.[24]

While we were touring the factory, I quipped to my grandson Korbin that maybe I would get him a pair of jeans for Christmas. But I thought differently when I learned that this pair sold for $195.00. Obviously, though, there is much more going on here than just a pair of jeans. The company website puts it this way:

> Bartle and Outland are asking that consumers look at the true value of the garments they wear. "If we all had the opportunity to visit some of the places where our things are made, then how we think about those things would change," Bartle says. "We hope to change this not only leading by example in how we treat and value our staff and give them a voice, but by contributing on a global level to the discussion about fashion ethics."[25]

James, Erica, and the team would never say they have arrived, because as a company with a unique brand, they see themselves to be on a journey. Every once in a while, though, they find it nice to stop and say, "Hey, how 'bout that duchess!" and reflect on that unexpected moment of success and the small inroads made by each and every one of their staff in the process. They know that God who called them and blessed them and gave them a cause of upmost importance with an unexpected marketing opportunity. They simply want to be obedient, as success is evidenced in improved and changed lives.[26] To God be the glory!

CHAPTER 9

We Are in This Together: Yesteryear, the Present, and the Future

Yesterday is gone. Tomorrow has not yet come. We have only today. Let us begin.

—Mother Theresa

Any review of the past would suggest that God works in a multitude of ways to bring "everything to its proper end," to accomplish "the Lord's purposes," and to conclude "plans to give a hope and a future" (Jer. 29:11). Think of how his purposes, plans, and procedures were very different in the created world, the patriarch period, the age of the kings, and the times of the prophets. What was God doing during the Roman Empire, the Middle Ages, the Ming Dynasty, or the Aztec Empire? How about during the years of the Protestant Reformation or the revolutions in Europe prior to modern times? Certainly, God raises up new strategies when new cultural and sociological transitions occur.

The early twentieth century was a stark contrast to the later part of the century, when God opened doors of opportunity for freely spreading the good news for decades after the Second World War. There has been plenty of disruption throughout the centuries, and that disruption continues today in our twenty-first world. And as we look to the future, we know that God is again moving in new ways.

It is the perspective of this book that the twentieth-century "missions" as understood and propelled by churches, agencies, and individuals was functionally accomplished by God's people working in obedience to the Great Commission. Churches and agencies were doing missionary work as they obeyed the command of Christ with a primary focus on eternity (the "not yet" of Luke 19:11–12 and Matt. 18:3). There was an urgency because of the times (such as the threat of Communism and nuclear war), the promised reward of peace with God (preached by Billy Graham), and the assurance of eternal salvation (John 3:16). In *Workship*, Patrick Lai suggests that times are changing again:

> In the past, the established methodologies and parachurch agencies could not adapt with the changing times. Often, they would adopt the new terminology of that day, but only as a veneer for keeping things the same. The question is, can parachurch agencies formed in the modern world of the 19th and 20th centuries make the deep root changes needed to adjust to the opportunities and needs of the postmodern 21st century?[1]

The purpose of this book is to establish the prominence of non-clergy professions, including business, in the fulfillment of God's Great Commandment and Great Commission purposes. We need to consider afresh how that can be accomplished in a spiritually, socially, and economically sustainable manner.

Earlier in this book, we established that in contrast to missionary efforts in the twentieth century, *missio Dei* shows us that it is God at work and that Christ's followers should join him in his "mission"—the mission of transforming the world in the "here and now" (Luke 17:20–21; Matt. 3:2; 6:10). It is less transactional (i.e., faith in Christ brings *eternal salvation*) and more focused on holistic transformation (i.e., living and loving like Jesus *in the present*). This is not to devalue missions as popularly defined in the twentieth century. Millions of people have come to believe in the Christian gospel and worship God today through the blessed efforts of thousands of his followers who served as missionaries in past decades.

As Bob Dylan puts it, however, "the times they are a-changin'," and it is only fair to recognize that the gospel is both "not yet" and "here and now." During the mid-twentieth century, there was a definite emphasis on the former, and seventy years later there is a definite emphasis on the latter.

As far as we can tell, God seems to be doing something different today than he did even in the recent past, and he will probably do something else that's new in the future for that time and culture. Some of the reasons for us in the twenty-first century are theological, like the interpretations of *missio Dei*; some are practical, like the closing of two-thirds of the world's population to traditional missionaries; some are cultural, like the differences among the younger generations as to what it means to be a Jesus-follower; and some are ecclesiastical, as we recognize and appreciate the variances of church doctrinal positions and perspectives. Perhaps no reasons, however, are as evident as the simple transformation of everyday believers in recognizing that they too can participate in God's mission, discarding traditional hierarchies of the evangelical church with its sacred-secular dichotomy.

All eras of Christian history have tended to emphasize certain key components of the gospel over another. For example, because of abuses in the Roman Catholic Church (such as the selling of indulgences to reduce time in purgatory) prior to Martin Luther's Ninety-Five Theses and John Calvin's *Institutes of the Christian Religion* in the sixteenth century, the main focus of these Reformers and others was on faith and faith alone. More recently, misunderstandings of the Social Gospel movement in the US between 1870 and 1920 resulted in conservative evangelicals swinging to the opposite pole of social concern, rejecting social enterprises as unnecessary to the mission of God. Thus, in the 1920s, the modernist/fundamentalist dichotomy (an evangelical partisan divide) emerged, resulting in "The Great Reversal."[2]

What is emerging now is a recognition again of the high value of the Great Commandment of Jesus to love our neighbor. That is something everyone can do, irrespective of profession, education, social status, race, ethnicity, language, or citizenship. Real Christians love their neighbor. The Great Commission of Jesus to make disciples is linked to the Great Commandment. As we love people, they will see Jesus living in us as we love them, which can then draw them to the cause and reason for the love. This reduces the need for professional missionaries, and there is less need to outsource the making of disciples to structures such as mission agencies or even church committees. There is even less need for an industry of missions as something unique and specialized. God's way is for *all of his followers to live missionally.*

God gave natural talents and abilities to everyone (Matt. 25:14–30; Acts 11:20); he gave the ability to learn and develop skills (Exod. 35:10; Prov. 22:29); he gave spiritual gifts (Rom. 12:6; 1 Pet. 4:10), and likewise experiences in life (Job 12:12; Eph. 5:1). All of these things contribute to who we are as we develop in character to be like Jesus. It is important that we understand and appreciate each of these domains as we seek to follow Jesus now and in the coming era. Only as we do so will we be able to contribute effectively to the growth of the kingdom of God on earth and maximize our part in where we go from here as it relates to *missio Dei*, disruptive innovation, and the creation of narratives not unlike those described in this book.

One of the business owners described earlier in this book wrote me during the writing process. He reminded me that the narrative of church history is similar to what he is doing in operating a profitable business for the glory of God. He asked "How can a business be called a mission?" and then cited the persecution of Christians in the first century when they were forced to flee to other parts of the Roman Empire. Those first-century Christians were just ordinary believers living as faithful followers of Jesus in the marketplace of life. Over the past two thousand years of church history, there are many such examples of times of upheaval that resulted in a renewed outpouring of the gospel.

The Importance of Partnerships

As we contemplate the future, desiring to live a kingdom lifestyle to the fullest, it is mandatory that we realize the importance of doing it together. Steven Spielberg says it well: "I love creating partnerships; I love not having to bear the entire burden. . . . It's really great—not only do I benefit, but the project is better for it."[3] Similarly, Bill Gates also gives credit to having good partnerships.

As we consider the propositions in this book, it is important to look around and determine how we might work together with others. As the history of *missio Dei* morphs further into the twenty-first century, we dare not forget the missional efforts of earlier centuries. Moving "from professional missionaries to missional professionals" does not suggest that we no longer value professional missionaries. Missional and pastoral professions are indeed one of the professions of the future, as they lead the majority of believers in preparing them for works of service (Eph. 4:12). They have contributed immeasurably to God at work over the past one hundred and fifty years; and while they will increasingly take a back seat to this emerging paradigm, there is much of high worth to value and come alongside in partnership.

Much of my career has been spent serving in mission agency leadership. In the later years of my tenure, my agency realized that times have drastically changed. Our response was to analyze the value of what our agency had to offer to cross-cultural missional people and place a monetary value on each element. That then became something that missional professionals could utilize and purchase. In essence, we were following Jim Collins's hedgehog concept, "What were we best in the world at?"[4]

As an agency, we believe we worked together well and helped our members with important factors such as learning a foreign language, developing cross-cultural competency, multicultural oversight, international crisis preparation and management, member care overseas, multinational legal and accounting savvy, and training and accountability for disciple-making. We were good at these. Many mission agencies will have a similar response. The difference between some and others is what is done with it.

Traditionally, a missionary joins an agency—which employs and cares for them with training, supervision, benefits, career development, contingency planning, and so on—but we believe that in the *missio Dei* of the future, although the agency as an entity and a package deal will be less required, many of the specific benefits will continue to be in high demand. In this case, benefits from an agency can be made available to other non-mission entities, cross-cultural kingdom-workers in multiple professions (see Appendix C).

For example, a missional engineer can take a job in a high-risk country in Africa or Asia and buy certain benefits from the agency. A missional entrepreneur can start a business in a faraway place and buy benefits from the agency. An attorney or an educator can form a contract abroad for his or her services and buy benefits from the agency. A world-class disciple-making musician can take an assignment with an Asian symphony and buy benefits from an agency. This may represent the best of agency partnerships of the future. The individual is fortified in his or her service with enhanced products and the agency still serves the grand purposes of God.

Churches are replete with a generous depository of human talent and experiences. As an entity they can and should mobilize that human resource for kingdom purposes, locally, nationally, and internationally, for the greater glory of God. I once had breakfast with a successful attorney who owned his own law firm. He was active in his church, loved Jesus, and sought to live like Jesus. One day, however, he said to me, "I don't think I have anything to offer God in this world." I wrote "What Do You Have to Offer?" (see Appendix B) for people like him. It is meant to help all believers see that they have something to bring to the kingdom-building experience.

On another occasion, I was teaching a graduate course at a college in Canada. On the third day, a businesswoman who owned a well-known and successful executive search business told me that this was the first time she had heard that her business is her ministry. She went on to tell me about all the involvement she has had in the church—teaching, short-term trips, tithing, giving, community involvement, and leadership—but never once did she get the message that her business was meant for her to bring glory to God and build his kingdom.

Such things are deplorable in light of Ephesians 4:12, where it mandates that the work of pastors and teachers in the church is "to prepare God's people for works of service." One of my mentors in graduate school, Merlin Brinkerhoff, a well-known sociologist of religion, revealed research that indicated that the majority of evangelicals attend church for the social function and that church pastors do not relate to the daily work world. How regrettable. The church should be a key partner with all believers so they can fulfill the work of Christ in their family, community, and workplace. The institutional church on Sunday should facilitate the life and work of each believer for Monday through Friday. They then would become proficient partners in a future destined to be reliant on missional professionals for the making of disciples.

Colleges and universities are important partners in these changing times. Academia is still esteemed as the pathway to success, and the minds of young people are impressionable and teachable. Every Christian institution should consider it mandatory to integrate principles of faith and work, ministry and marketplace, so its graduates can reflect on life experiences and be well on their way to living out their faith and mission within the profession God has prepared them.

When I joined the board of the Freedom Business Alliance, as I mentioned in the previous chapter, my wife and I took three of our teenage grandchildren to Southeast Asia to visit seven businesses committed to skill training and employing survivors of human slavery. Our oldest grandson was already about to start his studies at a well-known Christian university business school. After reflecting on the trip, he told me that this is what he wanted to do with his business degree. I couldn't have been happier! John Dewey is credited with stating, "We do not learn from experience; we learn from reflecting on experience." Good teaching, experience, and academia all partnered to propel him on his way toward serving with his God-given talents, earned skills, and life experience.

Much more could be said as God's people partner not only with agencies, churches, and colleges, but also with justice groups, micro-enterprise entities, professional certification bureaus, and Corporate Social Responsibility (CSR) programs, to name only a few.

CHAPTER 10

Where Do We Go from Here?

*I believe one of the next great moves of God is
going to be through believers in the workplace.*

—Billy Graham

In the 1989 movie *Back to the Future Part II*, Dr. Emmett Brown
creates a DeLorean time machine. He and the other protagonists
travel thirty years into the future to do a little fine-tuning and solve
a few problems. But as the movie unfolds, it is clear that there are
risks in thinking too much into the future.

Christiansen's Disruptive Innovation Theory is predicated on
theories of the future based on past experiences and innovations,
but with perhaps more accuracy than science fiction. Although at
times I envied Dr. Brown's DeLorean time machine, this final chapter will venture into the unknown in the spirit of Christiansen's
thoughtful analysis. Not only do we need to ask "Where do we go
from here?" but we also need to remember our history—as the
characters in *Back to the Future* remembered the past as they traveled into the future and vice versa. In my effort to value the missionary efforts of the past century, while digging into the meaning
of *missio Dei* as it was two thousand years ago, it is my hope that
this book can bring us to understand what the future of being a
missional professional might look like.

Although none of us knows what tomorrow will bring, we do
know that "Jesus Christ is the same yesterday and today and for-
ever" (Heb. 13:8). We also know that God is still working in the
world today for his good purposes; it's really a matter of finding out
what that means for each of us in whatever role he places us. This
calls for wisdom and discernment on our part:

All a person's ways seem pure to them,
but motives are weighed by the Lord.
Commit to the Lord whatever you do,
and he will establish your plans.
The Lord works out everything to its proper end—
even the wicked for a day of disaster. (Prov. 16:2–4)

Many are the plans in a person's heart,
but it is the Lord's purpose that prevails. (Prov. 19:21)

So we fix our eyes not on what is seen, but on what is unseen, since
what is seen is temporary, but what is unseen is eternal.

(2 Cor. 4:18)

Missionaries of yesteryear were sacrificial, purposeful, obedient, committed, honorable, and resourceful models for us all. I have
honored a few of them in *The Greatest Missionary Generation*. Their
characteristics are transcendent and worthy of replicating in every
other generation. Their fruit remains to this day.

But what about this generation and the next? Certainly, God
is not done, since more than two billion people still do not know
of Jesus and his love for them, and hundreds of millions live in
extreme poverty. Although two thousand years have passed, the
world really hasn't changed all that much for those of us who wish
to reach others with the good news of the gospel. There are still
frightening unknowns, risks, challenges, and even dangers. Persecution and martyrdom await followers of Jesus in multiple locations in this fallen world.

We now live in what has been termed "a liminal space." Here
is a good definition from "Liminal Space: Finding Life between
Chapters":

The word *liminal* comes from the Latin word "limen," meaning
threshold—any point or place of entering or beginning. A liminal
space is the time between the "what was" and the "next." It is a place
of transition, a season of waiting, and not knowing. Liminal space
is where all transformation takes place, if we learn to wait and let

it form us. Author and Franciscan friar Richard Rohr describes this space as: "where we are betwixt and between the familiar and the completely unknown. There alone is our old world left behind, while we are not yet sure of the new existence. That's a good space where genuine newness can begin. This is the sacred space where the old world is able to fall apart, and a bigger world is revealed. If we don't encounter liminal space in our lives, we start idealizing normalcy."[1]

Any individual or church alive and well today lives in liminal space with regard to how God is working in the world. I believe that all of us must approach this season of change with intention and with the help of others. It was my purpose with this book to help you boldly approach this liminal space and confidently move forward into your future as the Holy Spirit directs you.

New generations are among us, and there are others coming along fast behind them. Although they certainly have the capacity to meet various challenges, as did those who went before them, it will be different in most every way. Think of how technology, communications, transportation, medicine, and the sociopolitical environment have changed our world in only the past fifty years. Today, travel is easier than ever, immunizations can protect people from serious health risks, and modern hospitals exist in most developing world cities. In just the past couple of years during the COVID-19 pandemic, we have seen new and improved patterns of communication, education, and human interaction, much of which we hope will continue for years to come.

Indeed, world perspectives on anthropological, sociological, and missiological issues have also changed. As stated at the beginning of this book, when it was relatively easy for missionaries to receive visas between the 1940s and 1960s, we no longer have such privileges in the twenty-first century and two-thirds of the world is currently closed to missionary visas. But as Bob Roberts affirms in *Glocalization*, "The world is not closed; we just have to change our methods."[2] We know that God has not rescinded the Great Commission, which means that God still has a desire that all people worship and follow him and discover the love of Jesus.

So where do we go from here? In *Scatter: Go Therefore and Take your Job with You*, Andrew Scott reminds us of the parable of the talents. The master did not take kindly to the servant who did not use his talent wisely (Matt. 25:14–30), but he praised those who increased the value of what they had been given. Scott writes,

> The modern mission movement in the last few decades has pushed a doctrine that perpetuates a mindset of letting go of your vocation and the talents that put you there . . . so you can go reach the world. First, why would God take away what He has decided and allotted for you before the beginning of time—tools that He decided you should have for His purposes? In the same way, it would be ridiculous to think that part of forsaking all is giving up your spiritual gifts. So it is with talents as both are God-given.
>
> Second, I believe Jesus was not talking about giving up God-given things, rather things that we have put in the place of God and his purposes. Earthly relationships, security, safety, possessions, wealth, homes, retirement policies, and so on. None of these things are wrong in and of themselves. It is our attitude to them that gets us into trouble. The issue is when these are the things we hold on to and place as more important than our relationship and role with God.[3]

Whatever God's purpose for our lives, we are all called to follow Jesus using our existing God-given profession, abilities, skills, and experiences. The acronym S.H.A.P.E. helps us remember how God shaped us. He has given all of us:

Spiritual gifts
Heart (or passion)
Abilities
Personality
Experiences

Each of these five areas constitute who we are, and God wants to use that composite in its entirety to follow him as his disciple and for the making of new disciples.

Dale Losch is another author and leader who clarifies this topic in *A Better Way: Making Disciples Wherever Life Happens.* He notes that we do a disservice to the body of Christ when we refer to full-time ministry, negating the fact established in Scripture that every single believer is called to full-time ministry; it is not only the job of the clergy. He points out that the apostle Paul was one of the few religious professionals sent out by the early church as a missionary. The first-century missionary movement was carried out primarily by ordinary believers.[4]

While we have detailed the differences between twentieth-century missions and twenty-first-century mission as an attempt to understand *missio Dei* with the help of looking at Disruptive Innovation Theory, the case can be made that the twenty-first-century church looks much like the one of the first century. Jesus' followers left Jerusalem and were scattered abroad, proclaiming the good news wherever they went (Acts 8:4, 11:19–21). There is no indication that these believers had to be professional clergy. Indeed, there were no seminaries or Bible colleges, there was no institutional church or mission agency to support or provide professional care, and there was no historical or biblical reference indicating that it was normative to be a professional missionary. In fact, even the apostle Paul, whom some call the first missionary, was a professional tentmaker who "worked day and night in order not to be a burden to anyone while we preached the gospel" (1 Thess. 2:9). It would seem that the early Christians had livelihoods or work skills like everyone else, and they lived life with those occupations as they spread out to the world proclaiming Jesus. It was not until the second century that the clergy became professionalized and distinguished from the laity. It seems that in the first century, all Jesus' followers were priests (1 Pet. 2:9) before God as the gospel spread through the everyday believer in the marketplace of life.

The modus operandi of committed believers today is increasingly to take their skill and degree and work in the hard places of the world. All the while, they are the light of Jesus. They are invited to bring their company and/or skills to a country because they create value for the nation and for the people. While General

MacArthur once urged "Send missionaries," the battle cry today is "Send Christian professionals." That is indeed the *better way* for us in the twenty-first century, especially with our current technology that connects us around the world.

None of this negates challenges and risks of living in communities that are often politically, socially, and religiously antagonistic to the Western world. There are still kidnappings and murders of Westerners who risk everything to live out the gospel.

I recently met with about forty people doing business, humanitarian, and academic work in the most anti-Christian country in Asia. Why would anyone go to such a difficult place? Well, that is just the point. These people need God, they need Jesus, they need love, they need the technology or professional skill, they need jobs, they need someone who cares, and they need the good news of eternal salvation.

I want the generation of my grandsons and granddaughters to never ask "Why?" but always to ask "Why not?" I want them to serve like Liam and Sarah, who are helping a Middle Eastern country develop clean water for desperate people. I want them to serve like Phyllis and Joe in Central Asia: they are both medical doctors, listening to the needs of the people and helping them cope with disease in the name of Jesus. That's what engineers and physicians—*Christian* engineers and physicians—can do, even though it is high risk and uncomfortable.

Yes, the world has changed, and yet the world remains the same. Christians still are commanded to love their neighbor as Jesus stated in the Great Commandment and help people to follow him as called in the Great Commission, even though God's way of working in the future may have changed from how he has worked in the past.

May we never forget that the future calls us to new challenges and new technology though with the same goal: To serve a hurting world in the name of Jesus. It is disruptive, but that's a good thing. Like the times of our forefathers, it demands creativity, technology, dedication, sacrifice, and commitment, all of which will be unique for this and future generations. They too can "serve their generation by the will of God" (Acts 13:36).

Changes in Terminology

Old Terms	New Terms of More Effective Communication[1]
missions	blessing the nations, global engagement, God's global purposes, reconciliation, peacemaking
missionary	international staff, apostle, kingdom worker, cross-cultural worker, social entrepreneur, businessperson (relief and development, teacher, etc.), living an intentional Christian life
Christian	follower of Jesus, disciple
convert	follower of Jesus, disciple
church planting	gospel planting, forming communities of Jesus-followers
mission agency	faith-based organization, apostolic community, religious order
church	community of faith, community of Jesus-followers, community of hope, community of reconciliation
church missions department	global engagement, global relations, international task force, international peacemaking and justice department, international reconciliation task force
pagans, non-Christians	unbelievers, pre-believers, God-seekers
field	adopted homeland, host country

What Do You Have to Offer?

North American kingdom businesspeople who own or manage businesses sometimes wonder what they have to offer. They wonder what they can offer as a consultant, an advisor, a mentor, or a coach? It is a natural question for those who work in a very different context from a business start-up in Asia, Africa, or the Middle East.

What is business? It's an organization with appropriate management that provides a good or service and is created to earn a profit, serve customers, as well as create jobs, community value, and increase wealth. That is universal. Followers of Jesus have an integrated kingdom perspective in all that they do (1 Cor. 10:31) so that they operate their business for the glory of God. Faith is integrated into the daily work.

A person who owns a small- or medium-sized business or has worked in the management of such has likely learned a great deal about one or more of the following. This means they can teach what they have learned in a consulting, coaching, teaching, or mentoring venue.

The questions that follow can be used to stimulate thought for consideration by those planning to serve abroad, or by anyone who remains in their homeland contemplating sharing what they have learned.

Entrepreneurial Ability

1. What are the hurdles faced in starting something from nothing?
2. How did I find my niche in the business world?
3. How did I identify risk-takers—or how did I experiment and take risk?
4. Can I help someone know if they "have it or they don't"?

Strategic Thinking and Planning

1. Can I help a person think clearly and look for business opportunities?
2. How do I find the information I need for decision-making?
3. Can I help a person frame out their idea and develop a business model?
4. Can I walk through a simple business plan with someone who has never done it?
5. Can I help envision the customer base and what they might pay for this product?

Management of People

1. Do I know how to find good people? Can I teach that skill to someone?
2. What have I learned about HR laws that I can pass along?
3. Can I teach coaching practices or performance appraisal guidelines?
4. Do I know "best practices" for getting people to produce in a positive work environment?
5. Can I help someone with personal time management?

Product Development

1. In a changing world, can I teach someone to keep their product viable in the marketplace?
2. Have I learned to experiment without assuming too much financial loss?
3. Can I teach someone to produce and sell their particular product?
4. Can I teach someone the basics of business research and development?
5. Can I teach someone how to learn from the experience of others?

Marketing

1. Are there marketing principles I have learned that I can pass on?

2. Can I help someone understand the difference between marketing and sales?

3. Have I used media, sales reps, social media, ingenuity? How?

4. Can I teach someone how to promote their product?

5. How do I know what sells? How do I listen to the marketplace and establish pricing?

Operations

1. Can I ask key questions relative to insurance, benefits, salaries, accounting software, etc.?

2. Can I teach someone how to work with an assistant?

3. What are some tips for getting things done in a timely way?

4. Can I help someone who is struggling with keeping things organized?

5. What are signals in the business that I need to note to keep on top of things?

Financial Oversight

1. Can I give tips for keeping in touch with the financial situation of their business and financial reporting?

2. Can I teach someone the relevance and importance of a P&L, balance sheet, and cash flow?

3. How do I project out for one to three years? What indicators do I look at?

4. Do I have tips for a credit strategy? Amount to borrow? Payback schedules, etc.?

Technology

1. Do I appreciate and understand the value of technology to my business? Can I pass it on?
2. Where do I go for help when I need it?
3. How do I find, hire, and keep a trusted IT person?
4. How do I know when to implement a new IT strategy into my product line?

Legal Matters

1. What have I learned about how to structure things for my business? Can I pass it on?
2. Can I teach someone ownership options, tax relevance, where to go for help?
3. Can I teach someone how to negotiate?
4. Can I teach "Business Law for Dummies" to help a beginner down the right path?
5. Can I help the business start-up person ask the right questions?

Integration of Faith and Business

1. Have I learned ways to live out Jesus' kingdom values on the work site?
2. What have I learned about making disciples at work?
3. Do I see my business as a place of ministry 24/7?
4. Do my customers, suppliers, employees, competitors see Jesus in all I do?

Relationships

1. Sometimes, it's more about who you know than what you know. How can someone keep up effective and productive relationships?

2. How does a business owner keep a balance between the business detail and networking?

3. Do my beliefs and values look the same in the daily experience of life with people?

4. If I'm not a "people person," how have I learned to compensate for that in business?

You know more than you think! Business owners in overseas high-risk areas have lots of challenges, and many of them are the same challenges you face. You can help others with these questions. It will make a difference!

Missionary Agency Monetization of Value[1]

Agency Value (Billable Expertise)	Likely Recipient	Suggested Fee Structure
Assessment of potential, character, skills, etc.	Agency employed; non-member and non-employed	Standard cost of two-week session in person; on site
Cross-cultural training	Agency employed and non-member and non-employed	From one week to one month outsourced to CIT, MTI, or CultureBound
Crisis preparation and management	Non-employed and non-member	Monthly fee of $50 per person per month
Legal and logistics care	Non-employed and non-member	In-country legal documentation; $50 plus all real costs
Training in disciple-making cross-culturally	Agency employed and non-members; non-employed	Joint sessions on field with expenses shared equally
Disciple-making team oversight by director	Non-employed and non-member	Encouragement, counsel, accountability; $100 per month per person
Benefits	Non-employed and non-member	$200 for counsel and direction for best medical, life insurance, evacuation paid for separately
Member care: family and individual	Non-employed and non-member	Conflict resolution; emotional and spiritual counsel; MK counsel; $100 per person per month
Language learning	Non-employed and non-member	Arranged with reputable tutor at costs; $150 one-time fee

Notes

Preface

1. Os Guinness, *The Call* (Nashville: W Publishing Group, 2003), 31.
2. Denny Spitters and Matthew Ellison, eds., *Conversations on When Everything Is Missions: Recovering the Mission of The Church* (Albuquerque, NM: Sixteen:Fifteen, 2020), 18.

Introduction

1. Rick Love, "Following Jesus in a Glocalized World" (paper presented at the Society of Vineyard Scholars: "By the Renewal of Your Mind: Imagining, Describing, and Enacting the Kingdom of God" in Seattle, WA, February 2011).
2. Jeremy Bouma, "What Is Evangelism?," *Zondervan Academic* (blog), March 22, 2018, https://zondervanacademic.com/blog/evangelism.
3. "Amazon's Bezos: 'If You're Going to Invent, You Are Going to Disrupt,'" *MIT Sloan +Management Review*, November 30, 2011, https://sloanreview.mit.edu/article/amazons-bezos-if-youre-going-to-invent-youre-going-to-disrupt/.
4. For more on this, see Larry W. Sharp, *The Greatest Missionary Generation: Inspiring Stories from around the World* (Peabody, MA: Hendrickson, 2020).
5. Martin Luther, *The Babylonian Captivity of the Church* (1520).
6. Dorothy Leigh Sayers, "Why Work?" in *Creed or Chaos? And Other Essays in Popular Theology* (United Kingdom, Methuen: 1957), 53.
7. R. Paul Stevens, *Work Matters: Lessons from Scripture* (Grand Rapids: Eerdmans, 2012), 11.

Chapter 1

1. Tom Brokaw, *The Greatest Generation* (New York: Random House, 1998).
2. George M. Marsden, *Fundamentalism and American Culture* (New York: Oxford University Press, 2006), 231–57.

3. Spitters and Ellison, *Conversations on When Everything Is Missions*, 42–43.

4. David J. Bosch, *Transforming Mission* (Maryknoll: Orbis Books, 1991), 531.

5. Christopher J. H. Wright, *The Mission of God* (Downers Grove, IL: Intervarsity Press, 2006), 27.

6. J. Richard Middleton, "The Liberating Image? Interpreting the *Imago Dei* in Context," *Christian Scholars Review,* 24.1 (1994): 8–25.

7. R. Paul Stevens, *The Other Six Days: Vocation, Work and Ministry in Biblical Perspective* (Grand Rapids: Eerdmans, 1999), 197.

8. Stevens, *The Other Six Days,* 197.

9. Stevens, *The Other Six Days,* 202, 206.

10. Patrick Lai, *Workship: Recalibrate Work and Worship* (Mt. Clemens, MI: OPEN Worldwide, 2021).

11. Dallas Willard, *The Spirit of the Disciplines: Understanding How God Changes Lives* (New York: HarperOne, 1990), 214.

12. H. A. Snyder, "What Business Are You In—Church or Kingdom?," *Church Plants* (blog), https://churchplants.com/articles/5859-what-business-are-you-in-church-or-kingdom.html.

13. John Stott, *Christian Mission in the Modern World* (Downers Grove, IL: IVP, 2014), 30.

14. Stott, *Christian Mission in the Modern World,* 24.

15. David J. Bosch, *Transforming Mission,* (Maryknoll: Orbis Books, 1991), 389–90.

16. Jürgen Moltmann, *The Church in the Power of the Spirit: A Contribution to Messianic Ecclesiology* (London: SCM Press, 1977), 64.

17. Darrell L. Guder, ed., *Missional Church: A Vision for the Sending of the Church in North America* (Grand Rapids: Eerdmans, 1998), 4–5.

18. Bob Roberts Jr. "We Aren't About Weekends," *Christianity Today* (2007), https://www.christianitytoday.com/pastors/2007/winter/3.28.html.

19. Larry W. Sharp, "Why I Am Not a Missionary," *Evangelical Missions Quarterly* 48, no. 4 (2012): 478–84.

20. Bob Roberts Jr., *Glocalization: How Followers of Jesus Engage a Flat World* (Grand Rapids: Zondervan, 2007), 38.

21. Roberts Jr., *Glocalization,* 40.

22. Roberts Jr., *Glocalization,* 148.

23. Larry W. Sharp, "Are We Really about Church Planting?" *Missio Nexus,* July 1, 2005, https://missionexus.org/are-we-really-about-church-planting/.

24. William J. Danker, *Profit for the Lord* (Eugene, OR: Wipf & Stock, 2002), 102.

25. Data from the Joshua Project (2019), https://joshuaproject.net.

26. Patrick Lai, "Avodah—Work as Worship," *Business for Transformation*, April 1, 2014, https://b4tblog.com/avodah-work-is-worship/.

27. Andrew Kirk, *What Is Mission? Theological Explorations* (Minneapolis, MN: Fortress Press, 2000), 30.

28. Clark G. Fobes, "*Imago Dei* in *Missio Dei*: Biblical Foundations for Work and Mission" (paper presented at the EMS Southwest Regional Conference, March 23, 2018).

29. Stephen Neill quoted in Rod Mundy, "Missiology: *Missio Dei* (God's Mission)" *Global Ministries*, January 28, 2011, https://www.globalministries.org/college_of_mission_missio.

Chapter 2

1. Wayne W. LaMorte, "Diffusion of Innovation Theory," *Boston University School of Public Health*, last modified September 9, 2019, https://sphweb.bumc.bu.edu/otlt/MPH-Modules/SB/BehavioralChangeTheories/BehavioralChangeTheories4.html.

2. Everett Roges, "What Is Diffusion of Innovation?," *Diffusion of Innovation* (blog), https://corporatefinanceinstitute.com/resources/knowledge/other/diffusion-of-innovation/.

3. See more on Disruptive Innovation Theory at the Christensen Institute, https://www.christenseninstitute.org/.

4. The Acton Institute has produced some useful documentaries, the most powerful of which may be "Poverty Cure: From Aid to Enterprise." See https://www.acton.org.

5. Gea Gort and Mats Tunehag, *BAM Global Movement: Business as Mission Concepts and Stories* (Peabody, MA: Hendrickson, 2018).

6. For further reading on this subject, see Jeff Van Duzer, *Why Business Matters to God (and What Still Needs to Be Fixed)*, (Downers Grove, IL: Intervarsity Press, 2010).

Chapter 3

1. Tom Bassford, "Prophetic Imagination," *SAT Talks*, December 22, 2018, http://sattalks.org/prophetic-imagination-tom-bassford/.

2. Ken Eldred, *The Integrated Life: Experience the Powerful Advantage of Integrating Faith and Work* (Montrose, CA: Manna Ventures, 2010), 112.

3. A. W. Tozer, *The Pursuit of God* (Chicago: Moody, 2015), 121.

4. William Perkins, *Inspirational Stories*, https://www.inspirationalstories.com/quotes/t/william-perkins/.

5. Martin Luther, quoted in R. Paul Stevens, *The Other Six Days: Vocation, Work, and Ministry in Biblical Perspective* (Grand Rapids: Eerdmans, 1999), 75.

6. Gene Edward Veith, Jr., *God at Work: Your Christian Vocation in All of Life* (Wheaton, IL: Crossway, 2002), 19.

7. R. Paul Stevens, *Work Matters* (Grand Rapids: Eerdmans, 2012), 11.

8. Robert D. Lupton, *Toxic Charity* (New York: HarperOne, 2011).

9. Steve Corbett and Brian Fikkert, *When Helping Hurts: How to Alleviate Poverty Without Hurting the Poor . . . and Yourself* (Chicago: Moody, 2009).

10. Mark Deymaz, *The Coming Revolution in Church Economics* (Grand Rapids: Baker Books, 2019).

11. Jimmy Scroggins and Steve Wright, "Is the Future of Church Planting Bi-Vocational?," *9Marks*, August 22, 2014, https://www.9marks .org/article/is-the-future-of-church-planting-bi-vocational/.

12. Tentmaking is mission done in accordance with the model of the apostle Paul. He was a tentmaker by profession and made a living through his work when he was on his mission journeys (Acts 18:3; 1 Cor. 9; 1 Thess. 2: 8–9). Today the "tentmaking" label is used to describe those who seek to live missionally in other cultures through their profession. It includes businesspeople, professionals, and students bringing the gospel to new places.

Chapter 4

1. Matthew Parris, "As an Atheist, I Truly Believe Africa Needs God," *The New York Times,* December 27, 2008.

2. Art Lindsley, "Do Pastors Have a Higher Calling? Seven Key Points on Faith and Work," *Theology 101*, May 16, 2007, https://tifwe.org /do-pastors-have-a-higher-calling-seven-key-points-on-faith-and-work/.

3. "About," Barnhart Crane, https://www.barnhartcrane.com/about/.

4. "Our Story," *Hobby Lobby*, https://www.hobbylobby.com/about-us /our-story.

5. Jerry Bowyer, "What Makes Hobby Lobby a Christian Company? Hint: It's Not a Greed or a Misogyny Thing," *Forbes*, April 25, 2017, https://www.forbes.com/sites/jerrybowyer/2017/04/25/what-makes-hobby-lobby-a-christian-company-hint-its-not-a-greed-or-a-misogyny-thing/#794c217436d9.

6. Bowyer, "What Makes Hobby Lobby a Christian Company?"

7. Christian Ellis, "Chick-fil-A Founder's Daughter: We're in Business to Glorify God," *CBN News*, February 21, 2019, https://www1.cbn.com /cbnnews/us/2019/february/chick-fil-a-founders-daughter-were -in-business-to-glorify-god.

8. Trudy Cathy White, *Climb Every Mountain: Finding God Faithful in the Journey of Life* (Brentwood, TN: Forefront Books, 2019).

9. "Bringing New Life to Old Parts: Michael Cardone," *Faith-Driven Entrepreneur*, https://www.faithdrivenentrepreneur.org/video-stories/michael-cardone-of-cardone-industries.

Chapter 5

1. Mats Tunehag, "Deeply Rooted for the Future," *Transformational SME*, December 22, 2020, https://transformationalsme.org/deeply-rooted-for-the-future/.
2. George Weigel, "The Difference Christianity Made," *National Review*, December 16, 2021, https://www.nationalreview.com/magazine/2021/12/27/the-difference-christianity-made/.
3. J. D. Greear, "The Next Wave of Missions," *J. D. Greear Ministries*, December 2, 2011, https://jdgreear.com/blog/the-next-wave-of-missions/.
4. Greear, "The Next Wave of Missions."
5. https://www.youtube.com/watch?v=L6zEcW9dSJ4.
6. John Warton quoted in David and Lorene Wilson, *Pipeline: Engaging the Church in Missionary Mobilization* (Pasadena, CA: William Carey, 2018), 310–11.
7. Jeff Van Duzer, *Why Business Matters to God* (Downers Grove, IL: IVP, 2010), 46.
8. Ken Eldred, *The Integrated Life: Experience the Powerful Advantage of Integrating Your Faith and Work* (Montrose, CA: Manna Ventures, 2010), 45.
9. "Milton Friedman Update," *Gravity Payments*, https://gravitypayments.com/blog/milton-friedman.
10. John Mackey and Rajendra Sisodia, *Conscious Capitalism: Liberating the Heroic Spirit of Business* (Boston: Harvard Business Review, 2014), 33.
11. Wayne A. Grudem, *Business for the Glory of God* (Wheaton, IL: Crossway, 2003), 80–81.
12. Jim Clifton, *The Coming Jobs War* (Washington, DC: Gallup, 2013), 10.
13. Rakesh Kochhar, "Seven-in-ten people globally live on $10 or less per day," *Pew Research Center*, September 2, 2015, https://www.pewresearch.org.
14. "Lausanne Business as Mission Manifesto," *BAM Global Business as Mission*, October 2004, https://bamglobal.org/lop-manifesto/.
15. Mike Baer, *Business as Mission* (Seattle: YWAM, 2006), 43ff.
16. John E. Mulford and Ken Eldred, "Entrepreneurs Transforming Nations," *Global Business Review* 3, no. 2 (2009), https://www.regent.edu/acad/global/publications/rgbr/vol3iss2/Vol_3_Issue2.pdf.

17. Albert M. Erisman, *The ServiceMaster Story: Navigating Tension between People and Profit* (Peabody, MA: Hendrickson, 2020), 193.
18. Dale Losch, *A Better Way: Making Disciples Wherever Life Happens* (Kansas City: Crossworld. 2012), 123.
19. "Wealth Creation and the Stewardship of Creation," paper from the Global Consultation on Wealth Creation for Transformation, the Lausanne Movement and BAM Global in Chiang Mai, Thailand, March 2017, Lausanne Movement and BAM Global, 12–13, https://lausanne.org/content/wealth-creation-stewardship-creation.
20. "Wealth Creation Manifesto," *Lausanne Movement*, May 9, 2017, https://lausanne.org/content/wealth-creation-manifesto.
21. Mark Polet, "Wealth Creation and the Stewardship of Creation," Global Consultation on Wealth for Transformation Conference, December 2017.
22. Dorothy L. Sayers, "Why Work?," *Creed or Chaos* (New York: Harcourt Brace. 1949), 56.
23. Patrice Tsague, "What Is a Kingdom Business?" *Regent University Center for Entrepreneurship*, https://regententrepreneur.org/what-is-kingdom-business/.

Chapter 6

1. Timothy Keller with Katherine Leary Alsdorf, *Every Good Endeavor: Connecting Your Work to God's Work* (New York: Penguin Group, 2012), 48.
2. Jim Clifton, *The Coming Jobs War* (New York: Simon & Schuster, 2011), 83–97.
3. The word *Eurofragance* reflects the Spanish spelling and source of the company origins.
4. "History of Bethel Avodah," *Eurofragance,* www.eurofragance.com.ph.
5. "About," Sekolah Pelita Harapan, https://sph.edu/about-sph/vision-mission-history/.
6. For more details and stories, see *The Greatest Missionary Generation*, ch. 2.
7. Michael D. Robert, "Trinidad and Tobago at 51: The Evolution of the Steel Pan," *Los Angeles Sentinel*, September 20, 2013, https://lasentinel.net/trinidad-and-tobago-at-51-the-evolution-of-the-steel-pan.html.
8. "The History of Global Scholars," *Global Scholars*, https://global-scholars.org/who-we-are/history/.
9. AIC Kijabe Hospital, https://kijabehospital.org/.

10. Walter L. Larimore and William Carr Peel, *The Saline Solution: Sharing Christ in a Busy Practice* (Bristol, TN: Paul Tournier Institute, 2000).

11. "What We Do," IHS Global, https://www.ihsglobal.org/what-we-do.

12. "Ethiopia: World Health Organization," *Resource Mobilization for Health Action in Crisis*, https://www.who.int/hac/donorinfo/calls-formobilisation/ethiopia_resmob.pdf?ua=1.

13. "Our Story: Aravind Eye Care System," https://aravind.org/our-story/.

14. "About: Sight for Souls," *Sight for Souls*, https://www.sightforsouls.org/about.

15. Sarah Imtiaz, "A New Generation Redefines What It Means to Be a Missionary," *The Atlantic,* March 8, 2018, https://www.theatlantic.com/international/archive/2018/03/young-missionaries/551585/.

Chapter 7

1. Steve Rundle, "Do Economic Incentives Help or Hinder 'Business as Mission' Practitioners?," Crowell School of Business, 2013, https://www.biola.edu/blogs/business-ministry-life/2013/do-economic-incentives-help-or-hinder-business-as-mission-practitioners.

2. Remember the story of Dan in his large Asia city joining the chamber of commerce as the only foreigner and how it opened up amazing and fruitful opportunities.

3. Alan Moir, "Teaching English in Developing Countries," *The British Council*, December 5, 2014.

4. "The Benefits of the English Language for Individuals and Societies: Quantitative Indicators from Cameroon, Nigeria, Rwanda, Bangladesh and Pakistan," *Euromonitor International Ltd* (December 2010), 60–61.

5. Mats Tunehag, "Deeply Rooted for the Future," *Mats Tunehag* (blog), December 23, 2020, http://matstunehag.com/2020/12/23/deeply-rooted-for-the-future/.

6. The term "People Group" is defined to mean a group of people where (1) all individuals in the group understand each other reasonably well, and (2) cultural and relationship barriers are not so high that the transmission of the gospel message is seriously impeded. According to the Joshua Project, "An unreached people is a people group among which there is no indigenous community of believing Christians with adequate numbers and resources to evangelize this people group without outside assistance." There are few evangelical believers and little if any history of Christianity. Numerical statistics are a confusing and complicated milieu, highly dependent on

unique definitions, but the Joshua Project suggests there are 7,407 unreached people groups, most of which are in the missiological 10/40 window. They contain 41 percent of the world's population. The 10/40 window refers to the eastern hemisphere geographical area between 10 and 40 degrees north of the equator. The region is considered the most resistant to Christianity.

7. The flywheel is part of a concept of greatness developed by Jim Collins in his book *Good to Great.* The process is akin to pushing a large, heavy flywheel. It takes a lot of effort to get started and build energy, but with persistent pushing in a consistent direction over a long period, the flywheel builds momentum and eventually can't be stopped, and it achieves breakthrough results. The Jurassic team was determined to be the best in the world in this kind of tourism by making decisions and taking actions to reinforce Collins's hedgehog idea, which initiates positive momentum. This along with the grace and wisdom of God resulted in positive outcomes and an energized and loyal staff.

8. In 2006, the author founded IBEC Ventures as a consulting group for BAM startups. In 2014, Bob Bush became the managing director and grew the company to more than forty coaches and consultants, working in more than twenty-five countries.

9. Courtney Rountree relayed this story directly to the author.

10. Alexander Hill, *Just Business: Christian Ethics for the Marketplace* (Downers Grove, IL: IVP Academic, 2008).

11. Courtney Rountree Mills, "7 Markers for a Kingdom Business: A Framework for Entrepreneurs," *The BAM Review* (July 2016).

12. Claire Brenner, "Poverty in Mozambique: Challenges and Hope," *The Borgen Project* (July 2013).

13. This was a statement often heard at the ServiceMaster Company as noted by Albert Erisman, author of *The ServiceMaster Story* (page xiv).

14. Albert M. Erisman, *The ServiceMaster Story: Navigating Tension between People and Profit* (Peabody, MA: Hendrickson, 2020), 87.

15. https://www.cnn.com/2019/08/07/africa/zimbabwe-millions -starvation-intl/index.html.

16. Pastor Charles Shelton coined the question "What Would Jesus Do?" in his 1896 classic novel *In His Steps: What Would Jesus Do?* (repr., Peabody, MA: Hendrickson, 2003).

Chapter 8

1. "The History of Coffee," *National Coffee Association*, https://www .ncausa.org/about-coffee/history-of-coffee.

2. Astrid Eira, "Number of Starbucks Worldwide 2021/2022: Facts, Statistics, and Trends," *Finances Online*, https://financesonline.com /number-of-starbucks-worldwide/.

3. In the Business as Mission world, coffee shops have become quite common, with the story of the CDC representative of the many successful ones. Many have failed, however, making it incumbent on future start-up owners to study companies like CDC as informative and prescriptive.

4. "About Dignity Coconuts," *Dignity*, https://dignitycoconuts.com /pages/about.

5. Robert J. Marks, "The Exemplary Life and Legacy of Dr. Walter Bradley," *Discovery Institute*, https://centerforintelligence.org/about /walter-bradley/.

6. Jo Plummer, "The Power of Dignity Restored: Business in the Heart of a Community," *The BAM Review*, https://businessasmission.com /dignity-coconuts-story-part2/.

7. "Shirley," *Dignity Coconuts Blog*, https://dignitycoconuts.com/blogs /stories/meet-shirley.

8. Kate Shellnut, "Making Missions Count: How a Major Database Tracked Thailand's Church-Planting Revival," *Christianity Today* (March 15, 2019), https://www.christianitytoday.com/ct/2019/april /missions-data-thai-church-fjcca-reach-village.html.

9. Greg Garrison, "Former Birmingham CEO Helps Start 465 Churches in Asia; Flips Mission Model with Data," *Alabama Life & Culture*, https://www.al.com/life/2019/04/former-birmingham-ceo-helps-start-465-churches-in-asia-flips-mission-model-with-data.html.

10. Erisman, *The ServiceMaster Story*, 10.

11. "Don Flow: Ethics Flow at Flow Automotive," *Ethix* (April 1, 2014), https://ethix.org/2004/04/01/ethics-at-flow-automotive.

12. "The Victims," *National Human Trafficking Hotline*, https://human traffickinghotline.org/what-human-trafficking/human-trafficking /victims.

13. Anthony G. Craine, "Joseph Kony," *Britannica*, https://humantrafficking hotline.org/what-human-trafficking/human-trafficking/victims.

14. "What Are Trauma-Informed Workplaces?" The Market Project, https://marketproject.org.

15. "Aftercare," *Willow International*, https://www.willowinternational .org/aftercare/.

16. "Ten Steps for Business Creation," *The Market Project*, https://market project.org/ten-steps-for-business-creation.

17. For their story in their own words, watch a short video at https://www.facebook.com/EternityNews/videos/outland-denim-who-is-meghan-markle-wearing/336441890302338/.
18. "Our Origins," https://www.outlanddenim.com/pages/our-origins.
19. Roxanne Adamiyatt, "Meghan Markle Wore Outland Denim, Putting the Brand on the Map—And Changed Lives in the Process," *Town & Country* (July 21, 2019), https://www.townandcountrymag.com/style/fashion-trends/a28198319/meghan-markle-outland-denim-jeans-interview/.
20. David Bernstein and Susan Davis, *Social Entrepreneurship: What Everyone Needs to Know* (New York, NY: Oxford University Press, 2010), 1.
21. "The Triple Bottom Line," *Outland Denim*, https://www.outlanddenim.com/blogs/news/the-triple-bottom-line.
22. "Our Origins," https://www.outlanddenim.com/pages/our-origins.
23. "Our Origins," https://www.outlanddenim.com/pages/our-origins.
24. "Meghan Markle's Impact," *Outland Denim*, https://www.outlanddenim.com/blogs/news/meghan-markle-s-impact.
25. "Our Origins," https://www.outlanddenim.com/pages/our-origins.
26. "Outland Denim: Who Is Meghan Markle Wearing?" *Eternity News*, January 29, 2019, https://www.facebook.com/EternityNews/videos/outland-denim-who-is-meghan-markle-wearing/336441890302338/.

Chapter 9

1. Patrick Lai, *Workship: Recalibrate Work and Worship* (Las Vegas: Open Worldwide, 2021), 117.
2. For a fascinating and relevant discussion on personal evangelism versus social justice issues, see David O. Moberg, *The Great Reversal: Reconciling Evangelism and Social Concern* (Eugene, OR: Wipf & Stock, 2007).
3. Nicki Howell, "5 Powerful Lessons from Steven Spielberg on Content Marketing," B2C Brandviews, November 28, 2016, https://www.business2community.com/brandviews/act-on/5-powerful-lessons-steven-spielberg-content-marketing-01714775.
4. Jim Collins, *Good to Great: Why Some Companies Make the Leap . . . and Others Don't* (New York: Harper Business, 2001), 90–119.

Chapter 10

1. "What is Liminal Space?" *Liminal Space*, https://inaliminalspace.org/about-us/what-is-a-liminal-space/.
2. Bob Roberts Jr., *Glocalization: How Followers of Jesus Engage a Flat World* (Grand Rapids: Zondervan, 2007), 105.

3. Andrew Scott, *Scatter: Go Therefore and Take Your Job with You* (Chicago: Moody, 2016), 114ff.
4. Losch, *A Better Way*, 10–18.

Appendix A

1. Rick Love, "Following Jesus in a Glocalized World: Bearers of Blessing among Neighbors and Nations," paper presented at the Society of Vineyard Scholars, February 3–5, 2011, 17.

Appendix C

1. Courtesy of Crossworld global missions agency (2011) for use by workers who are not members of a mission agency.

About the Hendrickson Publishers/Theology of Work Line of Books

There is an unprecedented interest today in the role of Christian faith in "ordinary" work, and Christians in every field are exploring what it means to work "as to the LORD" (Col. 3:22). Pastors and church leaders, and the scholars and teachers who support them, are asking what churches can do to equip their members in the workplace. There's a need for deep thinking, fresh perspectives, practical ideas, and mutual engagement between Christian faith and work in every sphere of human endeavor.

This Hendrickson Publishers/Theology of Work line of books seeks to bring significant new resources into this conversation. It began with Hendrickson's publication of the *Theology of Work Bible Commentary* and other Bible study materials written by the TOW Project. Soon we discovered a wealth of resources by other writers with a common heart for the meaning and value of everyday work. The HP/TOW line was formed to make the best of these resources available on the national and international stage.

Works in the HP/TOW line engage the practical issues of daily work through the lens of the Bible and the other resources of the Christian faith. They are biblically grounded, but their subjects are the work, workers, and workplaces of today. They employ contemporary arts and sciences, best practices, empirical research, and wisdom gained from experience, yet always in the service of Christ's redemptive work in the world, especially the world of work.

To a greater or lesser degree, all the books in this line make use of the scholarship of the *Theology of Work Bible Commentary*. The authors, however, are not limited to the TOW Project's perspectives, and they constantly expand the scope and application of the material. Publication of a book in the HP/TOW line does not necessarily imply endorsement by the Theology of Work Project, or that the author endorses the TOW Project. It does mean we recognize the work as an important contribution to the faith-work discussion, and we find a common footing that makes us glad to walk side-by-side in the dialogue.

We are proud to present the HP/TOW line together. We hope it helps readers expand their thinking, explore ideas worthy of deeper thought, and make sense of their own work in light of the Christian faith. We are grateful to the authors and all those whose labor has brought the HP/TOW line to life.

William Messenger, Executive Editor, Theology of Work Project
Sean McDonough, Biblical Editor, Theology of Work Project
Patricia Anders, Editorial Director, Hendrickson Publishers

www.theologyofwork.org
www.hendrickson.com